LANDMARK
CONGRESSIONAL LAWS
ON EDUCATION

LANDMARK
CONGRESSIONAL LAWS
ON EDUCATION

DAVID CARLETON

STUDENT'S GUIDE TO
LANDMARK CONGRESSIONAL LAWS
John R. Vile, Series Editor

Greenwood Press
Westport, Connecticut • London

Library of Congress Cataloging-in-Publication Data

Carleton, David, 1959–
    Landmark congressional laws on education / David Carleton.
        p.   cm.—(Student's guide to landmark congressional laws)
    Includes bibliographical references and index.
    ISBN 0–313–31335–0 (alk. paper)
        1. Educational law and legislation—United States.   2. Educational law and
    legislation—United States—History.   I. Title.   II. Series.
    KF4119.C357   2002
    344.73'07—dc21   2001023851

British Library Cataloguing in Publication Data is available.

Library of Congress Catalog Card Number: 2001023851
ISBN: 0–313–31335–0

First published in 2002

Greenwood Press, 88 Post Road West, Westport, CT 06881
An imprint of Greenwood Publishing Group, Inc.
www.greenwood.com

Printed in the United States of America

The paper used in this book complies with the
Permanent Paper Standard issued by the National
Information Standards Organization (Z39.48–1984).

10 9 8 7 6 5 4 3 2 1

Contents

Series Foreword

Most of the Founding Fathers who met at the Constitutional Convention in Philadelphia in the summer of 1787 probably anticipated that the legislative branch would be the most powerful of the three branches of the national government that they created. For all practical purposes, this was the only branch of government with which the onetime colonists had experience under the Articles of Confederation. Moreover, the delegates discussed this branch first and at greatest length at the convention, the dispute over representation in this body was one of the convention's most contentious issues, and the Founding Fathers made it the subject of the first and longest article of the new Constitution.

With the president elected indirectly through an electoral college and the members of the Supreme Court appointed by the president with the advice and consent of the Senate and serving for life terms, the framers of the Constitution had little doubt that Congress— and especially the House of Representatives, whose members were directly elected by the people for short two-year terms—would be closest to the people. As a consequence, they invested Congress with the awesome "power of the purse" that had been at issue in the revolutionary dispute with Great Britain, where the colonists' position had been encapsulated in the phrase "no taxation without representation." The framers also entrusted Congress with the more general right to adopt laws to carry out a variety of enumerated powers and other laws "necessary and proper" to the implementation of these powers—the basis for the doctrine of implied powers.

Wars and the threats of wars have sometimes tilted the modern balance of power toward the president, who has gained in a media age from his position as a single individual. Still, Congress has arguably been the most powerful branch of government over the long haul, and one might expect its power to increase with the demise of the Cold War. Especially in the aftermath of President Franklin D. Roosevelt's New Deal and President Lyndon B. Johnson's Great Society program, the number and complexity of laws have increased with the complexity of modern society and the multitude of demands that citizens have placed on modern governments. Courts have upheld expansive interpretations of federal powers under the commerce clause, the war-powers provisions, and the power to tax and spend for the general welfare, and in recent elections Democratic and Republican candidates alike have often called for expansive new federal programs.

It has been noted that there are 297 words in the Ten Commandments, 463 in the Bill of Rights, 266 in the Gettysburg Address, and more than 26,000 in a federal directive regulating the price of cabbage. Although the U.S. Constitution can be carried in one's pocket, the compilation of federal laws in the *U.S. Code* and the *U.S. Code Annotated* requires many volumes, not generally available in high-school and public libraries. Perhaps because of this modern prolixity and complexity, students often consider the analysis of laws to be the arcane domain of lawyers and law reviewers. Ironically, scholars, like this author, who focus on law, and especially constitutional law, tend to devote more attention to the language of judicial decisions interpreting laws than to the laws themselves.

Because knowledge of laws and their impact needs to be made more widely accessible, this series on Landmark Congressional Laws presents and examines laws relating to a number of important topics. These currently include education, First Amendment rights, civil rights, the environment, the rights of young people, women's rights, and health and social security. Each subject is a matter of importance that should be of key interest to high-school and college students. A college professor experienced in communicating ideas to undergraduates has compiled each of these volumes. Each author has selected major laws in his or her subject area and has described the politics of these laws, considering such aspects as their adoption, their interpretation, and their impact.

The laws in each volume are arranged chronologically. The entry on each law features an introduction that explains the law, its significance, and its place within the larger tapestry of legislation on the issues. A selection from the actual text of the law itself follows the introduction. This arrangement thus provides ready access to texts that are often difficult for students to find while highlighting major provisions, often taken from literally hundreds of pages, that students and scholars might spend hours to distill on their own.

These volumes are designed to be profitable to high-school and college students who are examining various public policy issues. They should also help interested citizens, scholars, and legal practitioners needing a quick, but thorough and accurate, introduction to a specific area of public policy-making. Although each book is designed to cover highlights of the entire history of federal legislation within a given subject area, the authors of these volumes have also designed them so that individuals who simply need to know the background and major provisions of a single law (the Civil Rights Act of 1964, for example) can quickly do so.

The Founding Fathers of the United States devised a system of federalism dividing power between the state and national governments. Thus, in many areas of legislation, even a complete overview of national laws will prove inadequate unless it is supplemented with knowledge of state and even local laws. This is duly noted in entries on laws where national legislation is necessarily incomplete and where powers are shared among the three layers of government. The U.S. system utilizes a system of separation of powers that divides authority among three branches of the national government. Thus, while these volumes keep the focus on legislation, they also note major judicial decisions and presidential initiatives relating to the laws covered.

Although the subjects of this series are worthy objects of study in their own right, they are especially appropriate topics for students and scholars in a system of representative democracy like the United States where citizens who are at least eighteen years of age have the right to choose those who will represent them in public office. In government, those individuals, like James Madison, Abraham Lincoln, and Woodrow Wilson, who have acquired the longest and clearest view of the past are frequently those who can also see the farthest into the future. This series is presented in the hope that it will help students both to understand the past and to equip themselves for future lives of good citizenship.

This editor wishes to thank his friends at Greenwood Press, his colleagues both at his own university and at other institutions of higher learning who have done such an able job of highlighting and explaining the laws that are the focus of this series, and those students, scholars, and citizens who have responded by reading and utilizing these volumes. When the Founding Fathers drew up a constitution, they depended not only on a set of structures and rights but also on the public-spiritedness and education of future citizens. When Benjamin Franklin was asked what form of government the Founding Fathers had created, he reportedly responded, "A republic, if you can keep it." When we inform ourselves and think deeply about the government's role in major areas of public policy, we honor the faith and foresight of those who bequeathed this government to us.

John R. Vile
Middle Tennessee State University

Timeline of Milestones in U.S. Education

1635   Boston Latin Grammar School opens.

1636   Harvard College is founded, the first institution of higher education in what will become the United States.

1642   Massachusetts passes a law requiring parents to see that children learn to read and write.

1647   The Old Deluder Satan Act passes in Massachusetts, requiring schools in all towns with 50 families or more.

1648   Dedham, Massachusetts, establishes the first property tax to support schools.

1693   The College of William and Mary is founded, the first institution of higher education in the South.

1701   Yale University is founded.

1746   Princeton University is founded.

1779   Thomas Jefferson proposes the Bill for More General Diffusion of Knowledge, calling for free public education for all Virginians (excluding slaves).

1785   The Land Ordinance is passed, setting aside land in the Northwest Territory to support education.

1787   The Northwest Ordinance is passed, setting aside land for the support of schools and the establishment of a university in the Northwest Territory.

1789   The U.S. Constitution is adopted.

1794   The Society of Associated Teachers is founded in New York City, the first teacher association in the United States.

1795   The University of North Carolina is established, the first state university in the United States.

1802   The United States Military Academy at West Point is established, the first federally supported institution of higher education.

1812   New York establishes the first state superintendent of schools.

1819   The University of Virginia is founded.

1821   The first high school in the United States is founded in Boston.

1821   Emma Willard establishes the Troy Female Seminary, providing secondary education to women.

1827   Massachusetts requires high schools in all cities.

1837   Horace Mann, the "father of public education," is named secretary of the Massachusetts State Board of Education.

1837   Mary Lyon founds Mount Holyoke Female Seminary, the first institution of higher education for women in the United States.

1839   Massachusetts establishes the first state normal school to train teachers.

1845   United States Naval Academy is established.

1852   Massachusetts passes the first compulsory school attendance policy in the United States.

1854   Ashmun Institute, later to become Lincoln University, is founded, the first African American university in the United States.

1857   The National Teachers Association is founded, later to become the National Education Association, the largest teachers' union in the United States.

1862   The First Morrill Act is passed, providing for the endowment of the first land-grant colleges.

1865   The Freedmen's Bureau is established to provide education and other social services to newly freed slaves in Southern states.

1867   Howard Theological Seminary, later to become Howard University, is founded.

1867   The National Department of Education, later the Office of Education, is established.

1867   Henry Barnard is named the first U.S. commissioner of education.

1868   Samuel Chapman Armstrong founds Hampton Institute.

1881   Booker T. Washington founds Tuskegee Institute.

1890   The Second Morrill Act is passed, extending land-grant colleges into the Southern states, leading to the creation of many public black colleges and universities.

1894   National Education Association–sponsored "Committee of Ten" proposes a comprehensive secondary-education curriculum.

1896   *Plessy v. Ferguson* is decided by the U.S. Supreme Court, upholding the constitutionality of the "separate-but-equal" doctrine.

1896   John Dewey establishes the University of Chicago laboratory school.

1902   Illinois establishes the first public junior college in the United States.

1904   Mary McLeod Bethune founds the first "training school" for African American girls, the Daytona Normal and Industrial Institute for Negro Girls.

1906   The National Society for the Promotion of Industrial Education is founded.

1916   The American Federation of Teachers, an affiliate of the American Federation of Labor, is founded.

1917   The Smith-Hughes Act is passed, providing federal support for vocational education at the secondary-school level.

1918   *Cardinal Principles of Secondary Education* is issued by the Commission on the Reorganization of Secondary Education, impacting high-school curriculum.

1919   The Progressive Education Association is founded.

1925   Scopes "Monkey Trial" highlights the conflict between religion and science in public schools.

1925   *Pierce v. Society of Sisters* is decided by the U.S. Supreme Court, upholding parental rights to send their children to parochial schools.

1941   The Lanham Act is passed, providing temporary federal aid for schools impacted by federal activities.

1943   *West Virginia Board of Education v. Barnette* is decided by the U.S. Supreme Court, striking down a compulsory flag salute.

1944   The Servicemen's Readjustment Act, the G.I. Bill, is passed, providing broad educational benefits to returning World War II veterans.

1944   The United Negro College Fund is established.

1946   The National School Lunch Act is passed.

1947   *Everson v. Board of Education of the Township of Ewing* is decided by the U.S. Supreme Court, upholding the use of public funds for bus transportation for parochial-school students.

1950   The "impact laws" are passed, providing permanent federal aid to schools impacted by federal employees and activities.

1954   *Brown v. Board of Education of Topeka* is decided by the U.S. Supreme Court, declaring racial discrimination in public schools unconstitutional.

1954   The School Milk Program Act is passed.

1954   The United States Air Force Academy is established.

1954   The National Advisory Committee on Education is created to recommend studies needed to improve education.

1957   The *Sputnik I* satellite is launched, prompting concerns that U.S. schools are failing to keep pace with those in the Soviet Union.

1958   The National Defense Education Act is passed, providing federal aid to primary and secondary education, especially to promote math and science instruction.

1958   The Education of Mentally Retarded Children Act is passed, providing federal aid to train teachers for handicapped children.

1958   *Cooper v. Aaron* is decided by the U.S. Supreme Court, reaffirming support for the desegregation of education.

1962   *Engel v. Vitale* is decided by the U.S. Supreme Court, declaring state-organized or sponsored prayer in schools unconstitutional.

1963   *Abington School District v. Schempp* is decided by the U.S. Supreme Court, extending *Engel* to include the Lord's Prayer and Bible reading.

1964   The Civil Rights Act is passed, with one provision calling for a withdrawal of federal financial support from any discriminatory school districts.

1964   The Economic Opportunity Act is passed, establishing a variety of programs, including the college work-study program and Head Start.

1965   The Elementary and Secondary Education Act is passed, the first federal program of general financial aid to primary and secondary education.

1965   The Higher Education Act is passed, establishing a variety of programs, including guaranteed student loans and the Teacher Corps.

1968   The Bilingual Education Act is passed, the first federal legislation dealing explicitly with language and culture.

1971   *Swann v. Charlotte-Mecklenburg Board of Education* is decided by the U.S. Supreme Court, upholding the limited use of busing to achieve racial desegregation.

1971   *Lemon v. Kurtzman* is decided by the U.S. Supreme Court, establishing the three-pronged *Lemon Test* criteria for determining whether a government program violates the constitutional prohibition against establishing a religion.

1972   Title IX of the Education Amendments is passed, making discrimination in education on the basis of gender illegal.

1972   *Pennsylvania Association for Retarded Children v. The Commonwealth of Pennsylvania* consent agreement establishes the right of all disabled children to a free appropriate public education.

1972   *Mills v. Board of Education of the District of Columbia* is decided by the U.S. District Court, ruling that a lack of funds is not an acceptable reason to deny special education services for the District of Columbia.

1973   *San Antonio Independent School District v. Rodriguez* is decided by the U.S. Supreme Court, refusing to mandate equal educational funding nationwide.

1974   *Lau v. Nichols* is decided by the U.S. Supreme Court, ruling that non-English speaking students are entitled to special assistance in school.

1975   The Education for All Handicapped Children Act is passed, mandating free appropriate public education designed to meet the individual needs of all handicapped children.

1979   The Department of Education Organization Act is passed, establishing the modern Department of Education as a cabinet-level department.

1981   The Education Consolidation and Improvement Act is passed, consolidating 42 federal education programs into 7 programs.

1983   *A Nation at Risk* is published by the Department of Education, arguing for fundamental education reform.

1984   The Equal Access Act is passed, requiring that religious-oriented extracurricular and student-led activities be treated in the same manner as nonreligious activities.

1984   *Grove City College v. Bell* is decided by the U.S. Supreme Court, ruling that the Title IX prohibition against gender discrimination applies only to educational programs that receive direct aid from the federal government.

1986   The Drug Free Schools and Communities Act is passed, providing federal assistance for drug-abuse education and prevention.

1988   The Jacob K. Javits Gifted and Talented Students Act is passed, providing some federal funding for identification of and services for gifted and talented students.

1988   The Civil Rights Restoration Act is passed, largely reversing the 1984 *Grove City College* court decision regarding Title IX.

1989   The National Education Summit is held in Charlottesville, Virginia, at which the federal government and all 50 governors agree on six national education goals to guide reforms.

1993   The Student Loan Reform Act is passed, reforming the federal student loan system by adding a direct federal lending program.

1994   The Goals 2000: Educate America Act is passed, establishing institutions and funding to achieve national goals for education reform.

1994   The Safe Schools Act is passed, providing federal funding to help schools implement violence-prevention measures.

1998   The Charter School Expansion Act is passed, providing federal funding to promote and expand charter schools (public schools offering parents choices in curriculum and teaching methods).

Introduction

Education has played a central role in American politics and society. It has been a cornerstone of democratic government, an essential mechanism for integrating a diverse society, and a necessary component of economic development. The importance of education was understood from the founding of the United States, but the best and proper role of the federal government in education has been and remains a contentious issue. The federal role in education at first was very limited, a reflection of broad public preference for small government. While it has been hotly debated each step along the way, the federal role has expanded in response to changing social problems and circumstances. The evolution of the federal role began slowly, but quickened in the latter half of the 20th century. Today, while the states and their local school districts remain the primary players in education policy-making and funding, the federal role is very substantial. This volume examines the series of legislative landmarks that have shaped the changing federal role in American education.

THE ENDURING IMPORTANCE OF EDUCATION

Education has been a central feature—indeed, an indispensable feature—of American development. Noble prize-winning Swedish economist and sociologist Gunnar Myrdal, reflecting on the United States from a foreign perspective, concluded, "Education has in America's whole history been the major hope for improving the individual and society."[1] Broad access to quality education has always been seen as the key to social progress and advancement. Broad commitment to education was evident even in the earliest colonial period. In 1635 and 1636, respectively, the Boston Latin Grammar School and Harvard College were established. These were both private schools, but in 1647 Puritan Massachusetts enacted the Old Deluder Satan Act, the first law in America requiring public schooling:

> It being one chief object of that old deluder, Satan, to keep men from the knowledge of the scriptures . . . it is therefore ordered, that every township . . . after the Lord hath increased them to the number of fifty householders . . . shall . . . appoint one within their town to teach all children . . . to read and write. It is further ordered, that where any township shall increase to the number of one hundred families . . . they shall set up a grammar school.[2]

The American commitment to education began with the colonists and has endured, because access to schooling has been essential to sound political, social, and economic order.

Politically, education has been essential to democratic government. Effective and meaningful self-government demands a citizenry that is informed and capable, able to make sound decisions and judgments. The linkage between education and democracy was well understood by the Founding Fathers. Daniel Webster noted, bluntly, that "on the diffusion of education among the people rest the preservation and perpetuation of our free institutions."[3] Democratic governance demands a public broadly educated, a population that can both understand public issues and reject antidemocratic, demagogic appeals. Thomas Jefferson's 1779 fight for his Bill for More General Diffusion of Knowledge in Virginia and the insistence on schools and education in newly settled Northwest Territory, as embodied in the Land Ordinance of 1785 and the Northwest Ordinance in 1787, were rooted in the democratic imperative for an educated people.

Socially, education has been essential to pull a diverse and changing society together. A major part of the story of American education has been the continual expansion of educational opportunities to previously excluded groups. The 19th century saw the common-school movement, the Morrill Acts establishing a system of public colleges, and schools for freed slaves. The early 20th century saw the development of vocational education to reach those at lower socioeconomic levels. At midcentury, the United States extended unparalleled educational benefits to returning war veterans, and, more recently, a tremendous public commitment has been made to extend educational benefits to the poor, minority populations, those for whom English is not a native language, and, especially, for those with handicaps or disabilities.

Economically, education is essential to change and expansion. The economic changes experienced in the United States—from agriculture to industrialization to services and technology—could not have happened without a system committed to educating all children. Industrialization demanded a population with skills far beyond those needed on the farm. Today's information-based economy requires a population with skills far beyond those needed on the factory floor or in the front office. The linkage between education and economic progress is well understood: "In an information society, education is no mere amenity; it is the prime tool for growing people and profits."[4] Education is central to the economic well-being of each individual and to the economic well-being and progress of the nation.

From the earliest days of colonial settlement, there has been an enduring public commitment to education. A strong and broad system of education has served as a foundation for free, democratic political institutions, a social system working toward greater integration and inclusion, and an economy promoting growth and opportunity. The political question, from the colonial period to the present, is what role the federal government should play in promoting, designing, funding, and controlling the educational system.

THE RELIGION OF LOCALISM

The federal system of government in the United States has both complicated and enlivened policy-making in education. Whereas most countries clearly vest authority for education in the national government, there is always an argument in the United States over which level of government ought to make education decisions. There is long-standing sentiment, dating back to the founding of the country and still strongly espoused today, that education is properly a state and local concern. This belief or principle, strongly and consistently expressed, has often been termed the "religion of localism." Arguments for and against this sentiment are a regular feature of debates over all proposals to expand the role of the federal government in education.

The Constitution provided no direct, enumerated power to the federal government to act in the area of education. By this silence and the Tenth Amendment, which reserves powers not delegated to the federal government to the states, the Constitution was generally seen as granting broad powers to the states and their local school districts to control education. Both public sentiment and the reality of education at the start of the country were captured by the notion that in the United States "education is a local responsibility, a state function, and a national concern."[5] Education was seen as a legal function of the states, which delegated day-to-day responsibility to local school districts, but it remained a national concern. Education was essential to national development, and national leaders felt strongly about the importance of education, but national concern did not equal federal control. The federal structure in the United States led to the creation of a uniquely decentralized system of education.

First and always, therefore, as the federal government passed landmark legislation dealing with education, the political debate involved criticism from defenders of localism. From the First Morrill Act in 1862 to passage of Goals 2000 in 1994, the first question proponents have had to answer is why the federal government should act instead of the states. This issue runs through the politics of nearly all the legislation discussed in this volume. In the 1860s, Congressman Justin Morrill (R-VT) had to convince people of the propriety of federal involvement in establishing public colleges and universities. In the early 20th century, Senator Hoke Smith (D-GA) and Congressman Dudley Hughes (D-GA) had to convince people of the propriety of federal involvement in vocational education. In the 1960s, President Lyndon Johnson had to convince people of the propriety of federal involvement in funding education for poor children. In the 1990s, President Bill Clinton had to convince people of the propriety of federal involvement in establishing national education standards and testing.

The federal role in education has expanded considerably since the 1780s, but because of the political belief in and broad appeal of localism in education, the expansion has been slow and evolutionary. The federal government has only been able to expand its role when a compelling case could be made or a compelling need could be demonstrated. The debate between those who adhere to the religion of localism and those who wish to match national concern with national action and responsibility, between those who favor relatively more decentralized and relatively more centralized education, is the enduring political fight in American education.

THE EVOLVING FEDERAL ROLE

Proposals for comprehensive federal involvement in education have always failed. In 1870, Congressman George Hoar (R-MA) introduced and fought for legislation to provide general federal financial aid to all primary and secondary schools, as well as grant the federal government authority to appoint school superintendents at both the state and school district level. Two years later, in 1872, Congressman Legrand Perce (D-MS) proposed the creation of a permanent federal fund to help finance local schools on the basis of community population. In 1879, Senator Ambrose Burnside (R-RI) proposed the sale of federal lands to provide regular funding for primary and secondary schools. Finally, Senator Henry Blair (R-NH) repeatedly proposed legislation in the 1880s to establish federal aid for common schools. These efforts, however structured and however well argued, always failed. Several similar efforts were made in the 20th century, always with the same result. Calls for the general involvement of the federal government in education, in every instance, have lacked political support.

The federal role in education has only been expanded, therefore, in particular areas of clear need; to bend the principle of localism, federal expansion must be strongly justified. Over the years, only four rationales or areas of national concern have consistently justified federal expansion: the promotion of higher education, the needs of national defense, civil rights and expanded access to education, and improving educational quality. The federal role in education has evolved through the passage of legislation related to these four particular areas of national need, and nearly all of the landmark legislative acts discussed in this volume were initiated and justified on one or more of these grounds.

The Federal Government and Higher Education

The land grant colleges were founded on the idea that a higher and broader education should be placed in every State within the reach of those whose destiny assigns them to, or who may have the courage to choose industrial vocations where the wealth of nations is produced; where advanced civilization unfolds its comforts, and where a much larger number of the people need wider educational advantages, and impatiently await their possession.[6]

Senator Justin Morrill

The public commitment to localism in education has always centered on primary and secondary education; there has always been less political resistance to federal involvement in higher education. Consequently, many of the first steps taken by the federal government in education dealt with colleges and universities. Today, the federal role in higher education still remains greater than in other parts of the educational system. Federal assistance has regularly contributed to the establishment of new institutions, the funding and promotion of research, and, especially, providing financial assistance to ensure broader access to higher education.

The Northwest Ordinance, passed in 1787, established the provision of education and schools as a national priority in the settlement of new territories. The Ohio Land Contracts, adopted concurrently with and based on the Northwest Ordinance, guaranteed proceeds from the sale of federal lands to create a university in each territory. The two Morrill Acts, adopted in 1862 and 1890, provided for the sale of additional federal land to fund the establishment of public colleges and universities in each state. The Freedmen's Bureau, established in 1865, provided crucial funding for a number of black colleges and universities. The 1944 G.I. Bill provided unprecedented levels of federal financial aid to help World War II veterans attend college, and subsequent bills extended similar benefits to Korean War, Vietnam War, and post-Vietnam veterans. In the National Defense Education Act of 1958, the federal government extended substantial funding to promote university research, particularly in the sciences. In the wide range of federal education legislation passed in the 1960s, funding was provided for the college work-study and guaranteed student loan programs, to support both community colleges and historically black colleges, and for the expansion and improvement of college programs to train new teachers.

Higher education has clearly and consistently provided the broadest arena for federal action, and the federal government has acted strongly. Today, the United States has the largest system of higher education in the world and sends the highest percentage of students on to postsecondary education. Federal actions are not solely responsible for these accomplishments, to be sure, but federal legislative action has certainly made a significant positive contribution.

National Defense and Education

> The Congress hereby finds and declares that the security of the Nation requires the fullest development of the mental resources and technical skills of its young men and women. . . . The national interest requires . . . that the Federal Government give assistance to education for programs which are important to our defense.[7]
>
> National Defense Education Act, 1958

The needs of war and national defense have also served as a strong basis for expanding federal involvement in education. Indeed, up to Lyndon Johnson's Great Society education legislation in the 1960s, national defense was the primary justification for federal involvement in education at the primary and secondary levels. Legislation was passed to ensure that the country was prepared for and could prosecute wars effectively, to deal with the effects of war, and to thank and compensate veterans for their sacrifices.

The 1865 Freedmen's Bureau was created, in large measure, to deal with educational needs of former slaves following emancipation and the Civil War. The 1917 Smith-Hughes Act represented the first federal involvement in vocational education at the secondary level. President Woodrow Wilson and many in Congress supported the act because it would play a role in national war preparedness. Wilson told Congress, "There are two sides to the question of [war] preparation. There is not merely the military side; there is the industrial side."[8] Federal involvement in vocational education was justified because of the national need for adequately trained technicians for war production and modern warfare. The 1941 Lanham Act and the far more ambitious "impact laws" passed in 1950 provided very substantial federal funding to support primary and secondary schools in communities with defense installations. The G.I. Bill and related veterans' aid bills were an obvious response to U.S. involvement in foreign conflicts. Finally, the 1958 National Defense Education Act represented a major expansion of the federal role in primary and secondary education all across the country. It provided federal funds to support math and science programming, teachers, and libraries, as well as new plant and equipment. The act was a direct response to the Cold War, intended to ensure that the United States remained scientifically and technologically competitive with the Soviet Union.

National-defense concerns have thus played an ongoing role in federal education policy. The country remained committed, overall, to localism in primary and secondary education, but the defense of the nation was a higher priority. The need adequately to prepare for war, the need to ensure the education of the children of servicemen serving at bases around the country, and the need to offer educational opportunities to civilians and veterans after the sacrifices of war have consistently justified federal education initiatives.

Education and Opportunity

> Congress hereby declares it to be the policy of the United States to provide financial assistance . . . to local educational agencies serving areas with concentrations of children from low-income families to expand and improve their educational programs by various means . . . which contribute particularly to meeting the special educational needs of educationally deprived children.[9]
>
> Elementary and Secondary Education Act, 1965

The federal government has consistently played an active role in expanding educational opportunities to excluded classes and particular groups of students. The educational system at the founding of the country was exclusive and elitist; beyond the primary level, only a small segment of the American population had meaningful access to education. Today, by contrast, the United States arguably has the most accessible education system in the world, and the federal government has been responsible for much of this change. In the 19th and early 20th centuries, several steps were taken to broaden access, but the major legislative steps taken by the federal government began in the 1960s.

The first steps taken vis-à-vis educational opportunity included the Freedmen's Bureau (to aid freed slaves), the land-grant colleges, and vocational education, which extended new educational opportunities to millions of African Americans, millions of students previously excluded from elite colleges, and working- and lower-class students. The National School Lunch Act, adopted in 1946, was intended to ensure that poor children were adequately nourished so they could learn effectively. The major federal push to expand opportunity, however, began in the Johnson administration. The Economic Opportunity Act and the Elementary and Secondary Education Act, adopted in 1964 and 1965, respectively, provided very substantial federal funding to expand and improve education for poor Americans. The 1968 Bilingual Education Act reached millions of students with limited English proficiency. Finally, the Education for All Handicapped Children Act of 1975 mandated major changes in school policies at the local level to ensure full educational opportunities for children with disabilities.

The national concern for education has thus involved a strong civil rights component—a concern that all children be included and receive equal educational opportunity. The Supreme Court's *Brown v. Board of Education* decision in 1954 declared segregated schools unconstitutional, creating an environment where access to equal educational opportunity is expected. Since *Brown*, the federal government has repeatedly acted to ensure access and has committed substantial resources to the goal. Much of this legislation, predicated on the notion that a child's early years are crucial to lifelong educational attainment, focused federal efforts for the first time on primary education. Localism has always been strongest with regard to primary schooling, but the national concern for educational equality has provided a strong political rationale for federal involvement.

Quality and Reform

> Our Nation is at risk. . . . the educational foundations of our society are presently being eroded by a rising tide of mediocrity. . . . If an unfriendly foreign power had attempted to impose on America the mediocre educational performance that exists today, we might well have viewed it as an act of war. As it stands, we have allowed this to happen to ourselves.[10]
>
> National Commission on Excellence in Education, 1983

The most recent and evolving area of federal expansion in education involves the quality of American schools. The National Commission on Excellence in Education was sponsored by the federal government, and its 1983 report *A Nation at Risk* galvanized public opinion that American schools needed improvement. The states responded with major reforms, with the federal government as a partner in the effort. Federal concern over school quality has focused on the importance of good education for both individual and national economic well-being. The federal role to date has consisted of efforts to raise awareness of the issue, fund academic research, and fund work to create national standards and assessments.

The George Bush administration developed a coordinated quality-reform strategy with the states in 1989, establishing the first national education goals and funding model or experimental schools across the country. The Bill Clinton administration built upon this approach, passing the Goals 2000: Educate America Act in 1994. Under Goals 2000, the federal government commits resources to develop national curricular standards for primary and secondary education, as well as tests to measure individual student attainment of the standards. This is a cooperative effort with the states, but it is a wholly new area of federal involvement in education.

School performance as a national concern is the most recent political rationale for bending the principle of localism in education. It is a concern that is likely to lead to further federal legislation in the future. The 2000 presidential campaign saw both major-party presidential nominees advocating federal action to improve school quality. Vice President Al Gore proposed federal funding to hire primary- and secondary-school teachers to reduce class sizes, and Governor George W. Bush proposed the use of some federal funds to promote school choice as a spur to quality improvement. Federal involvement in education has evolved in particular areas in response to particular national concerns—first, higher education, followed by the needs of national defense and equal opportunity. For the foreseeable future, quality reform is the likeliest area for further evolution and expansion of the federal role in American education.

THE STRUCTURE OF THIS BOOK

This volume examines the principal legislation that has moved the federal government from the sidelines to the center of American education. The legislation discussed deals with a very diverse set of issues—the sale of land for school funding, the promotion of colleges, schools for ex-slaves, vocational education, school lunches and nutrition, college loans, veterans' benefits, preschool programs, bilingual education, national standards, special education, and administrative structure. While federal courts have issued rulings impacting different areas of education, this volume examines federal legislative action—each act discussed was passed by both the House of Representatives and Senate, and signed by the president. A piece of legislation was selected if it represented a major step in the direction of expanding and formalizing the federal presence in education. The entire educational system was considered, from preschool through graduate school. Taken together, the acts discussed demonstrate the pattern of evolution toward an activist federal education policy, moving education from a national concern to both a concern and a responsibility.

Rather than being grouped by topic—acts dealing with higher education here, those with secondary education there—the laws are presented in chronological order (the dates in the chapter titles refer to the date of final approval). Spanning the period from 1785 to 1994, the chronological presentation makes clear the evolutionary and simultaneous expansion of federal activity in each educational area.

The discussion of each landmark law is intended to convey the substance of the act, the purpose and rationale for the act, and the practical and political effects of the act. To this end, each discussion begins with a summary of the legislative language—the specific policies, programs, and agencies created. This is followed by a lengthier discussion of the legislative history of the act—the politics, individuals, groups, and issues involved in the fight for congressional approval. Next, there is a discussion of the impacts produced by the legislation—funding, students served, successes and failures, and, especially, political ramifications. Finally, each discussion ends with the text of an excerpt from the text of the actual legislation.

NOTES

1. Laurence J. Peter, *Peter's Quotations: Ideas for Our Time* (New York: William Morrow and Company, 1977), p. 178.

2. Quoted in John D. Pulliam and James Van Patten, *History of Education in America*, 7th ed. (Upper Saddle River, NJ: Merrill, 1999), p. 51.

3. Address made in Madison, Indiana, June 1, 1837, quoted in George Seldes, *The Great Quotations* (Secaucus, NJ: Castle Books, 1966), p. 729.

4. Corporate leader John Naisbitt, quoted at *CreativeQuotations.com* (http://www.creativequotations.com), 2000.

5. Norman C. Thomas, *Education in National Politics* (New York: David McKay Company, 1975), p. 19.

6. U.S. Department of Health, Education, and Welfare, *Land-Grant Colleges and Universities, 1862–1962* (Washington, DC: U.S. Government Printing Office, 1962), p. 2.

7. National Defense Education Act, *United States Statutes at Large*, vol. 72 (Washington, DC: U.S. Government Printing Office, 1958), p. 1581.

8. Quoted in Layton S. Hawkins, Charles A. Prosser, and John C. Wright, *Development of Vocational Education* (Chicago: American Technical Society, 1951), p. 87.

9. Elementary and Secondary Education Act, *United States Statutes at Large*, vol. 79 (Washington, DC: U.S. Government Printing Office, 1965), p. 27.

10. National Commission on Excellence in Education, *A Nation at Risk: The Imperative for Educational Reform* (Washington, DC: U.S. Government Printing Office, 1983), p. 5.

1

The Land Ordinance of 1785

May 20, 1785

The Land Ordinance of 1785 was the first in a series of congressional land ordinances regulating the incorporation of new western lands into the United States. The ordinance drew attention to the importance of providing for education and common schools in new territories and states. Among its provisions, the ordinance laid out how new lands were to be surveyed and sold. Included in the survey plan was a stipulation that education must be supported: "There shall be reserved the lot No. 16, of every township, for the maintenance of public schools, within the said township."[1] These words made clear the important role education was to play in the new territories and, indeed, in the new country as a whole.

In conjunction with the other land ordinances that followed, the Land Ordinance of 1785 encouraged westward expansion, ensured the creation of common schools in new lands, and established the precedent of using land sales to finance education. This approach was to prove crucial in establishing a system of public colleges and universities in the 1860s and 1890s. More broadly, and of ongoing importance, the Land Ordinance made it clear that at this very early stage of national development, Congress and the national government would play a role in education.

BACKGROUND

The Land Ordinance of 1785 was passed under the original Articles of Confederation and was intended to regulate the sale of lands in the Northwest Territory, that is, those areas that today roughly make up Ohio, Indiana, Illinois, Michigan, Wisconsin, and parts of Minnesota. At the time, the borders of these lands were uncertain; it was not always clear where U.S. territory left off and colonial territories of European powers began. The new U.S. government was faced with enormous debts as a result of the Revolutionary War. Settlement in these territories was haphazard and unregulated. Thus Congress was interested in surveying and clarifying boundaries, encouraging the settlement of these lands, raising revenue from the sales of these lands, and ensuring that the process was orderly.

The ordinance called for the Northwest Territory to be surveyed and laid out in a grid pattern. The basic building blocks of the survey system were to be "lots" and "townships." Each individual lot was to comprise an area of one square mile. Each township was to comprise a six-mile-by-six-mile area, or 36 lots. Land was to be sold either by township or by individual lot. The Land Ordinance required that lot 16 of the 36 lots in each township be reserved for the maintenance of schools. Lot 16 would constitute a land grant; that is, it would be sold, and the proceeds would be used to establish and operate a common, public school for children in the township.

While this provision for education in the ordinance had real and lasting impact, it was not the primary purpose or intent of the legislation. This was fundamentally a land ordinance; passage was the culmination of several years of effort in Congress to determine how to manage new territories. Congress was focused on how lands would be laid out, how land would be bought and sold, who would hold deeds, and how these areas would be governed.[2] Education was simply not the focus of this debate.

Facing uncertainty over how to organize the Northwest Territory in the early 1780s, Congress authorized a committee headed by Thomas Jefferson to draft an ordinance. Reported out in March 1784, the draft made no provisions for schools or education of any kind. This is unexpected, given Jefferson's deep, lifelong commitment to education, but speaks to the fact that the primary focus of the whole legislative effort was governance and settlement of the territories. Jefferson's draft drew considerable criticism, however, particularly from representatives of the New England states. One of the main complaints about the ordinance as presented by Jefferson was the absence of any reference to or provision regarding education.

As congressional debate proceeded, the changes made to the Jefferson draft reflected New England concerns and experiences. For instance, the size of new townships was reduced to the six-mile-by-six-mile standard, as this was the existing practice in New England territories. The use of land grants to support education was also a long-standing tradition in the New England territories. They had relied on land sales to support new schools for over a century, and the "lot No. 16" clause added to the Land Ordinance reflected this regional experience.

Commentators have inferred that the intent of the New Englanders in adding the provision on education was a belief in common education as a means to bind the new nation together. The actual rationale, however, was far more pragmatic: the education clause was "designed more to encourage development of the Western lands (by making them seem more attractive to Eastern investors) than as any evidence of concern for education as such."[3] Most of the prospective buyers of land in the territories were from the Northeast; the Ohio Company, founded in 1786, was largely composed of investors from Massachusetts. Schools were an inducement to attract buyers and, ultimately, settlers to these lands: "In the early negotiations between land buyers and Congress, grants for schools seemed more a bargaining chip than a fixed entitlement for novel republican purposes. . . . If land buyers wanted school subsidies, that was part of the contract in a buyer's market."[4]

When the Land Ordinance was passed by Congress on May 20, 1785, therefore, education was hardly the first priority. Jefferson had ignored it altogether. The education provision had been added late in the legislative process, and then as an inducement to buyers. Yet the provision that lot 16 be reserved for schools—regardless of motivation or intention—was finally included, and with lasting effect.

IMPACT

The effects of the educational provision in the Land Ordinance of 1785 fall into four areas. First, the provision for schools did help in encouraging settlement in the Northwest Territory, as intended. Schools were viewed as a "civilizing" influence on wild, new territories. As such, they made settlement in the territories more attractive and made the integration of settler communities into the broader nation smoother.[5]

Second, the Land Ordinance helped firmly root the idea of common schools, that is, public schools for grades one through eight. In colonial America, much of education remained in the hands of exclusive, private academies, and, further, the Revolutionary War and loss of support from British institutions had seriously hurt existing American schools.[6] To the extent that the ordinance contributed to establishing common schools as a national principle, it promoted the equality of all citizens and the revolutionary notion that true democratic government demands an educated citizenry.

Third, the Land Ordinance set the precedent for national land grants to support education. This was a crucial step in the development of the system of public education in the United States at all levels. It was essential to primary and secondary education and even more so to higher education. With the precedent laid down in 1785, educational land grants expanded very rapidly; by the 1850s, more than six million acres of public land had been reserved for educational grants.[7] Further, the two Morrill Acts of 1862 and 1890, which promoted the development of much of the country's system of public colleges and universities, were based on broad land grants. The land-grant idea of 1785 proved indispensable in building American education.

Fourth, and finally, the Land Ordinance of 1785 set a clear marker, early in U.S. political development, that the national government would play a role in education. This was a time of very considerable apprehension about active central government. The United States was still governed under the Articles of Confederation, which provided for a particularly weak national government. Even the later Constitution makes no reference to education. Yet even under these circumstances, the national government asserted a role in education, and, in a sense, the Land Ordinance of 1785 was thus the forerunner for all federal actions in education to follow, from the Morrill Acts in the 1800s, to the G.I. Bill in the 1940s, to Head Start in the 1960s, and charter schools in the 1990s.

These effects of the Land Ordinance were real and lasting, but implementation of the ordinance was not without controversy and problems. The ordinance, as drafted, left important questions unanswered. For instance, while the assumption was that lot-16 land would be sold to raise funds, this was not explicit in the ordinance, and several leasing arrangements were attempted. These efforts to lease the land proved unsuccessful; given the vast expanses of land available in the territories, leasing was simply unprofitable. Even when the land was sold, moreover, there was a question of how fast to proceed. To sell land quickly would allow for more rapid settlement, but would drive prices down and leave few resources to support subsequent generations of settlers. Congress never provided guidance to townships and states in these matters, and land sales were ultimately managed using a wide variety of approaches.

A second problem was the fact that the ordinance failed explicitly to designate which level of government would have responsibility for managing the educational land and proceeds. Ohio was the first state created out of the territories, in 1803, and responsibility for land and monies was given to local townships. This very decentralized system was followed in many other territories and ultimately led to practical and administrative problems because lot 16 in one township might be far more valuable than in another and because of poor record keeping, incompetence, and, in some instances, fraud. In response to these problems, there was a gradual move to centralize control of school land and monies in state government. In 1837, Michigan was the first state created with state control. The goal was to ensure that all townships were treated fairly and to bring a measure of expertise and professionalism to management of the funds. This shift in authority over education from the local to the state level of government helped establish the key role of the states in educational policy-making.[8]

The entire education provision of the Land Ordinance consists of no more than a line or two in legislation intended to deal in great detail with land surveys and sales. Education was only an afterthought in the drafting of the legislation and was ultimately added for strictly practical reasons. Intended or not, however, the educational provision of the Land Ordinance had real, meaningful, and lasting impacts on the course of American public education.

1. The Land Ordinance of 1785

An Ordinance for Ascertaining the Mode of Disposing of
Lands in the Western Territory[9]

Be it ordained by the United States in Congress assembled, that the territory ceded by individual states to the United States, which has been purchased of the Indian inhabitants, shall be disposed of in the following manner:

A surveyor from each state shall be appointed by Congress or a Committee of the States. . . .

The surveyors. . . . shall proceed to divide the said territory into townships of 6 miles square. . . .

The plats [maps] of the townships respectively, shall be marked by subdivisions into lots of one mile square . . . and numbered from 1 to 36. . . .

There shall be reserved the lot No. 16, of every township, for the maintenance of public schools, within the said township. . . .

Done by the United States in Congress assembled, the 20th day of May, in the year of our Lord, 1785, and of our sovereignty and independence the ninth.

NOTES

1. Howard Cromwell Taylor, *The Educational Significance of the Early Federal Land Ordinances* (New York: Arno Press and The New York Times, 1969), p. 131.

2. Lawrence A. Cremin, *American Education: The National Experience, 1783–1876* (New York: Harper and Row, 1980), p. 10.

3. Homer D. Babbidge, Jr. and Robert M. Rosenzweig, *The Federal Interest in Higher Education* (New York: McGraw-Hill, 1962), p. 2.

4. David Tyack, Thomas James, and Aaron Benavot, *Law and the Shaping of Public Education, 1785–1954* (Madison: University of Wisconsin Press, 1987), p. 32.

5. Peter S. Onuf, "The Founders' Vision: Education in the Development of the Old Northwest," in *". . . Schools and the Means of Education Shall Forever Be Encouraged:" A History of Education in the Old Northwest, 1787–1880*, ed. Paul H. Mattingly and Edward W. Stevens, Jr. (Athens, Ohio University Libraries, 1987), pp. 5–16.

6. John D. Pulliam and James Van Patten, *History of Education in America*, 7th ed. (Upper Saddle River, NJ: Merrill, 1999), pp. 81–83.

7. Roger L. Williams, *The Origins of Federal Support for Higher Education: George W. Atherton and the Land-Grant College Movement* (University Park: Pennsylvania State University Press, 1991), p. 35.

8. For a discussion of this centralizing tendency, see Tyack, James, and Benavot, *Law and the Shaping of Public Education, 1785–1954*, p. 42.

9. For the full text, see Taylor, *The Educational Significance of the Early Federal Land Ordinances*, pp. 129–133.

2

The Northwest Ordinance

July 13, 1787

The Northwest Ordinance was the necessary corollary to the Land Ordinance of 1785. The latter had provided for the sale of lands in the Northwest Territory—what would become Ohio, Indiana, Illinois, Michigan, and Wisconsin—but had not laid out in any detail the manner in which these lands would be governed. The purpose of the Northwest Ordinance was to answer questions of governance, of how, when, and under what conditions new territories would gain statehood. Article III of the ordinance included one simple sentence dealing with education: "Religion, morality, and knowledge, being necessary to good government and the happiness of mankind, schools and the means of education shall forever be encouraged."[1] This brief clause made clear the integral role education was to play in the new republic.

The Northwest Ordinance was adopted under the Articles of Confederation and was so vague that it was not really enforceable in any meaningful sense. Its importance, however, lies in its clarity as a statement of national principle. It led the national government to take steps to in fact encourage the means of education. As a statement of principle it did not itself mandate action, but it spurred the national government to act nonetheless. In particular, it affected what provisions were actually written into land contracts in the territories, with lasting impact on the resources dedicated to education at all levels. Indeed, in considering the education clause, Daniel Webster wrote, "I doubt whether one single law or any lawgiver, ancient or modern, has produced effects of more distinct, marked, and lasting character than the Ordinance of 1787."[2] The

Northwest Ordinance included only one sentence on education, but that sentence had a marked impact on the development of education in the United States.

BACKGROUND

Issues of governance in the Northwest Territory were crucial, and Congress struggled with the matter throughout the 1780s. Tremendous land speculation was occurring in the territories. Sale of the lands would play a major role in defraying the war debts of the young government. The creation and addition of new states would affect the power and influence of existing states. These were not easy issues. Congress understood that it needed to establish and clarify set rules and regulations for the governance of the territories—to help bring speculation under control, promote sales for national debt payments, and head off potential sectional fights over the creation of new states. The Northwest Ordinance was the culmination of congressional efforts to address these issues. It did so for the Northwest Territory directly and, by precedent and extension, for all other territories as the United States expanded westward.

Various efforts or proposals were made to deal with the governance questions. Maryland, in 1779, called for the nationalization of all western territories, with independent governments to be established by Congress as it saw fit. In 1782 and 1783, the so-called Army Plan and Financiers Plan were proposed, with the former endorsed by George Washington, the latter by Alexander Hamilton. Each, in its own way, called for the creation of a new state or states in the West and relied on Revolutionary War veterans as the core of new settler communities.[3] Congress then established a committee, headed by Thomas Jefferson, to address these issues; the work of this committee resulted in the adoption of the Ordinance of 1784. This provided for the nationalization of western lands and established a temporary government. What it did not do was make any provision for the actual sale of land in the territories to settlers and for any means of establishing a permanent government. The former issue was therefore addressed in the Land Ordinance of 1785 (see chapter 1) and the latter in the Northwest Ordinance of 1787, which thus repealed and replaced the Ordinance of 1784.

The 1784 legislation provided a means to govern the Northwest Territory prior to statehood, but had not established rules for establishing new states and permanent governments. Congress appointed a new committee in 1786 to draft legislation for the establishment of a permanent government in the Northwest. Originally chaired by James Monroe, the committee was later led by William Johnson of Connecticut. It was the work of this committee that ultimately resulted in the Northwest Ordinance. While the Northwest Ordinance was not technically a land ordinance itself, it was of a part with the Ordinance of 1784 and the Land Ordinance of 1785 and completed the legislative process of bringing the Northwest Territory fully into the United States in an orderly fashion. It did so in a manner that had lasting impact on the country, primarily by ensuring that these territories would achieve statehood on an equal basis with the original states and by committing the federal government to support public education in these lands. While the education clause was very brief, it was one of the essential features of the ordinance, precisely because it went to the basic principles of the nation. Further, it clearly built upon the specific land-grant provision in the Land Ordinance of 1785. The addition of the clause to the ordinance, however, was not inevitable, and owes much to the Ohio Company and, in particular, the Reverend Manasseh Cutler.

Cutler led the Ohio Company, and the intention of the company to purchase a large tract of land in the Northwest was known throughout the legislative process. Informal negotiations between Cutler and the government shaped the final form of the Northwest Ordinance. The Ohio Company had certain needs in order to make the purchase and settlement of the land successful, and Congress worked with Cutler to try and meet these needs. It is clear that Cutler and the Ohio Company were primarily responsible for the education clause.

In negotiations with Congress, the Ohio Company was interested in a system of governance that would attract settlers. Without sufficient settlers, the company would fail. Cutler worked through contacts with Nathan Dane and Rufus King, both members of the Continental Congress from Massachusetts, to shape the Northwest Ordinance in a beneficial manner. He pushed for the equality of newly created states and a prohibition on slavery in any new states and was almost wholly responsible for the form and substance of Article III on education. Cutler understood that if the territories were to attract large numbers of settlers from New England, which was the intention, governance in them needed to be rooted in basic

American principles, and settlers had to be assured that they would not lose any of their rights when they moved from established states to new states.[4]

In the end, a number of related concerns led to the adoption of the Northwest Ordinance. It was necessary to complete the unfinished work of the Ordinance of 1784, to promote sales of federal lands to bring needed monies into the national treasury, and to attract settlers and make the Ohio Company's purchase of land financially sound. The result was a fundamental piece of legislation that transformed the frontier and laid the principled basis for much of public education.

IMPACT

The Northwest Ordinance was intended to establish permanent and stable governments in the territories, establish new states and incorporate them into the United States, promote the sale of land, and induce settlement in the territories. In each respect, the ordinance succeeded. It succeeded not only in the Northwest, but, as a model for the future, for all other territories incorporated into the United States. The education clause was not solely responsible for this level of success, but it certainly contributed to the overall success of the ordinance.

Beyond this, the education clause had the tangible impact of fostering the creation of actual schools, particularly in higher education. On July 23, 1787, just 10 days after the adoption of the Northwest Ordinance, Congress approved the sale of five million acres in the Northwest to Cutler's Ohio Company. The two acts were and are inextricably linked: "The Northwest Ordinance is remembered for its language and the concept it espoused, while the Ohio contract actually accomplished a great deal more of real significance."[5] The Ohio contract put the Northwest Ordinance into action.

In negotiations with Congress, Cutler originally asked for a whole series of land grants: lot 16 of each township for common schools, one complete township to support religion, and four complete townships in the Ohio lands to establish a university. This proved too generous for Congress, however. The final contract included the lot 16 provision as called for in 1785, but reduced Cutler's request of land to support religion to lot 29 of each township. Most significantly, however, it provided that "not more than two complete townships . . . be given perpetually for the purpose of an University . . . to be applied to the intended object by the legislature of the State."[6] This stipulation was extended and expanded in later land sales; by the time of the Civil War, more than four million acres of federal lands had been granted to newly created states to support universities.[7] The practical effect of the Northwest Ordinance was to foster the establishment of public higher education in the United States.

The final impact of the Northwest Ordinance can be found in its role as a statement of national principle and purpose. It is one of the basic foundation documents of the United States and places education in a prominent place within the nation. The effect is difficult to measure, but is certainly real. Time and again, as the federal government debated whether to move into new areas of education—land-grant colleges, vocational education, educational benefits for veterans—the language of the Northwest Ordinance was invoked in the House and Senate. Public education has been a central feature and tenet in building a single, cohesive American nation. The Northwest Ordinance represents a clear statement of this principle, made at the founding of the country.

As with the Land Ordinance of 1785, the education-related language of the Northwest Ordinance is brief and was added to address practical concerns. Its effect, however, was significant—helping to settle the Northwest Territory, promoting land sales to help defray national debts, laying the foundation for public higher education, and elevating education as a guiding principle of the nation.

2a. The Northwest Ordinance

An Ordinance for the government of the Territory of the
United States northwest of the River Ohio[8]

Be it ordained by the United States in Congress assembled . . .

Article III. Religion, morality, and knowledge, being necessary to good government and the happiness of mankind, schools and the means of education shall forever be encouraged. . . .

Article V. There shall be formed in the said territory, not less than three nor more than five States; . . . And, whenever any of the said States shall have sixty thousand free inhabitants therein, such State shall be admitted, by its delegates, into the Congress of the United States, on an equal footing with the original States in all respects whatever. . . .

Be it ordained by the authority aforesaid, That the resolution of the 23rd of April, 1784, relative to the subject of this ordinance, be, and the same are hereby repealed and declared null and void.

2b. Powers to the Board of Treasury to Contract for the Sale of Western Territory [authorization for the first Ohio land contract][9]

The report of a committee, consisting of Mr. Carrington, Mr. King, Mr. Dane, Mr. Madison, and Mr. Benson, amended to read as follows, viz:

That the Board of Treasury be authorized and empowered to contract with any person or persons for a grant of a tract of land which shall be bounded by the Ohio. . . .

The purchaser or purchasers, within seven years of the completion of this work, to lay off the whole tract, at their own expense, into townships and fractional parts of townships, and to divide the same into lots, according to the land ordinance of the 20th of May, 1785; complete returns whereof to be made to the Treasury Board. The lot No. 16, in each township or fractional part of a township, to be given perpetually for the purposes contained in the said ordinance. The lot No. 29, in each township or fractional part of a township, to be given perpetually for the purposes of religion. The lots Nos. 8, 11, and 26, in each township or fractional part of a township, to be reserved for the future disposition of Congress. Not more than two complete townships to be given perpetually for the purposes of a University, to be laid off by the purchaser or purchasers, as near the center as may be, so that the same shall be of good land, to be applied to the intended object by the legislature of the State. The price to be not less than one dollar per acre for the contents of the said tract. . . . Not less than 500,000 dollars of the purchase-money to be paid down upon closing of the contract, and the remainder upon the completion of the work to be performed by the geographer or other officer on the part of the United States. . . .

Ordered, that the above be referred to the Board of Treasury, to take order, July 23, 1787.

NOTES

1. "The Northwest Ordinance," University of Oklahoma Law Center (http://www.law.ou.edu/hist/ordinanc.html, 2000).

2. Quoted in Edward Danforth Eddy, Jr., *Colleges for Our Land and Time: The Land-Grant Idea in American Education* (New York: Harper and Brothers 1957), p. 21.

3. For discussions of the Maryland, "Army," and "Financiers" proposals, see George N. Rainsford, *Congress and Higher Education in the Nineteenth Century* (Knoxville: University of Tennessee Press, 1972), pp. 30–32; and Howard Cromwell Taylor, *The Educational Significance of the Early Federal Land Ordinances* (New York: Arno Press and The New York Times, 1969), pp. 30–36.

4. For a detailed discussion of the role Cutler played in negotiating key language, see Taylor, *The Educational Significance of the Early Federal Land Ordinances*, pp. 42–52.

5. Rainsford, *Congress and Higher Education in the Nineteenth Century*, p. 113.

6. Quoted in Eddy, *Colleges for Our Land and Time*, p. 21.

7. Eddy, *Colleges for Our Land and Time*, p. 22.

8. For the full text, see "The Northwest Ordinance," pp. 1–5.

9. For the full text, see Taylor, *The Educational Significance of the Early Federal Land Ordinances*, pp. 133–134.

3

The First Morrill Act

July 2, 1862

The Morrill Act of 1862 was central to the emergence and development of public higher education in the United States. It built and expanded on the significant efforts made in the 1700s. While the Northwest Ordinance and the resulting Ohio land grants for higher education laid the foundation for a system, it was the Morrill Act that provided the framework for building real institutions. The Morrill Act provided grants of federal land to the states, which they could then sell and use the proceeds to fund colleges and universities. The Morrill Act, in the end, was responsible for the establishment or support of more than one hundred such land-grant colleges and universities, including many of the country's leading academic institutions (see Table 1). The course of American higher education was profoundly impacted by this legislation.

The act was the result of years of legislative effort and both political and sectional competition. Legislative games and machinations were needed to avoid hostile committees and get the bill to a vote in Congress. When the act was first passed in 1858, it was successfully vetoed by President James Buchanan, with nearly uniform Southern opposition, due largely to constitutional concerns. It took the election of President Abraham Lincoln and the secession of the Southern states to create a political climate where the Morrill Act could become law. Even after passage, early implementation of the Morrill Act was very difficult and troubled. Its educational potential and significance were not realized until many years after its enactment in 1862. The Morrill Act traveled a very long and difficult road, but its final impact was and is enormous.

Table 1
Land-Grant Colleges and Universities

Alabama
Alabama A&M University
Auburn University
Tuskegee University

Alaska
University of Alaska System

American Samoa
Community College of American Samoa

Arizona
Navajo Community College
University of Arizona

Arkansas
University of Arkansas-Fayetteville
University of Arkansas-Pine Bluff

California
D-Q University
University of California System

Colorado
Colorado State University

Connecticut
Connecticut Agricultural Experimentation Station
University of Connecticut

Delaware
Delaware State University
University of Delaware

District of Columbia
University of the District of Columbia

Florida
Florida A&M University
University of Florida

Georgia
Fort Valley State College
University of Georgia

Guam
University of Guam

Hawaii
University of Hawaii

Idaho
University of Idaho

Illinois
University of Illinois

Indiana
Purdue University

Iowa
Iowa State University

Kansas
Haskell Indian Nations University
Kansas State University

Kentucky
Kentucky State University
University of Kentucky

Louisiana
Louisiana State University System
Southern University System

Maine
University of Maine

Maryland
University of Maryland-College Park
University of Maryland-Eastern Shore

Massachusetts
Massachusetts Institute of Technology
University of Massachusetts

Michigan
Bay Mills Community College
Michigan State University

Micronesia
Community College of Micronesia

Minnesota
Fond Du Lac Community College
Leech Lake Tribal College
University of Minnesota

Table 1 (continued)

Mississippi
Alcorn State University
Mississippi State University

Missouri
Lincoln University
University of Missouri System

Montana
Blackfeet Community College
Dull Knife Community College
Fort Belknap Community College
Fort Peck Community College
Little Big Horn College
Montana State University
Salish Kootenai College
Stone Child College

Nebraska
Nebraska Indian Community College
University of Nebraska System

Nevada
University of Nevada

New Hampshire
University of New Hampshire

New Jersey
Rutgers University

New Mexico
Crownpoint Institute of Technology
Institute of American Indian Arts
New Mexico State University
Southwest Indian Polytechnic Institute

New York
Cornell University

North Carolina
North Carolina A&T State University
North Carolina State University

North Dakota
Fort Berthold Community College
Little Hoop Community College
North Dakota State University
Standing Rock College
Turtle Mountain Community College
United Tribes Technical College

Northern Marianas
Northern Marianas College

Ohio
Ohio State University

Oklahoma
Langston University
Oklahoma State University

Oregon
Oregon State University

Pennsylvania
Pennsylvania State University

Puerto Rico
University of Puerto Rico

Rhode Island
University of Rhode Island

South Carolina
Clemson University
South Carolina State University

South Dakota
Cheyenne River Community College
Oglala Lakota College
Sinte Gleska University
Sisseton Wahpeton Community College
South Dakota State University

Tennessee
Tennessee State University
University of Tennessee

Texas
Prairie View A&M University
Texas A&M University

Utah
Utah State University

Vermont
University of Vermont

Virgin Islands
University of the Virgin Islands

29

Table 1 (continued)

Virginia
Virginia Polytechnic Institute and State
  University
Virginia State University

Washington
Northwest Indian College
Washington State University

West Virginia
West Virginia University

Wisconsin
College of the Menominee Nation
Lac Courte Oreilles Ojibwa Commu-
  nity College
University of Wisconsin-Madison

Wyoming
University of Wyoming

Source: National Association of State Universities and Land-Grant Colleges (NASULGC). The
    Land Grant Tradition: The 105 Land Grant Colleges and Universities at http://
    www.nasulgc.org/publications/Land_Grant/Schools.htm

BACKGROUND

With the Morrill Act, the federal government committed itself to
"providing for the endowment, support and maintenance of colleges of agriculture and mechanic arts."[1] To this end, the act provided to each state 30,000 acres of federal lands for each
representative and senator it had, based on the 1860 census. States
that did not have sufficient federal lands for this within their own
borders received "land scrip," in essence, a voucher to sell federal
lands in other states. Revenue generated from this land grant was
to be used to support and maintain colleges and universities providing instruction in agriculture, mechanical arts, and, given events
of the day, military tactics.

The Morrill Act land grants were far more regulated than those
in the Land Ordinance of 1785 and the Ohio company contracts.
No state then in rebellion, quite naturally, was eligible.[2] There were
limits on how much land scrip could be used to sell land in any
one state. The states were required to cover all costs associated with
managing the lands prior to sale and managing the monies after
the sale. There were limits on how monies could be invested, and
the capital generated could never be spent. Any of the capital spent
or lost needed to be replaced by the state. Monies were intended
for support and maintenance of programs and could not be used
to build or maintain buildings. Up to 10 percent of proceeds could

be used to purchase land on which to locate the colleges. States were required to pass legislation formally accepting the land grant and all of the conditions. Within five years of acceptance, states were required to have established or be supporting at least one college that provided instruction in agriculture, mechanical arts, and military tactics (these colleges could provide classical and other studies as well). Finally, each participating state was required to provide an annual written report regarding progress at the land-grant colleges.

The legislation was sponsored and shepherded by Congressman Justin S. Morrill of Vermont. In a speech made in 1887, he summarized the intended purpose of the act:

> The land grant colleges were founded on the idea that a higher and broader education should be placed in every State within the reach of those whose destiny assigns them to, or who may have the courage to choose industrial vocations where the wealth of nations is produced; where advanced civilization unfolds its comforts, and where a much larger number of the people need wider educational advantages, and impatiently await their possession. . . . It would be a mistake to suppose it was intended that every student should become either a farmer or a mechanic when the design comprehended not only instruction for those who may hold the plow or follow a trade, but such instruction as any person might need—with "the world all before them where to choose"—and without the exclusion of those who might prefer to adhere to the classics.[3]

The motivations for the act—for the federal government actively promoting higher education, particularly as it related to agriculture—were several. Higher education in colonial America was exclusive and elitist. Few citizens had access or opportunity to anything beyond common or primary-level schooling. Further, existing academies, colleges, and universities almost exclusively offered classical education. They did not offer practical education useful for common citizens, or, in Morrill's words, those "needing higher instruction for the world's business, for industrial pursuits and professions of life."[4] They were largely closed, traditional institutions, "fortresses of knowledge, termed such because little of the changing times passed over the drawbridge."[5] In the early 1800s, in other words, institutions of higher education were increasingly out of step with the times.

This was the time of the "Jacksonian revolution," the movement headed by President Andrew Jackson that, at root, was an impulse to open institutions, some measure of egalitarianism, and opportunities for common citizens. Traditional, elitist academies were not easily reconciled with this populist impulse. As early as 1806, President Thomas Jefferson had asked Congress to provide land grants to establish a national university. As Jacksonianism increasingly set the tenor of the times in the first half of the 1800s, there was growing interest in opening educational opportunities beyond the social and economic elite.[6]

Another driving influence was the increasing role of science and technology, generally, and their application to agriculture, in particular. Growing industrialization increasingly put a premium on broad access to technical or mechanical education. The educational system needed to change and adjust to new, evolving economic needs. In particular, there was growing interest in the application and use of science in the agricultural sector. Several European countries had established institutions for the study and research of modern agricultural techniques. There was concern over the lack of progress in American agriculture.[7]

A number of efforts were made, both public and private, to develop schools focused on agricultural development. The first was the Gardine Lyceum, which operated in Maine from 1823 to 1832. The University of Michigan was created in 1837 with an explicit mandate to offer study in farming and agriculture. In 1855, Pennsylvania created the Farmers' High School, later to become Pennsylvania State University. Calls were made to establish a federal department of agriculture and education and to create a national agricultural college. A congressional report in 1858 concluded that U.S. farmers were "notoriously less instructed in those branches of scientific knowledge directly connected with the proper and economic management of their own pursuits than any other class of citizens."[8] In short, there was a growing need and interest in modernizing and professionalizing agricultural research and development, and a growing expectation that the federal government would contribute to this process.[9]

Beyond these concerns, but no less important, there was a political motivation for the Morrill Act as well. Congressman Morrill was a Republican, and he and his party had passed new tariff legislation that protected and aided commercial and industrial interests, sometimes at the expense of farmers. Morrill noted that "all direct encouragement to agriculture has been rigidly withheld,"[10] and he understood that his land-grant legislation would help his party appeal to rural interests and build a winning political coalition. In the words of one commentator, Morrill's "concern for the farmer was a mixture of honest desire and political wisdom."[11]

The legislative enactment of the Morrill Act was difficult; the process revolved around sectional differences, North and South, East and West. Congressman Morrill first introduced land-grant legislation on December 14, 1857. This original bill called for 20,000 acres of public land to be given to the states for each congressional representative and senator, based upon the 1850 census. Morrill, knowing that the House Committee on Public Lands was likely to be hostile to the idea, asked the House leadership to send the bill instead to a "committee of friends." This request was denied, and in April 1858 the Committee on Public Lands made a strong recommendation that the bill be rejected by the full House. The committee argued that the Morrill Act would be an unconstitutional intrusion of the federal government into the affairs and responsibilities of state governments. Further, it argued that the act would irresponsibly squander public lands that should be safeguarded for future generations.

When it appeared that the bill would not be brought to a vote, Morrill creatively employed parliamentary rules to force a floor vote. The bill narrowly passed the House by a 105–100 vote. The vote made the North-South sectional divide clear, with Northern Republicans voting overwhelmingly in favor of the bill, Southern Democrats almost universally against. Southern representatives saw the expanded domestic role of the federal government envisioned by the Morrill Act as an erosion of states' rights generally, with clear implications for the intense slavery-abolition debate.

The bill went to the Senate, where it passed by a close 25–22 vote on February 7, 1859. The Senate vote showed the same North-South sectional divide seen in the House and added a clear East-West divide as well. The eastern states were populous and had little public land. Since the Morrill Act land grants were tied to representation and, hence, population, the eastern states would receive the bulk of the benefits. Since they had little public land themselves, the eastern states would receive scrip to sell land in the western states. The western states clearly saw in this a blatant transfer of wealth from the West to the East and further worried that putting so much land on the market at one time would depress land prices all across the West.

President James Buchanan immediately vetoed the Morrill Act, with his veto message mirroring the concerns of both the South and the West. He argued that the Morrill Act was an unconstitutional federal intrusion into state responsibilities; the federal government had no power to enforce compliance with the regulations on the states; land prices in the West would be severely depressed; and, further, the viability of existing colleges and universities would be threatened. Given the closeness of the votes in both House and Senate, Buchanan's veto could not be overridden, and the bill died.

Morrill reintroduced his legislation on December 16, 1861, increasing the land grant to 30,000 acres per representative and senator, changing the benchmark to the 1860 census, and adding the requirement that the study of military tactics be supported. Abraham Lincoln was president, the Southern states had seceded, and the political landscape was very different. Still, in the House, the Committee on Public Lands again recommended against passage. Morrill was unable to maneuver the bill to the floor as he had in 1858, and the legislation appeared dead. Morrill fought on, though, and convinced Senator Benjamin Wade of Ohio to introduce identical legislation in the Senate. There, it passed 32 to 9, with largely western opposition. Having passed the Senate, it returned to the House, where it could go straight to a floor debate without passing through committee. In this manner, Morrill got the bill to a vote, where it passed easily, given the absence of southern votes, 90 to 25. President Lincoln signed the Morrill Act into law, without comment, on July 2, 1862.

The educational effects of the Morrill Act proved enormous, yet the educational implications received virtually no attention in the legislative debate. The debate in Congress was over the Constitution and states' rights and the sound and proper management of public lands. These were the issues of concern to Congress at the time, but the act's educational impact secured its place in history. With the passage of the Morrill Act, the United States "was the first nation in the world, whether in peace or war, systematically to commit its resources for the support of higher education."[12] The existence and prominent role of land-grant colleges and universities over a century and a quarter after passage is ample evidence of the importance of the Morrill Act to American higher education.

IMPACT

The educational impact of the Morrill Act was not immediately realized. Indeed, the early implementation of the act was troubled and its success very much in doubt. The newly established land-grant colleges were weak institutions—"The best called for apology; the worst [were] . . . appalling."[13] The facts are clear:

> The colleges did not fail in the sense of having to close their doors—indeed, by 1870 all thirty-seven states had founded or had laid the groundwork for establishing a land-grant college. But the colleges did not flourish. Enrollments . . . grew slowly, and student attrition remained high. Professors were asked to endure low salaries, heavy workloads, and primitive facilities. State support was slim, if forthcoming at all.[14]

The land-grant colleges, for a generation at least, were ridiculed for poor facilities, an inadequate number of students, poor-quality students, focusing on secondary and unprestigious fields of study, and as mere "cow colleges."[15] This was a wholly new system of public higher education, and it was not easily born. The land-grant colleges only slowly emerged as serious, reputable, and appealing institutions of learning. These institutions needed to be built and to prove themselves, and, ultimately, they did so beyond expectations.

Land-grant institutions, by definition, are those institutions designated by the states as meeting the requirements of the Morrill Act (and subsequent amendments and expansions) and receive funding under the act. Some of the Morrill Act land-grant colleges were created whole and new by the states for the purpose, but in some cases, state support was extended to existing institutions. The vast majority were public colleges and universities, but several, most notably Cornell University, were private. The basic Morrill Act system has been continually expanded by the federal government through the 1887 Hatch Act supporting agricultural experimentation stations, the Second Morrill Act in 1890 greatly expanding the number of institutions, the 1914 Smith-Lever Act creating cooperative extension services, and the inclusion of the District of Columbia in 1967, remaining U.S. territories in 1971, and tribal colleges in 1994. More than 17 million acres of federal lands have been transferred under the act. There are today 105 land-grant colleges and universities, and the federal government directs more than

$500 million in direct appropriations to further support these institutions each year.

Despite the difficult start, over time the land-grant colleges did in fact prove themselves. In facilities and libraries, faculty and teaching, in areas of both pure and applied research, they became fully competitive with existing institutions.[16] In so doing, they redirected higher education better or more fully to meet changing social and economic times. They significantly raised the curricular standards and educational importance of most technical fields. Finally, and most important, they made higher education accessible to a far broader segment of American society.

On the latter point, the Morrill Act greatly expanded educational opportunity across socioeconomic lines, extending access beyond the social elite. Further, as written, it was neutral with respect to both gender and race. The Morrill Act did not require that states admit women to land-grant colleges, but neither did it prohibit admission. In application, while women did not receive equal opportunities under Morrill, many women unquestionably received greater opportunities. The effects of providing higher education to a broader segment of women were real and diverse. Many of the women afforded these opportunities went on to leadership positions in politics, journalism, and a variety of social movements. The expansion of educational opportunities helped fuel social progress in many areas of American society.

The Morrill Act was similarly neutral with regard to race, but, in practice, provided unequal and segregated institutions. Under the Second Morrill Act (see Law 5, chapter 5), 17 segregated black land-grant colleges were created. While the provision of such institutions fell far short of equal educational opportunity, these few Morrill-related institutions provided at least some access to higher education for African Americans.

Finally, the Morrill Act continued the evolution of federal involvement in education. Most clearly, it expanded and deepened the federal role in higher education first directed in the Northwest Ordinance and the Ohio contracts. Beyond this, however, it established a precedent for the design and implementation of future federal education-related activities. Under the Morrill Act, the federal government provided resources to the states to pursue a public goal, outlined or regulated the basic uses for these resources, and then left the implementation and much of the day-to-day decision-making authority to the states. States could create new institutions or support existing ones, work through public or private colleges, and focus exclusively on agriculture, mechanical arts, and military tactics or include classical studies as well. This type of shared or cooperative federal-state relations would characterize later federal involvement in areas such as primary and secondary education, education for disadvantaged children, and education of special-needs children.

The congressional debate over the Morrill Act barely mentioned its educational purposes and was consumed rather by sectional concerns and advantages. The lasting importance of the act, however, is the crucial role it played in shaping public higher education—scores of new institutions, restructuring curriculum in accord with developing industrialization and mass society, and setting down the road to equal educational opportunity. The Morrill Act created the potential that, over the course of years and decades, the actual work of the land grant colleges and universities largely realized. "Nothing did more *eventually* for mass or democratized education. . . . They were committed, they opened their doors, and they pressed fate with action. Their early contribution was the ardent conviction and the provision of opportunity, the expectation, and the ideal, not the actual achievement. They were ahead of their times. . . . When the ideal did blossom, it did so magnificently."[17] The uniqueness and significance of the Morrill Act are difficult to overstate. As Andrew D. White, cofounder and first president of Cornell University, once remarked about the Morrill Act: "In all the annals of republics, there is no more significant utterance of confidence in national destiny out from the midst of national calamity."[18]

3. The First Morrill Act

An Act Donating Public Lands to the several States and Territories which may provide Colleges for the Benefit of Agriculture and Mechanic Arts[19]

Be it enacted by the Senate and House of Representatives of the United States of America in Congress assembled, That there be granted to the several States, for the purpose hereinafter mentioned, an amount of public land, to be apportioned to each State a quantity equal to thirty thousand acres for each senator and representative in Congress to which the States are respectively entitled by the apportionment under the census of eighteen hundred and sixty; Provided, That no mineral lands shall be selected or purchased under the provisions of the act.

Section 2. And be it further enacted, That the land aforesaid, after being surveyed, shall be apportioned to the several States in sections or subdivisions of sections, not less than one quarter of a section; and wherever there are public lands in a State, subject to sale at private entry at one dollar and twenty-five cents per acre, the quantity to which said State shall be entitled shall be selected from such lands, within the limits of such State; and the Secretary of Interior is hereby directed to issue to each of the States, in which there is not the quantity of public lands subject to sale at private entry, at one dollar and twenty-five cents per acre, to which said State may be entitled under the provisions of this act, land scrip [voucher] to the amount in acres for the deficiency of its distributive share; said scrip to be sold by said States, and the proceeds thereof applied to the uses and purposes prescribed in this act, and for no other purposes whatsoever; Provided . . . That not more than one million acres shall be located by such assignees in any one of the States. . . .

Section 3. And be it further enacted, That all the expenses of management, superintendence, and taxes from date of selection of said lands, previous to their sales, and all expenses incurred in the management and disbursement of moneys which may be received therefrom, shall be paid by the States to which they may belong, out of the treasury of said States, so that the entire proceeds of the sale of said lands shall be applied, without any diminution whatever, to the purposes hereinafter mentioned.

Section 4. That all monies derived from the sales of lands aforesaid by the States to which lands are apportioned . . . shall be invested in bonds of the United States or of the States or some other safe bonds; or the same may be invested by the States having no State bonds in any manner after the legislatures of such States shall have assented thereto and engaged that such funds shall yield a fair and reasonable rate of return, to be fixed by the State legislatures, and that the principal thereof shall forever remain unimpaired; Provided, That the moneys so invested or loaned shall constitute a perpetual fund, the capital of which shall remain forever undiminished (except so far as may be provided in section 5 of this Act), and the interest of which shall be inviolably appropriated, by each State which may take and claim the benefit of this act, to the endowment, support, and maintenance of at least one college where the leading object shall be, without excluding other scientific and classical studies and including military tactics, in such manner as the legislatures of the States may respectively prescribe, in order to promote the liberal and practical education of the industrial classes on the several pursuits and professions in life.

Section 5. And be it further enacted, That the grant of land . . . hereby authorized shall be made on the following conditions, to which, as well as to the provisions hereinbefore contained, the previous assent of the several States shall be signified by legislative acts:

First. If any portion of the fund invested, as provided by the foregoing section, shall, by any action or contingency, be diminished or lost, it shall be replaced by the State to which it belongs, so that the capital of the fund shall remain forever undiminished; . . .

Second. No portion of said fund, nor the interest thereon, shall be applied, directly or indirectly, under any pretense whatever, to the purchase, erection, preservation, or repair of any building or buildings;

Third. Any State which may take and claim the benefit of the provisions of this act shall provide, within five years, at least not less than one college, as prescribed in the fourth section of this act, or the grant to such State shall cease; . . .

Fourth. An annual report shall be made regarding the progress of each college . . .

Sixth. No State, while in a condition of rebellion or insurrection against the Government of the United States, shall be entitled to the benefit of this act;

Seventh. No State shall be entitled to the benefits of this act unless it shall express its acceptance thereof by its legislature within two years from the date of its approval by the President.

Approved July 2, 1862.

NOTES

1. U.S. Department of Health, Education, and Welfare, *Land-Grant Colleges and Universities, 1862–1962* (Washington, DC: U.S. Government Printing Office, 1962), p. 54.

2. Following the Civil War, all of the provisions of the Morrill Act were fully extended to the former Confederate States.

3. U.S. Department of Health, Education, and Welfare, *Land-Grant Colleges and Universities, 1862–1962,* p. 2.

4. Quoted in Edward Danforth Eddy, Jr., *Colleges for Our Land and Time: The Land-Grant Idea in American Education* (New York: Harper and Brothers, 1957), p. 28.

5. Eddy, *Colleges for Our Land and Time,* p. 2.

6. For a discussion of the Jacksonian influence, see Eddy, *Colleges for Our Land and Time,* pp. 1–7.

7. For discussions of these developments, see George N. Rainsford, *Congress and Higher Education in the Nineteenth Century* (Knoxville: University of Tennessee Press, 1972), pp. 72–82; Eddy, *Colleges for Our Land and Time*, pp. 8–20; and U.S. Department of Health, Education, and Welfare, *Land-Grant Colleges and Universities, 1862–1962*, p. 1.

8. Quoted in Rainsford, *Congress and Higher Education in the Nineteenth Century*, p. 79.

9. For discussions of these issues, see Eddy, *Colleges for Our Land and Time*, pp. 12–13; and Rainsford, *Congress and Higher Education in the Nineteenth Century*, pp. 79–80.

10. Quoted in Eddy, *Colleges for Our Land and Time*, p. 30.

11. Eddy, *Colleges for Our Land and Time*, p. 30.

12. Harold M. Hyman, *American Singularity: The 1787 Northwest Ordinance, the 1862 Homestead and Morrill Acts, and the 1944 G.I. Bill* (Athens: University of Georgia Press, 1986), p. 36.

13. Quoted in Hyman, *American Singularity*, p. 54.

14. Roger L. Williams, *The Origins of Federal Support for Higher Education: George W. Atherton and the Land-Grant College Movement* (University Park: Pennsylvania State University Press, 1991), p. 3.

15. For a discussion of these criticisms, see Hyman, *American Singularity*, pp. 53–55.

16. For a discussion of the gradual improvement in land-grant colleges, see Hyman, *American Singularity*, pp. 53–56.

17. Eldon L. Johnson, "Misconceptions about the Early Land Grant Colleges," *Journal of Higher Education* 52 (1981): 391.

18. Quoted in Eddy, *Colleges for Our Land and Time*, p. 45.

19. *The Land-Grant Tradition: Text of Federal Legislation Relating to Land-Grant Colleges and Universities*, National Association of State Universities and Land-Grant Colleges (http://www.nasulgc.org/publications/Land_Grant/LandMorrill.htm).

4

The Freedmen's Bureau

March 3, 1865

The Freedmen's Bureau—officially, the Bureau of Refugees, Freedmen, and Abandoned Lands—was created to manage the wide-ranging problems associated with Civil War refugees and freed slaves. During and after the war, millions of freed men and women suffered severe housing, food, medical, and educational needs. Prior to the creation of the bureau, to the extent that these issues were dealt with, responsibility necessarily fell on the Union Army. The bureau was intended to relieve occupying armies of these duties and deal with the problems in a more concerted and comprehensive fashion. The Freedmen's Bureau existed for only seven years, from 1865 to 1872, and the bulk of its work was completed by 1870. While it undertook actions across a whole spectrum of social problems, much of the bureau's most lasting work was in education. The bureau was responsible for the creation of thousands of primary and secondary schools for blacks and a series of teacher-training schools to train black teachers all across the South.

The creation, continuation, and work of the Freedmen's Bureau were all politically contentious. The creation of the bureau was very strongly opposed by Southern political leaders, who viewed it as a means of Northern control and domination of the South. Subsequent legislation continuing the existence and expanding the mandate of the bureau was the subject of intense presidential-congressional conflict, with repeated vetoes and votes to override these vetoes. The work of the bureau fueled Southern political opposition and was the subject of repeated charges and investigations into corruption and misuse of public funds. The bureau itself was short lived and contentious, but its work, especially in education, had lasting importance.

BACKGROUND

The Emancipation Proclamation in 1863, freeing slaves in the Confederate states, coupled with the usual effects of war, had created a huge social challenge. More than four million freed slaves and refugees were in need, to varying degrees, of housing and food, medical care, land and employment, and training and education. They faced the challenge of building new lives, starting with little or nothing, in a largely hostile environment after generations of enslavement. Occupying Union armies struggled to deal with refugees who fled toward military encampments, and private aid societies petitioned the federal government for a more sustained and coherent response to the situation.[1] The case for federal action was made on the House floor, with the tone demonstrating both the humanitarian and paternalistic impulses of the day:

> We have four million people in poverty because our laws have denied them the right to acquire property; in ignorance because our laws have made it a felony to instruct them; without organized habits because war has broken the shackles which bound them. . . . We are to organize them into society; we are to guide them, as the guardian guides his wards, for a brief period, until they can acquire habits and become confident and capable of self-control; we are to watch over them, and, if we do, we have, from their conduct in the field and in the school, evidence that they will more than repay our labor. . . . If we do not, we will doom them to vagrancy and pauperism.[2]

This was the sense and sentiment behind the proposition to create the Freedmen's Bureau. The intent was to create a temporary agency to address the wide-ranging social problems confronting freed slaves all across the Southern states.

Legislation was first proposed by Congressman T. D. Eliot (R-MA) in early 1863. The bill died, however, for lack of action, and he introduced a new bill to create, in this permutation, a bureau of emancipation in the next session of Congress. The bill was intensely debated. Eliot and other supporters argued that such an agency was needed to deal with the existing human problems, to protect the safety and new freedom of the refugees, and successfully to integrate freed slaves into society. Opponents, largely Democrats, argued that the bureau was not needed, exceeded the federal government's limited constitutional powers, discriminated against needy poor white Southerners, would promote patronage and corruption, and would result in a new form of servitude for blacks under federal masters.

Given this contentiousness, the House vote was very close, with the bill passing 69 to 67. In the Senate, debate followed similar lines, although with the addition of a bureaucratic fight that ultimately delayed creation of the Freedmen's Bureau by a year. The issue was which federal department should house the new bureau, with arguments made for the army, the Treasury Department, the Justice Department, and a wholly new department patterned after the Bureau of Indian Affairs. This debate had a significant impact. The House bill had granted administrative responsibility to the War Department. In the Senate, the bill was amended to move the bureau to the Treasury Department. The House then refused to concur with the change, and so, despite majority support for the creation of the Freedmen's Bureau in both chambers, action had to be postponed to the next session of Congress.

In the next session, it took several House-Senate conference committees to work out a successful compromise bill, with the final version returning control to the War Department. During debate, the hostility of the opposition—which would only build among Democrats and Southerners and fuel corruption charges in later years—was clearly evident. Senator Lazarus Powell (D-KY), for instance, one of the leading opponents, argued that "the men who are to go down there and become overseers and negro-drivers will be your broken-down politicians and your dilapidated preachers; that description of men who are too lazy to work and just a little too honest to steal. That is the kind of crew you propose to fasten on these poor negroes."[3] Despite the intensity of the opposition, however, the bill passed both the Senate and the House on March 3, 1865. President Abraham Lincoln signed it into law on the same day; it was one of his last official acts before he was assassinated.

Operating within the War Department, the new Freedmen's Bureau was authorized "to continue during the present war of rebellion, and for one year thereafter."[4] While it was given this short tenure, it was granted a very broad mandate: "the supervision and management of all abandoned lands, and the control of all subjects relating to refugees and freedmen from rebel states."[5] The commissioner of the bureau was given nearly total control over huge tracts of land and property and the lives of more than four million freed men and women. The commissioner could exercise legislative, executive, and judicial authority over nearly all issues pertaining to the lives and conditions of ex-slaves.

The first and only commissioner of the Freedmen's Bureau was General Oliver O. Howard, who was detached from the command of General William Sherman to assume the position. Upon Howard's appointment, Sherman wrote, "I can not imagine that matters that involve the fate of 4,000,000 souls could be put in more charitable hands."[6] From Maine, and a graduate of both Bowdoin College and West Point, Howard was only 34 at the time of his appointment. A colonel at the start of the Civil War, he rose quickly to the rank of general—he fought at the first battle of Bull Run, lost an arm in the Battle of Fair Oaks, and commanded Sherman's right wing in the "March to the Sea." General Howard provided strong, forward-looking leadership to the bureau in the face of tremendous adversity and hostile opposition.

Howard quickly organized the bureau into ten districts, each with an assistant commissioner, all military officers. Headquartered in Washington, D.C., the central office was organized into four divisions: Records, Land, Finance, and Medical. The original legislation creating the bureau made no explicit mention of schools or education for freedmen, but Howard had every intention of moving in that direction. Thus the Records Division was given administrative responsibility over school issues.[7]

Howard made his intentions regarding education known within the bureau almost immediately. In a circular distributed just 16 days after the creation of the bureau, he wrote: "The education and the moral conditions of the people will not be forgotten and the utmost facility will be offered to benevolent and religious organizations and state authorities in the maintenance of good schools for refugees and freedmen until a system of free schools can be supported by the reorganized local governments. It is not my purpose to supersede the benevolent agencies already employed in the work of education but to sympathize with and facilitate them."[8] Many Northern religious aid societies had formed during the Civil War and were active in creating schools and supporting teachers for freedmen. With or without explicit legislative authority, Howard intended to assist these efforts, and, in the end, he dedicated substantial public resources to "facilitate" their work.

Howard almost immediately confronted a debate over the proper life span of the bureau as well. The legislation called for the Freedmen's Bureau to terminate one year after the end of the war. It was unclear, however, when the war was officially over. For some, it was over with the surrender of Southern armies; for others, it required the lifting of martial law and reinstatement of the writ of habeus corpus; for others, it required an affirmative declaration from Congress and the president.[9] New legislation was requested by Howard and introduced in Congress to expand the bureau's mandate over education and both clarify and extend its life. This step initiated intense congressional-presidential conflict. In all, Congress passed four bills; President Andrew Johnson (who succeeded the slain Lincoln) vetoed all four, but Congress successfully overrode three of the vetoes.

The first piece of legislation was introduced in early 1866 and responded to Howard's requests by extending the life of the bureau indefinitely and directing the bureau to provide for the education of the freedmen. The bill was easily passed by Congress, but, in a surprise move, was vetoed by President Johnson, who argued that the bill was unnecessary because the bureau was still authorized to operate for some time, it was a war measure at a time when the country was rapidly returning to peace, and portions of the bill were unconstitutional. Congress attempted to override the veto, but could not.

A second bill was then introduced in May 1866, addressing the same basic issues. It quickly passed Congress and was again vetoed. This time, however, the veto was overridden, and the bill became law. Under it, the Freedmen's Bureau was given an explicit mandate over education, and its life was extended roughly two years, to July 1868.

The following year, in 1867, General Howard recommended to Congress that the Bureau's aid activities in fact terminate in 1868, but that the educational work should continue. He recommended that authority for education programs be transferred to the Department of Education and ownership of school buildings and property be transferred to the private aid societies. Congress responded by passing legislation extending the life of the bureau an additional year, to July 1869. This too was vetoed by Johnson and became law only through a congressional override.

Finally, Congress overrode a third presidential veto in 1868 on a bill that authorized the continuation of the bureau's education work until Congress ordered its termination. This it did in early

1872, setting the final day of the Freedmen's Bureau as June 30 of that year. Thus the bureau existed through seven extremely tumultuous years. It was created amid conflict, was repeatedly amended, and was the focus of an intense struggle between the legislative and executive branches of government. Amid this environment, it undertook the massive effort to house, care for, and educate the millions of refugees and freed men and women all across the South.

IMPACT

The Freedmen's Bureau did a great deal of work in a short period of time. Its work spanned the full range of social services needed by refugees and freed people. The most lasting work of the bureau, however, was clearly in education. Two main areas of educational impact can be identified. First, the bureau was responsible for the creation or promotion of literally thousands of common or primary-level schools—day schools, night schools, technical schools for women, and Sunday schools—for African Americans of all ages. Second, the bureau was responsible for the creation or promotion of normal schools to train African American teachers all across the South.

The most immediate educational need was clearly for common schools. The intention of the bureau was to promote and build upon the work already begun by the private aid societies. The latter had created many schools and could recruit Northern teachers, but were hampered by limited contributions and a pressing need for land and buildings to house schools. The Freedmen's Bureau had access to many buildings that had been confiscated for military purposes but that the army no longer needed. Early on, it made these buildings available anywhere there was interest and a teacher could be found to form a school. Later, as many of these buildings were returned to their previous owners, the bureau took a different approach to school promotion.

The bureau was prohibited from constructing buildings, but it could rent or lease buildings, and it could pay to repair buildings. It was also prohibited from paying salaries for teachers. Howard and his staff found creative ways—that is, ways that were technically legal, even if they violated the spirit of the law—to work around restrictions on the bureau and continue to promote the development of new common schools. Examples of this creativity included encouraging benevolent societies to buy inexpensive buildings and using bureau funds to repair them; working with the societies to start new construction, with the bureau completing construction under the banner of "repairs"; and transferring ownership of buildings to the societies and then leasing them back at a rate sufficient to allow teachers to be paid their salaries.[10] The Freedmen's Bureau had an enormous and important task to complete, and under Howard's leadership it found ways—legal ways—to act and to get the job done.

In the end, the bureau spent more than five million dollars on the schools, money that leveraged and expanded on the work and resources of the private aid societies. Together, the bureau and the societies created a system of schools to serve freed men and women across the South, affecting thousands of communities. By the end of the bureau's tenure, "there were under its direction 2,677 day and night schools with 3,300 teachers and 149,581 pupils; 1,562 Sabbath schools with 6,007 teachers and 97,752 pupils, or a grand total of 4,239 schools, 9,307 teachers, and 247,333 pupils."[11] This was a huge accomplishment for such a short time, but its impact was tempered by the fact that even with this effort, when the bureau was closed, only about 10 percent of freed men and women of school age were actually attending school.[12] Beyond this, many of the teachers in these schools had little training and were of limited quality, reducing the effectiveness of the schools. Still, the Freedmen's Bureau undertook a massive job under extraordinary circumstances and succeeded in offering common schooling to hundreds of thousands of freed persons.

In creating the common schools, it quickly became apparent that there was a multifaceted teacher problem that also needed to be addressed. First, there was a general shortage of teachers to staff all of the new schools envisioned. Second, the aid societies were bringing Northerners south to teach, and this generated considerable political backlash and local resentment. There were many instances of intimidation, harassment, ostracism, and sometimes violence against Northern teachers.[13] In part, this was due to the obvious resentments of the lost war. Beyond this, however, was a concern on the part of many Southerners that Northern teachers would teach blacks social and political ideas they opposed or feared:

On February 10, 1867, *Flake's Bulletin* voiced the widespread white southern suspicion of northern teachers and suggested what might be done: ". . . besides teaching the freedman to says his abc's, these teachers from abroad put foolish notions in his head, and destroy the usefulness of his labor, . . . [and] perhaps inculcate notions not exactly in accordance with our social customs, and with the necessities of our situation."[14]

At the very least, Northern teachers might have been a vehicle for socializing freedmen to Republican politics and voting patterns.

To deal with the teacher shortage and the hostility, the Freedmen's Bureau determined that it needed to promote the development of black normal schools. These schools could train generations of Southern black teachers to staff new black schools. The bureau provided assistance to existing institutions and encouraged private groups to found new normal schools to which it would provide financial aid. About two dozen normal schools received substantial assistance.[15] Many of these institutions are extremely prominent today—Hampton University, Howard University,[16] Morehouse College, and Fisk University, for instance—demonstrating the effectiveness and meaningfulness of the bureau's role.

It should be noted that throughout the tenure of the Freedmen's Bureau, it generated intense hostility and opposition, which only grew with its effectiveness. There were repeated charges of corruption, misuse of authority, and malfeasance. President Johnson initiated an investigation. The House of Representatives completed an investigation after charges were filed by Congressman Fernando Wood (D-NY) in 1870. Finally, General William Sherman presided over a military court of inquiry. While some minor accounting problems were found, none of these investigations concluded that there were any serious or systemic problems in the administration of the bureau.[17]

The Freedmen's Bureau was created to deal with massive problems under extraordinarily difficult circumstances—having to build its administrative structure whole, serve the needs of more than four million persons, operate in a war and immediate postwar environment, function in a region where the majority population was hostile to it and its mission, and operate as an executive agency when the president opposed its existence. These are circumstances where failure would be likely, and yet the Freedmen's Bureau succeeded, in education above all else. An evaluation of the bureau's efforts in education, written in the 1860s, is just as cogent today: "The great work performed by the Bureau, is that of education.

Though this work is usually credited to the Benevolent Societies, yet the Bureau has been the foundation of it all, and all these Societies would long since have been compelled to close, or to carry on very small undertakings, if they had been deprived of the aid of the Bureau."[18] In pursuing and legitimizing the idea of African American schools, by creating thousands of actual schools, and by creating key African American colleges and universities, the Freedmen's Bureau in its few years of existence had a lasting educational effect.

4. The Freedmen's Bureau

An Act to establish a Bureau for the Relief of Freedmen and Refugees[19]

Be it enacted by the Senate and House of Representatives of the United States of America in Congress assembled, That there is hereby established in the War Department, to continue during the present war of rebellion, and for one year thereafter, a bureau of refugees, freedmen, and abandoned lands, to which shall be committed, as hereinafter provided, the supervision and management of all abandoned lands, and the control of all subjects relating to refugees and freedmen from rebel states, or from any district or county within the territory embraced in the operations of the army, under such rules and regulations as may be prescribed by the head of the bureau and approved by the President. The said bureau shall be under the management and control of a commissioner to be appointed by the President, by and with the advice and consent of the Senate, whose compensation shall be three thousand dollars per annum, and such number of clerks as may be assigned to him by the Secretary of War, not exceeding one chief clerk, two of the fourth class, two of the third class, and five of the first class. And the commissioner and all persons appointed under this act, shall, before entering upon their duties, take the oath of office prescribed. . . .

Section 2. And be it further enacted, That the Secretary of War may direct such issues of provisions, clothing, and fuel, as he may deem needful for the immediate and temporary shelter and supply of destitute and suffering refugees and freedmen and their wives and children, under such rules and regulations as he may direct.

Section 3. And be it further enacted, that the President may, by and with the advice and consent of the Senate, appoint an assistant commissioner for each of the states declared to be in insurrection, not exceeding ten in number, who shall, under the direction of the commissioner, aid in the execution of the provisions of this act. . . . Each of said commissioners shall receive an annual salary of two thousand five hundred dollars in full compensation for all his services. And any military officer may be detailed and assigned to duty under this act without increase of pay or allowances. The commissioner shall, before the commencement of each regular session of congress, make full report of his proceedings with exhibits of the state of his accounts to the President, who shall communicate the same to congress, and shall also make special reports whenever required to do so by the President or either house of congress; and the assistant commissioners shall make quarterly reports of their proceedings to the commissioner, and also such other special reports as from time to time may be required.

Section 4. And be it further enacted, That the commissioner, under the direction of the President, shall have authority to set apart, for the use of loyal refugees and freedmen, such tracts of land within the insurrectionary states as shall have been abandoned, or to which the United States shall have acquired title by confiscation or sale, or otherwise, and to every male citizen, whether refugee or freedman, as aforesaid, there shall be assigned not more than forty acres of such land, and the person to whom it was so assigned shall be protected in the use and enjoyment of the land for the term of three years at an annual rent not exceeding six per centum upon the value of such land. . . . At the end of such term, or at any time during said term, the occupants of any parcels so assigned may purchase the land and receive such title thereto as the United States can convey, upon paying therefor the value of the land. . . .

Section 5. And be it further enacted, That all acts and parts of acts inconsistent with the provisions of this act, are hereby repealed.

Approved, March 3, 1865.

NOTES

1. For a discussion of the refugee problems and the lobbying efforts of private aid societies, see Paul Skeels Peirce, *The Freedmen's Bureau: A Chapter in the History of Reconstruction* (New York: Haskell House, 1971), pp. 25–32; and Dwight Oliver Wendell Holmes, *The Evolution of the Negro College* (New York: AMS Press, 1970), pp. 31–32.

2. Congressman William D. Kelley (R-PA) quoted in Holmes, *The Evolution of the Negro College*, pp. 31–32.

3. Quoted in Peirce, *The Freedmen's Bureau*, p. 43.

4. Freedmen and Southern Society Project, "The Freedmen's Bureau Act,

March 3, 1865" (University of Maryland: http://www.inform.umd.edu/ARHU/ Depts/History/Freedman/fbact.htm, 2000).

5. Freedmen and Southern Society Project, "The Freedmen's Bureau Act, March 3, 1865," p. 1.

6. Quoted in Holmes, *The Evolution of the Negro College*, p. 35.

7. For discussions of the organizational structure and responsibilities within the Freedmen's Bureau, see Holmes, *The Evolution of the Negro College*, pp. 35–39; and Peirce, *The Freedmen's Bureau*, pp. 46–54.

8. Quoted in Holmes, *The Evolution of the Negro College*, p. 39.

9. Peirce, *The Freedmen's Bureau*, p. 55.

10. For a discussion of bureau actions, see George R. Bentley, *A History of the Freedmen's Bureau* (Philadelphia: University of Pennsylvania Press, 1955), pp. 172–174.

11. Peirce, *The Freedmen's Bureau*, pp. 82–83.

12. Peirce, *The Freedmen's Bureau*, p. 83.

13. See, for instance, Ward M. McAfee, *Religion, Race, and Reconstruction: The Public School in the Politics of the 1870s* (Albany: State University of New York Press, 1998), pp. 13–17.

14. Bentley, *A History of the Freedmen's Bureau*, p. 181.

15. For discussions of the normal schools, see Horace Mann Bond, *The Education of the Negro in the American Social Order* (New York: Prentice-Hall, 1934), pp. 30–32; and Bentley, *A History of the Freedmen's Bureau*, pp. 175–178.

16. Founded in 1867 as Howard Theological Society and later named the Howard Normal and Theological Institute for the Education of Teachers and Preachers and, finally, Howard University, the school is named in honor of General Oliver Otis Howard for all he did for education in leading the Freedmen's Bureau from 1865 to 1872.

17. For a discussion of the charges and investigations, see Holmes, *The Evolution of the Negro College*, pp. 48–49.

18. Bentley, *A History of the Freedmen's Bureau*, p. 231.

19. For a complete copy of the text, see Freedmen and Southern Society Project, "The Freedmen's Bureau Act, March 3, 1865," pp. 1–2.

5

The Second Morrill Act

August 30, 1890

The Second Morrill Act expanded significantly on the work begun by Justin Morrill in 1862 (see the First Morrill Act, July 2, 1862, Law 3, chapter 3).[1] It led to the creation of many new institutions, the most important of which were black land-grant colleges in the South. Historian Edward Danforth Eddy, Jr., writing in the 1950s, concluded that the act "accomplished for the Negroes of the South what the first act in 1862 had accomplished for the men and women of other races."[2] While this may overstate the case, the act certainly broadened opportunities for higher education in America. Beyond this, the act provided further support for existing land-grant colleges and thereby helped to stabilize their difficult financial condition. Finally, the act expanded and deepened federal oversight of state administration of the land-grant colleges. The Second Morrill Act thus successfully addressed many of the weaknesses and shortcomings of the First Morrill Act. In so doing, it greatly helped secure the full development of public higher education in the United States.

The act was not easily achieved. Morrill first introduced legislation to expand aid to the land-grant colleges in 1872, by which time he had moved from the House of Representatives to the U.S. Senate. His legislative efforts, however, were defeated year after year. In all, Senator Morrill proposed legislation in 12 of the 18 years from 1872 to final success in 1890. As with the First Morrill Act, he confronted forceful opposition, made on both constitutional and practical grounds. It took persistence, patience, and some considerable political skill on the part of Morrill to see the proposal through to enactment.[3]

BACKGROUND

The purpose of the Second Morrill Act was to provide for "the more complete endowment and support of the colleges for the benefit of agriculture and the mechanic arts."[4] With monies generated through the sale of additional public land, the act appropriated an endowment of $15,000 for each state that agreed to the terms of the original 1862 act. This would be an annual payment and would increase by $1,000 per year to a maximum of $25,000. Thus, while the First Morrill Act provided for a one-time transfer of resources from the federal government to state governments, the Second Morrill Act provided for ongoing, annual support.

The funding provided under the act could only be used for "instruction in agriculture, the mechanic arts, the English language and the various branches of mathematical, physical, natural, and economic sciences, with special reference to their applications in the industries of life."[5] While this language was in keeping with the basic thrust of the 1862 act, it was added to the bill in an effort to limit and narrow the discretion of the states and colleges. In operation, it was later interpreted by the land-grant institutions as a broader mandate, allowing them room to transform over time from fairly narrow agricultural colleges to broad, general universities.

Like the 1862 legislation, the Second Morrill Act prohibited expenditures for the construction or maintenance of any buildings. Federal monies were intended to support programming, teaching, and research activities. The individual states were expected to provide for and support the physical plant. With the commitment of the federal government to annual payments in 1890, the willingness of the states to appropriate their own funds for the colleges increased significantly.

Most important, the Second Morrill Act provided "that no money shall be paid out . . . to any State or Territory for the support and maintenance of a college where a distinction of race or color is made in the admission of students."[6] African Americans could not be excluded from the benefits of the act; states that prohibited admission of blacks to existing land-grant colleges were required either to allow admission or to create a separate black institution. By 1890, the Southern states that had been excluded from the original act had been brought into the system and had created land-grant colleges, and this provision regarding race was mainly aimed at them.

The provision was at once both forward-looking and troubling. In purposefully including African Americans, the Second Morrill Act was undoubtedly progressive for its day—under the act, black institutions could be funded at the secondary as well as post-secondary level. At the same time, however, it represents one of the few cases where the "separate-but-equal" doctrine was explicitly endorsed in federal law:

> The establishment and maintenance of such colleges separately for white and colored students shall be held to be a compliance with the provisions of this act if the funds received in such State or Territory be equitably divided as hereinafter set forth: Provided, that . . . the legislature of such a State may propose and report to the Secretary of Interior a just and equitable division of the fund to be received under this act between one college for white students and one institution for colored students established as aforesaid, which shall be divided into two parts and paid accordingly.[7]

Despite the odious nature of the separate-but-equal language and the fact that the funds were never actually divided equitably by the states, the 1890 act was nevertheless directly responsible for the creation of 17 black land-grant colleges. These institutions have contributed and continue to contribute significantly to educational opportunity in America.

Finally, the Second Morrill Act provided for heightened federal oversight of state activities. The land-grant colleges were required to submit annual, detailed reports on their activities and finances to both the U.S. Department of Agriculture and the U.S. Department of Interior. If the Interior determined that a state had failed to comply with the requirements of either Morrill Act, it could decertify the state and thereby cut off annual payments. President James Buchanan, in vetoing the First Morrill Act, had argued that the federal government lacked the constitutional authority to follow funds into the states and regulate what they did with the monies. The Second Morrill Act, however, provided for a regulatory regime far beyond the one that had concerned Buchanan, and it set the precedent for subsequent federal educational grant programs.

Again, the road to passage for the legislation was long and hard.

It also took a politically circuitous route. Morrill's first legislative effort in 1872 passed in the U.S. Senate, but failed in the House. At the same time, Congressman George Hoar of Massachusetts was pushing legislation to provide federal financial aid to common schools, that is, primary and secondary education. His bill passed in the House in 1872, but failed in the Senate. Morrill concluded from this that he needed to build a political coalition with those in Congress seeking common-school aid. In 1873 and subsequent years, therefore, his legislative proposals included the additional aid he wanted for the land-grant colleges and aid to common schools. He hoped to entice House support due to members' desire for the common-school aid and Senate support due to members' desire for the college aid.

Throughout the years of legislative struggle that followed, Morrill continuously tinkered with his proposal, trying to find a politically winning formula. In some years, the common-school aid was discussed first and prominently; in other years, the college aid came first. Different amounts and sources of revenue were proposed. Despite the coalition building and all of these efforts, however, Morrill's bills were defeated again and again.

Morrill's original 1890 proposal appeared headed for the same fate. As with all the proposals from 1873 on, it included aid to common schools. Senator Henry Blair of New Hampshire, however, a strong common-school proponent and chair of the Committee on Education and Labor, convinced Morrill that this political strategy was wrong. Rather than building a coalition in the House and Senate, linkage of common-school and college aid was only ensuring the defeat of both. Morrill therefore submitted a substitute bill in April 1890, omitting all references to common schools.[8] Blair's advice proved sound; Morrill's substitute bill was quickly recommended by Blair's committee and passed the whole Senate easily.

The bill encountered more opposition when it moved to the House. While the opposition was not nearly as broad or vehement as in the debate over the original Morrill Act, some still viewed the whole land-grant enterprise as constitutionally suspect. The primary opposition, however, was rooted in a criticism of the actual workings of the colleges. Farm interest groups and their allies in the House felt that the land-grant colleges did little to help agriculture, their intended purpose. Rather, they felt that the colleges emphasized, and funds were diverted toward, more traditional fields of study. One unidentified congressman, for instance, argued that

"the trouble is that in some of the States there is very little difference between an agricultural college and a literary college."[9] Farm
interests saw no purpose in expanding a system they felt provided
them little practical benefit.

This opposition was overcome in two ways. First, the House
amended the bill to limit funding to support, as quoted earlier,
certain fields related to agricultural and mechanical arts. Again, this
language was later interpreted by the colleges very broadly, but its
inclusion successfully tamped down farm-group opposition. Second,
unlike in 1862, dozens of land-grant colleges actually existed in
1890 to lobby their congressional delegations on behalf of the bill.
Once it passed the Senate, the presidents of the colleges organized
and lobbied very hard for final passage. The extent of this lobbying
effort was described on the House floor:

> I tell you, Mr. Speaker, that the only lobby I have seen at this session of
> Congress was the education lobby, composed of the presidents of the
> agricultural institutions. They have haunted the corridors of the Cap-
> itol; they have stood sentinel at the door of the Committee on educa-
> tion; they have even interrupted the solemn deliberations of that body
> by imprudent and impudent communications. . . . My God, if there is
> any eagerness in the world it is possessed by these gentlemen.[10]

With this very strong political support and the compromise language on the uses of the funds, the Second Morrill Act passed the
House and became law on August 30, 1890. After 18 years of legislative effort and varying permutations of language, it was passed
as originally envisioned—a straight endowment package for the
land-grant colleges.

IMPACT

The areas of impact of the Second Morrill Act mirror those areas,
discussed earlier, in which it differed from the 1862 legislation. The
act thus impacted four areas: the amount and form of federal assistance to the colleges, the amount of state assistance to the colleges, expanding some opportunity to African Americans in higher
education, and establishing a new level of federal regulation in
grant programs to the states.

The most obvious impact, and the central purpose as envisioned
by Morrill, was to provide a recurring source of financial assistance

for the colleges. The Second Morrill Act provided annual payments, guaranteeing the colleges at least a minimum yearly cash flow, and payments that far exceeded federal support from the first act. "The first is estimated to have produced $8.5 million by 1887, which, invested at 7 percent, would have realized $600,000 annually. In the first year the second act provided $570,000 and by 1900 over $1 million annually."[11] The land-grant colleges had encountered many problems in their early years, especially in attracting students and a faculty of both an adequate number and high quality. The infusion of federal resources after 1890 allowed the colleges to address these issues. As they did so, the colleges began to come into their own as institutions of higher learning—"contemporary official reports and college histories alike emphasize the [1890] act as the turning point for that particular institution."[12]

Contributing to this was the fact that the new federal aid promoted significant new aid from the states to the colleges as well. With the act, the colleges looked more stable and long-lasting. States gradually ceased to view them as federal institutions and more and more as "their" colleges. As a result, state support increased very rapidly. In 1889–1890, the states provided $506,254 to the colleges; by 1899–1900, state assistance reached nearly $1 million.[13] The combined effect of new federal and growing state aid secured the financial condition of the colleges and helped them move from the margin to the center of higher education.

Socially, the act took a step in the direction of equality with its provisions regarding institutions for African Americans. As noted, however, the accomplishment was severely tempered by the fact that it promoted separate racial institutions. The clearest effect was on the establishment and state recognition of black land-grant colleges, with five states designating existing state institutions as black land-grant colleges, six designating private institutions, and six states creating wholly new black public colleges or universities. These institutions were separate and, most assuredly, unequal. Despite the language in the act, the black colleges never received a just or equitable share of federal revenue.[14] Moreover, the increased level of state support generated for the land-grant colleges was overwhelmingly directed to white institutions. The result, well into the 20th century, was black colleges that were grossly underfunded and with poor facilities. The impact of the Second Morrill Act for African Americans was thus mixed. The creation of institutions, some federal aid, and expansion of educational opportunity for some citizens were steps forward, but, as historian Roger

Williams has noted, "they could hardly do for their race what civil disobedience, freedom marches, federal troops, and civil rights legislation would begin to do seventy years later."[15]

Finally, as referenced earlier, the Second Morrill Act began to reshape federal regulation of grants to the states. The land grants provided or implied by the Land Ordinance of 1785 and the Northwest Ordinance left the individual states with very broad discretion over how to use transferred funds. The First Morrill Act was more specific, but still left the states very broad latitude. The Second Morrill Act, however, embodied far more restrictions and held the states accountable for meeting the regulations. Indeed, the act was the first federal grant program, in education or any policy area, with a withholding provision.[16] If states failed to follow federal grant regulations, future monies would be withheld and frozen. Given this new level of federal regulation and state accountability, one historian has said that the act "resembles more a twentieth- than a nineteenth-century piece of federal legislation, and it serves well to illustrate changes in attitude and governmental practice between these two centuries."[17] This new federal-state relationship presaged the pattern evident in all contemporary federal grant programs in education.

While the 1890 legislation was intended as a mere expansion of the original Morrill Act, its scope and impact allow it to stand on its own. The 1862 act took the bold step of creating the land-grant colleges, but they struggled to survive for a generation. The Second Morrill Act not only ensured their survival, it expanded their reach and allowed them to thrive. The changes brought by the act helped propel the struggling agricultural colleges to their later status as large, successful public universities and, in the case of many of the institutions, universities with world-class reputations.

5. The Second Morrill Act

An act to apply a portion of the proceeds of the public lands to the more complete endowment and support of the colleges for the benefit of agriculture and the mechanic arts established under the provisions of an act of Congress approved July second, eighteen hundred and sixty-two.[18]

Be it enacted by the Senate and House of Representatives of the United States of America in Congress assembled, That there shall be and hereby is, annually appropriated [spent or financed], out of any money in the Treasury not otherwise appropriated, arising from the sales of public lands; to be paid as hereinafter provided to each State and territory for the more complete endowment and maintenance of colleges for the benefit of agriculture and mechanic arts now established or which may be hereafter established, in accordance with an act of Congress approved July second, eighteen hundred and sixty-two, the sum of fifteen thousand dollars . . . and an annual increase of the amount of such appropriation thereafter for ten years by an additional sum of one thousand dollars over the preceding year, and the annual amount to be paid thereafter to each State and Territory shall be twenty-five thousand dollars to be applied only to instruction in agriculture, the mechanic arts, the English language and the various branches of mathematical, physical, natural, and economic science, with special reference to their applications in the industries of life, and to the facilities for such instruction: Provided, That no money shall be paid out under this act to any State and Territory for the support and maintenance of a college where a distinction of race or color is made in the admission of students, but the establishment and maintenance of such colleges separately for white and colored students shall be held to be a compliance with the provisions of this act if the funds received in such State or territory be equitably divided as hereinafter set forth: Provided, That in any State in which there has been one college established in pursuance of [adherence with] the act of July second, eighteen hundred and sixty-two, and also in which an educational institution of like character has been established, or may be hereafter established, and is now aided by such State from its own revenue for the education of colored students in agriculture and the mechanic arts, however named or styled, or whether or not it has received money heretofore under the act to which this act is an amendment, the legislature of such a State may propose and report to the Secretary of Interior a just and equitable division of the fund to be received under this act between one college for white students and one institution for colored students established as aforesaid, which shall be divided into two parts and paid accordingly, and thereupon such institution for colored students shall be entitled to the benefits of this act and subject to its provisions, as much as it would have been if it had been included under the act of eighteen hundred and sixty-two, and the fulfillment of the foregoing provisions shall be taken as a compliance with the provisions in reference to separate colleges for white and colored students. . . .

Section 3. That if any portion of the moneys received by the designated officer of the State or Territory for the further and more complete endowment, support, and maintenance of colleges, or of institutions for colored students, as provided in this act, shall, by any action or contingency, be diminished or lost, or be misapplied, it shall be replaced by the State or Territory to which it belongs, and until so replaced no subsequent appropriation shall be apportioned or paid to such State or Territory; and no portion of said moneys shall be applied, directly or indirectly, under any pretence whatever, to the purchase, erection, preservation, or repair of any building or buildings. An annual report by the president of each of said colleges shall be made to the Secretary of Agriculture, as well as the Secretary of Interior, regarding the condition and progress of each college, including statistical information in relation to its receipts and expenditures, its library, the number of its students and professors, and also to any improvements and experiments made under the direction of any experiment stations attached to said colleges, with their costs and results, and such other industrial and economical statistics as may be regarded as useful. . . .

Section 4. That on or before the first day of July in each year, after the passage of this act, the Secretary of the Interior shall ascertain and certify to the Secretary of the Treasury as to each State and Territory whether it is entitled to receive its share of the annual appropriations for colleges, or of institutions for colored students, under this act, and the amount which thereupon each is entitled, respectively, to receive. If the Secretary of the Interior shall withhold a certificate from any State or Territory of its appropriation, the facts and reasons therefor shall be reported to the President, and the amount involved shall be kept separate in the Treasury until the close of the next Congress, in order that the State or Territory may, if it should so desire, appeal to Congress from the determination of the Secretary of the Interior. . . .

Section 5. That the Secretary of the Interior shall annually report to Congress the disbursements which have been made in all the States and territories, and also whether the appropriation of any State or territory has been withheld, and if so, the reasons therefor.

Section 6. Congress may at any time amend, suspend, or repeal any or all of the provisions of this act.

Approved, August 30, 1890.

NOTES

1. The act is sometimes referred to by different names—the Second Morrill Act, as used here, as well as the Morrill Act of 1890 and the Morrill-McComas Act.

2. Edward Danforth Eddy, Jr., *Colleges for Our Land and Time: The Land-Grant Idea in American Education* (New York: Harper and Brothers, 1957), p. 258.

3. See, for instance, the discussion in William B. Parker, *The Life and Public Services of Justin Smith Morrill* (New York: Da Capo Press, 1971), pp. 272–273.

4. U.S. Department of Health, Education, and Welfare, *Land-Grant Colleges and Universities, 1862–1962* (Washington, DC: U.S. Government Printing Office, 1962), p. 59.

5. Ibid.

6. Ibid.

7. Ibid.

8. George N. Rainsford, *Congress and Higher Education in the Nineteenth Century* (Knoxville: University of Tennessee Press, 1972), pp. 107–108.

9. Quoted in Eddy, *Colleges for Our Land and Time*, p. 101.

10. Quoted in Roger L. Williams, *The Origins of Federal Support for Higher Education: George W. Atherton and the Land-Grant College Movement* (University Park: Pennsylvania State University Press, 1991), p. 141.

11. Rainsford, *Congress and Higher Education in the Nineteenth Century*, p. 113.

12. Earle D. Ross, *Democracy's College: The Land-Grant Movement in the Formative Stage* (Ames: Iowa State College Press, 1942), p. 277.

13. Williams, *The Origins of Federal Support for Higher Education*, pp. 154–155.

14. For a discussion and some data, see Rainsford, *Congress and Higher Education in the Nineteenth Century*, p. 111.

15. Williams, *The Origins of Federal Support for Higher Education*, p. 156.

16. V.O. Key, Jr., *The Administration of Federal Grants to States* (Chicago: Public Administration Service, 1937), p. 161.

17. Rainsford, *Congress and Higher Education in the Nineteenth Century*, p. 114.

18. For a complete copy of the text, see U.S. Department of Health, Education, and Welfare, *Land-Grant Colleges and Universities, 1862–1962*, pp. 59–61.

6

The Smith-Hughes Act

February 23, 1917

The Smith-Hughes Act was central to the development of vocational education in the United States; indeed, it is often referred to as the Magna Carta of vocational education. It initiated a system of federal involvement in vocational education that remained largely unchanged until the 1960s and, in broad outline, continues today. It was the first permanent legislation authorizing federal involvement in education below the college level.[1] It was one of the first education bills to mandate matching funds from the states. It represented a very significant increase in federal oversight and regulation of state educational policies. Finally, the Smith-Hughes Act created the only national board of education that has ever existed in the United States.

When the Smith-Hughes Act was voted on in 1917, it received nearly unanimous support. This level of support was not in any way inevitable, however. It was the result of years of lobbying by a uniquely broad coalition of business, labor, and educational leaders. It was the result of patient coalition building by Senator Hoke Smith of Georgia, its principal congressional sponsor. It was the result, finally, of President Woodrow Wilson coming to see the act as a necessary part of war preparedness on the eve of U.S. involvement in World War I. The unanimity of 1917 was thus a reflection of the effective political work leading up to the final vote.

BACKGROUND

The Smith-Hughes Act was intended to create a cooperative program with the states to promote, expand, and improve vocational education. The vocational focus of the act was narrowly drawn to aim assistance at schools below the college level, serving students aged 14 and older, and providing training in or teachers for subjects related to agriculture, trade, industry, and home economics—the act specifically limited assistance to those "who are preparing to enter upon the work of the farm or of the farm home . . . [or] who are preparing for a trade or industrial pursuit."[2] The act had a twofold purpose: to ensure that Americans had meaningful employment opportunities and the possibility of economic mobility, and to ensure that the country had a ready supply of trained labor.

The Smith-Hughes Act provided federal financial assistance to the states for three substantive activities related to vocational education:

1. Section 2 of the act created a permanent appropriation to assist states in paying for salaries of teachers, supervisors, or directors of agricultural subjects. Beginning with $500,000 in 1918 and rising gradually to annual payments of $3,000,000 in 1926, this was the first significant appropriation of federal funds for teacher salaries below the college level.

2. Section 3 of the act mirrored the second, providing a permanent appropriation to assist states in paying for salaries of teachers of trade, industrial, and home-economics subjects. The amounts and graduated schedule of payments were the same as those provided for agricultural subjects.

3. Section 4 of the act provided a permanent appropriation to assist the states in training teachers of the covered vocational subjects. Beginning with $500,000 in 1918, funding rose in steps to an annual rate of $1,000,000 in 1921.

In all, therefore, once the Smith-Hughes Act was fully implemented, it provided permanent appropriations of $7 million per year to the states to support secondary-level vocational education. Subsequent legislation—particularly the George-Reed Act of 1929, the George-Deen Act of 1936, and the George-Barden Act of 1946—increased the appropriated amounts and broadened the definitions of the vocational subjects covered, but the basic structure of federal support for vocational education laid out in the Smith-Hughes Act remained fully in place for nearly half a century.

In addition, the act created the Federal Board for Vocational

Education. The board existed from 1917 to 1933, when its responsibilities were transferred by executive order to the Office of Education in the Department of Interior.[3] This is the only national board of education that has ever existed in the United States, and it was given broad powers to oversee and implement the act, review and approve state vocational-education plans, and certify state compliance with the act's rules and regulations. Further, the board was given a mandate to undertake or sponsor research into job requirements in vocational fields, effective vocational schooling, effective vocational teaching and teacher training, and effective administration of vocational programs. For this, the board was given an annual appropriation of $200,000.

More so than any education legislation that had preceded it, the Smith-Hughes Act provided tight federal regulation and oversight of how the states used the appropriated monies. States were given the option of choosing one, two, or all three forms of federal aid, but with each, extensive regulations were attached. The most significant regulations were as follows: states were required to create a state board to carry out the provisions of the act; states were required to submit detailed plans covering types of schools, courses, fields of study, teacher qualifications, teaching methods, and other matters for approval by the Federal Board for Vocational Education; states were required to submit annual financial reports on how federal monies were used; states were required to set minimum qualifications, with federal approval, for teachers of vocational subjects; and states were required to match federal spending, dollar for dollar, for both teacher salaries and teacher training. With respect to these regulations, the Federal Board for Vocational Education had to certify that each state was in compliance each year, and it could withhold future monies from any state found to be out of compliance.

The Smith-Hughes Act, in both its provisions and level of federal oversight, went well beyond any previous education bill. The legislative history of the bill exhibited growing support and shrewd politics. As the U.S. economy became increasingly industrialized and specialized, there was considerable sentiment in favor of practical, useful vocational education. The leading proponent of federal action was the National Society for the Promotion of Industrial Education (NSPIE). It played an essential role in the form, passage, and, ultimately, the execution of the Smith-Hughes Act.

In 1912, Senator Carroll Page of Vermont introduced a bill to provide federal aid to support secondary-level vocational education. Also introduced in Congress was the Smith-Lever bill to provide federal aid to support agricultural extension training for farmers and home economics. The two bills competed for support, with the Republican Senate supporting the Page bill, the Democratic House the Smith-Lever bill. In 1913, Senator Hoke Smith broke the deadlock by striking a "gentlemen's agreement" with the Page supporters. They would provide sufficient support to pass Smith-Lever, and Senator Smith would sponsor the creation of a commission to study the issues addressed by the Page bill.[4]

The Commission for National Aid to Vocational Education was thus created on January 20, 1914. The nine-member commission included both Senators Page and Smith, as well as Charles Prosser, then executive secretary of the NSPIE. The commission was intended to recommend action, and it did. It filed its report in June 1914, concluding with a draft of proposed federal legislation supporting vocational education. It is well established that the proposed legislation was drafted almost entirely by Prosser.[5] The proposal was copied verbatim and submitted to Congress by two of the commission members: Senator Smith, then chairman of the Senate Committee on Education, and Congressman Dudley Hughes, chairman of the House Committee on Education.

Senator Smith guided the bill through Congress. He was criticized at the time for moving too slowly, but he argued that it was essential to build support and a broad coalition behind the legislation. By and large, Smith's legislative strategy worked. While the National Education Association (NEA) opposed passage due to concerns over creating a dual system of schools, and educational theorist John Dewey was concerned that the bill was aimed at addressing the needs of industry rather than general education, a broad coalition was built to encourage passage.[6] Leading the lobbying effort was the NSPIE, which worked tirelessly on behalf of the Smith-Hughes bill. It was joined, moreover, by the U.S. Chamber of Commerce, the National Association of Manufacturers, the American Federation of Labor, and a wide range of educational leaders.[7] The coalition thus included leaders in industry, labor, and education, a powerful combination. Finally, as U.S. involvement in World War I became more and more likely, President Wilson repeatedly and publicly lobbied for the passage of the Smith-Hughes bill. Wilson argued that it was an essential part of war preparedness: "There are two sides to the question of preparation. There is not merely the military side; there is the industrial side. An ideal I have in mind is this: We ought to have in this great country a system of industrial and vocational education under federal guidance and federal aid."[8] Demonstrating the urgency of Wilson's appeals, the United States entered the war just four months after passage of the Smith-Hughes Act.

With this broad support in place, the bill was finally brought to a vote in early 1917, nearly three years after the National Commission had made its recommendation. The bill received nearly unanimous support in both houses of Congress and was signed into law by President Wilson on February 23, 1917. It is clear that several important factors came together to reach this result. Passage certainly required the acknowledged parliamentary skill of Senator Smith. The support of labor, industry groups, and educators, as well as the realities of World War I and President Wilson's lobbying, all contributed to the passage of the act. Historians, however, increasingly give strong emphasis to the role played by Charles Prosser in leading the NSPIE.[9] He served on the National Commission that recommended action, there is considerable evidence that he drafted the proposed legislation, and he spearheaded the intense lobbying effort of the NSPIE for final passage. It is instructive, as well, that Prosser went on to serve as the first chairman of the new Federal Board for Vocational Education. In the end, Prosser, Smith, Wilson, and the various private groups accomplished the passage of a path-breaking piece of education legislation, one that guided vocational education largely unchanged for the next half century.

IMPACT

The actual impacts of the Smith-Hughes Act are quite clear and thus widely accepted. The act clearly affected the size, funding, shape, and oversight of vocational education. Where there is disagreement is over the evaluation of these impacts; that is, did the effects of the act improve or harm both vocational and general education? Here there has been considerable debate, and when the Smith-Hughes approach to vocational education was substantively amended in the 1960s and again in the 1990s, efforts were made to address the concerns of the act's critics.

The most obvious effect of the Smith-Hughes Act was on the funding for and students enrolled in vocational education. When the act was fully in force, it called for appropriations of $7 million to the states. Through periodic amendments, mentioned earlier, these appropriations were repeatedly increased, such that by the early 1950s federal grants for vocational education exceeded $25 million per year. The act also spurred increased state funding. The states, in fact, went well beyond the requirement to match federal expenditures. By the early 1950s, the states collectively were spending more than $85 million per year on vocational education, more than three times the federal expenditures. With this rise in spending, student enrollments in the vocational fields covered by the act increased steadily and significantly.[10]

Second, as noted, the Smith-Hughes Act also greatly increased the level of federal oversight. It completed the pattern of increasing federal regulation of educational grants and programs. The Land and Northwest ordinances of the 1780s provided very broad discretion to the states over all issues of implementation. The First Morrill Act in 1862 provided for more federal controls, but still left much of the decision making in state hands. The Second Morrill Act in 1890 provided for far more federal control than the First, and the Smith-Hughes Act went further still. The level of oversight required by the act—detailed state plans requiring federal approval, annual financial reports, annual certification of compliance, matching requirements, and so on—established a model for all subsequent educational grants well into the 1990s.

Finally, the Smith-Hughes Act was path-breaking due to its creation of the Federal Board for Vocational Education. There has always been strong public and political sentiment in favor of very limited federal direction of primary and secondary education— what has been termed a "religion of localism." As recently as the 1990s, there was very significant opposition even to voluntary national standards and testing for K–12 education. While the Federal Board was relatively short lived, it stands out for having been created at all; there was no precedent for it, nor has there since been a national board of education responsible for any part of primary or secondary education in the United States.

These are the clear impacts of the Smith-Hughes Act—more funding, more students, more federal oversight, and a first-ever national board. There have been differing evaluations of these effects. On the positive side, it is argued that the act promoted a more rapid and fuller development of vocational education than would have otherwise been the case. Further, by significantly increasing student enrollments and student access to vocational education, it provided both opportunity to millions of individual Americans and a skilled labor pool for ongoing industrial expansion. Finally, due largely to the efforts of Prosser and his activist leadership of the Federal Board for Vocational Education, the act was responsible for increasing the standards for both vocational programs and teaching. The act thus led not only to more, but to higher-quality vocational education.[11]

By contrast, there are two main criticisms of the Smith-Hughes Act. First, beginning with the "Russell Report," an evaluation prepared by the Advisory Committee on Education in 1938, there was a serious concern that the Smith-Hughes system was too rigid and inflexible. It was so specific with regard to vocational subjects covered, what needed to be in state plans, and other requirements that state experimentation and adaptation were largely stifled—it established "grooves that became ruts." Even if the economy changed and new job fields emerged, for instance, training was limited to those areas covered by the act.[12]

Second, there was long-standing and repeated criticism of the Smith-Hughes Act for fostering a dual track or separate educational systems for vocational and general education. Under the act, vocational education was governed by a separate state board, received separate funding, and followed a separate curriculum. The concern was that to the extent that vocational education supplanted rather than augmented general education, the educational system would work to divide people into classes rather than serve a unifying and egalitarian purpose.[13]

Both supporters and critics agree that the Smith-Hughes Act had a significant impact on vocational education in the United States. It came about due to the exigencies of the day and effective lobbying and coalition building. It governed vocational education in the United States for nearly 50 years. When it was substantively amended or replaced—by the Vocational Education Act of 1963, the Carl D. Perkins Vocational and Applied Technology Act of 1990, and the School to Work Opportunity Act of 1994—the concerns of the act's critics were largely addressed. In vocational education today, states have far greater room to experiment, and it is more clearly integrated with general education. Even after these substantive changes, however, it is clear that the Smith-Hughes Act set a course that continues, a course of active federal involvement in funding vocational training in secondary schools across the country.

6. The Smith-Hughes Act

An Act to provide for the promotion of vocational education;
to provide for cooperation with the States in the promotion of
such education in agriculture and the trades and industries; to
provide for cooperation with the States in the preparation of
teachers of vocational subjects; and to appropriate money and
regulate its expenditure.[14]

Be it enacted by the Senate and House of Representatives of the United
States of America in Congress assembled, That there is hereby annually
appropriated . . . the sums provided in sections two, three, and four of this
act, to be paid to the respective States for the purpose of cooperating with
the States in paying the salaries of teachers, supervisors, and directors of
agricultural subjects, and teachers of trade, home economics and industrial subjects, and in the preparation of teachers of agriculture, trade,
industrial, and home economics subjects; and the sum provided for in
section seven for the use of the Federal Board for Vocational Education. . . .

Section 2. That for the purpose of cooperating with the States in paying
the salaries of teachers, supervisors, or directors of agricultural subjects
there is hereby appropriated for the use of the States, subject to the provisions of this act, for the fiscal year ending June thirtieth, nineteen hundred and eighteen, the sum of $500,000; for the fiscal year ending June
thirtieth, nineteen hundred and nineteen, the sum of $750,000; for the
fiscal year ending June thirtieth, nineteen hundred and twenty, the sum
of $1,000,000; for the fiscal year ending June thirtieth, nineteen hundred
and twenty-one, the sum of $1,250,000; for the fiscal year ending June
thirtieth, nineteen hundred and twenty-two, the sum of $1,500,000; for
the fiscal year ending June thirtieth, nineteen hundred and twenty-three,
the sum of $1,750,000; for the fiscal year ending June thirtieth, nineteen
hundred and twenty-four, the sum of $2,000,000; for the fiscal year ending
June thirtieth, nineteen hundred and twenty-five, the sum of $2,500,000;
for the fiscal year ending June thirtieth, nineteen hundred and twenty-
six, and annually thereafter, the sum of $3,000,000. Said sums shall be
allotted to the States in the proportion which their rural population bears
to the total rural population in the United States. . . .

Section 3. That for the purpose of cooperating with the States in paying
the salaries of teachers of trade, home economics, and industrial subjects
there is hereby appropriated for the use of the States, for the fiscal year
ending June thirtieth, nineteen hundred and eighteen, the sum of

$500,000; for the fiscal year ending June thirtieth, nineteen hundred and nineteen, the sum of $750,000; for the fiscal year ending June thirtieth, nineteen hundred and twenty, the sum of $1,000,000; for the fiscal year ending June thirtieth, nineteen hundred and twenty-one, the sum of $1,250,000; for the fiscal year ending June thirtieth, nineteen hundred and twenty-two, the sum of $1,500,000; for the fiscal year ending June thirtieth, nineteen hundred and twenty-three, the sum of $1,750,000; for the fiscal year ending June thirtieth, nineteen hundred and twenty-four, the sum of $2,000,000; for the fiscal year ending June thirtieth, nineteen hundred and twenty-five, the sum of $2,500,000; for the fiscal year ending June thirtieth, nineteen hundred and twenty-six, the sum of $3,000,000; and annually thereafter, the sum of $3,000,000. Said sums shall be allotted to the States in the proportion which their urban population bears to the total urban population in the United States. . . .

That not more than twenty per centum of the money appropriated under this act for the payment of salaries of teachers of trade, home economics, and industrial subjects, for any year, shall be expended for the salaries of teachers of home economic's subjects.

Section 4. That for the purpose of cooperating with the States in preparing teachers, supervisors, and directors of agricultural subjects and teachers of trade and industrial and home economic's subjects there is hereby appropriated for the use of the States, for the fiscal year ending June thirtieth, nineteen hundred and eighteen, the sum of $500,000; for the fiscal year ending June thirtieth, nineteen hundred and nineteen, the sum of $700,000; for the fiscal year ending June thirtieth, nineteen hundred and twenty, the sum of $900,000; for the fiscal year ending June thirtieth, nineteen hundred and twenty-one, and annually thereafter, the sum of $1,000,000. Said sums shall be allotted to the States in the proportion which their population bears to the total population of the United States. . . .

Section 5. That in order to secure the benefits of the appropriations provided for in sections two, three, and four of this act, any State shall, through the legislative authority thereof, accept the provisions of this act and designate and create a State board, consisting of not less than three members, and having all necessary power to cooperate, as herein provided, with the Federal Board for Vocational Education in the administration of the provisions of this act. . . .

Any State may accept the benefits of any one or more of the respective funds herein appropriated . . . and shall be required to meet only the conditions relative to the fund or funds the benefits of which it has accepted. . . .

Section 6. That a Federal Board for Vocational Education is hereby created, to consist of the Secretary of Agriculture, the Secretary of Commerce, the Secretary of Labor, the United States Commissioner of Education, and three citizens of the United States to be appointed by the President, by and with the advice and consent of the Senate. One of said three citizens shall be a representative of the manufacturing and commercial interests, one a representative of the agricultural interests, and one a representative of labor. . . .

The board shall have the power to cooperate with State boards in carrying out the provisions of this act. It shall be the duty of the Federal Board for Vocational Education to make, or cause to have made, studies, investigations, and reports, with particular reference to their use in aiding the States in the establishment of vocational schools and classes and in giving instruction in agriculture, trades, and industries, commerce and commercial pursuits, and home economics. . . .

Section 7. That there is hereby appropriated to the Federal Board for Vocational Education the sum of $200,000 annually, to be available from and after the passage of this act, for the purpose of making or cooperating in making the studies, investigations, and reports provided for in section six of this act. . . .

Section 8. That in order to secure the benefits of the appropriations for any purpose specified in this act, the State board shall prepare plans, showing the kinds of vocational education for which it is proposed that the appropriation shall be used; the kinds of schools and equipment; courses of study; methods of instruction; qualifications of teachers; and, in the case of agricultural subjects, the qualifications of supervisors or directors; plans for the training of teachers; and, in the case of agricultural subjects, plans for the supervision of agricultural education, as provided for in section ten. Such plans shall be submitted by the State board to the Federal Board for Vocational Education, and if the Federal Board finds the same to be in conformity with the provisions and purposes of this act, the same shall be approved. The State board shall make an annual report to the Federal Board for Vocational Education, on or before September first of each year, on the work done in the State and the receipts and expenditures of money under the provisions of this act.

Section 9. . . . The moneys expended under the provisions of this act, in cooperation with the States, for the salaries, teachers, supervisors, or directors of agricultural subjects, or for the salaries of teachers of trade, home economics, and industrial subjects shall be conditioned that for each dollar of Federal money expended for such salaries, the State or local community, or both, shall expend an equal amount for such salaries;

and that appropriations for the training of teachers of vocational subjects, as herein provided, shall be conditioned that such money be expended for maintenance of such training, and for each dollar of Federal money so expended for maintenance, the State or local community, or both, shall expend an equal amount for the maintenance of such training.

Section 10. . . . That in order to receive the benefits of such appropriation for the salaries of teachers, supervisors, or directors of agricultural education such education shall be that which is under public supervision or control; that the controlling purpose of such education shall be to fit for useful employment; that such education shall be of less than college grade and be designed to meet the needs of persons over fourteen years of age who have entered upon or who are preparing to enter upon the work of the farm or of the farm home; that the State or local community, or both, shall provide the necessary plant and equipment determined upon by the State board, with approval of the Federal Board for Vocational Education, as the minimum requirement for such education. . . .

Section 11. That in order to receive the benefits of the appropriation for the salaries of teachers of trade, home economics, and industrial subjects the State board of any State shall provide in its plan for trade, home economics, and industrial education that such education shall be given in schools or classes under public supervision or control; that the controlling purpose of such education shall be to fit for useful employment; that such education shall be of less than college grade and shall be designed to meet the needs of persons over fourteen years of age who are preparing for a trade or industrial pursuit or who have entered upon the work of a trade or industrial pursuit; that the State or local community, or both, shall provide the necessary plant and equipment determined upon by the State board, with approval of the Federal Board for Vocational Education, as the minimum requirement in such State for education of any given trade or industrial pursuit. . . .

Section 14. That the Federal Board for Vocational Education shall annually ascertain whether the several States are using, or are prepared to use, the money received by them in accordance with the provisions of this act . . . [and] shall certify to the Secretary of the Treasury each State which has accepted the provisions of this act and complied therewith, certifying the amounts which each State is entitled to receive under the provisions of the act. . . .

Section 16. That the Federal Board for Vocational Education may withhold the allotment of moneys to any State whenever it shall be determined that such moneys are not being expended for the purposes and under the conditions of this act. . . .

Section 17. . . . No portion of any moneys appropriated under this act for the benefit of the States shall be applied, directly or indirectly, to the purchase, erection, preservation, or repair of any building or buildings or equipment, or for the purchase or rental of lands, or for the support of any religious or privately owned school or college.

Section 18. That the Federal Board for Vocational Education shall make an annual report to Congress, on or before December first, on the administration of this act and shall include in such report the reports made by the State boards on the administration of the act by each State and the expenditure of the money allowed to each State.

Approved February 23, 1917.

NOTES

1. The Freedmen's Bureau, discussed in chapter 4, provided federal assistance to primary and secondary schools, but was always intended to be a temporary measure, as it proved to be.

2. See Sections 10 and 11 of the act in the excerpt from the text of the act.

3. Once the board was transferred, it served in an advisory capacity until its final abolition in 1946.

4. On the relationships among the Smith-Lever, Page, and Smith-Hughes bills, see Layton S. Hawkins, Charles A. Prosser, and John C. Wright, *Development of Vocational Education* (Chicago: American Technical Society, 1951), pp. 80–83; and Arthur G. Wirth, *Education in the Technological Society: The Vocational–Liberal Studies Controversy in the Early Twentieth Century* (Scranton, PA: Intext Educational Publishers, 1972), pp. 91–92.

5. See, for instance, the discussion in Wirth, *Education in the Technological Society,* p. 162.

6. For a discussion of the concerns of both the NEA and Dewey, see Wirth, *Education in the Technological Society,* pp. 137, 215–216.

7. Harvey Kantor, "Vocationalism in American Education: The Economic and Political Context, 1880–1930," in *Work, Youth, and Schooling: Historical Perspectives on Vocationalism in American Education,* ed. Harvey Kantor and David B. Tyack (Stanford: Stanford University Press, 1982), pp. 14–44; and Wirth, *Education in the Technological Society,* p. 40.

8. Quoted in Hawkins, Prosser, and Wright, *Development of Vocational Education,* p. 87.

9. See, for instance, Neville B. Smith, "A Tribute to the Visionaries, Prime Movers, and Pioneers of Vocational Education, 1892–1917," *Journal of Vocational and Technical Education* 16, no. 1 (Fall 1999): 67–76.

10. Hawkins, Prosser, and Wright, *Development of Vocational Education,* pp. 350–366.

11. For a discussion of the views of supporters, see Larry Cuban, "Enduring Resiliency: Enacting and Implementing Federal Vocational Education Legislation," in *Work, Youth, and Schooling: Historical Perspectives on Vocationalism in American Ed-*

ucation, ed. Harvey Kantor and David B. Tyack (Stanford: Stanford University Press, 1982), p. 51.

12. For a discussion, see Cuban, "Enduring Resiliency," p. 50.

13. "Smith-Hughes Act of 1917," Prentice Hall Documents Library (http://hcl.chass.ncsu.edu/garson/dye/docs/smith917.htm, 1998).

14. North Carolina State University College of Agriculture and Life Sciences "The National Vocational Education (Smith-Hughes) Act" (http://www.cals.ncsu.edu/agexed/sae/smithugh.html, 2000).

7

The Servicemen's Readjustment Act

June 22, 1944

The Servicemen's Readjustment Act, far more commonly known as the G.I. Bill, has been described as the most significant piece of federal legislation in the 20th century.[1] It provided comprehensive readjustment benefits in health care, housing, unemployment compensation, and education to millions of returning World War II veterans. Far more veterans took advantage of the education benefits than had been anticipated, with profound effect. One historian has said that the G.I. Bill made America the best-educated country in the world.[2] The G.I. Bill played a significant role, perhaps an indispensable role, in developing the American middle class; it opened the doors of higher education to millions who otherwise would have been denied such opportunity. The bill, moreover, remade colleges and universities, which changed curricula, admissions procedures, and housing arrangements to meet the needs of a huge influx of nontraditional students. The G.I. Bill, finally, set the standard for veterans' affairs in the United States, laying the groundwork for the Korean G.I. Bill, the Vietnam Era G.I. Bill, and the post-Vietnam Montgomery G.I. Bill.

The G.I. Bill was motivated by a concern that the United States not repeat the problems it had encountered with veterans' readjustment after World War I and by concerns about mass unemployment among returning veterans. The educational portions of the bill faced significant opposition from several influential educational leaders, and passage required extraordinary efforts to get the legislation to a final vote. In the end, however, the G.I. Bill gained unanimous support in Congress. The single largest educational bill to date was enacted, and the United States was permanently changed.

BACKGROUND

As noted, the G.I. Bill offered wide-ranging benefits to veterans. In addition to the education benefits discussed here, it offered health care to injured or disabled veterans, loan guarantees for purchasing homes, farms, and businesses, job-search assistance, and unemployment compensation. The educational component was sweeping in nature, but simple in design. It provided the means to pay tuition and other educational costs, as well as a monthly living allowance, to all World War II veterans. All other decisions, particularly regarding courses of study and institutions to attend, were left to veterans themselves.

The stated purpose of the bill was to compensate veterans for interruptions or delays in their education or training caused by their military service to the country. Any veteran who served between September 16, 1940, and the end of the war, and who was not dishonorably discharged, was eligible. All veterans received one year of education or training, plus additional time equal to their time served, up to four years. They were free to choose whatever form of training they desired—finishing a high-school diploma, vocational training, apprenticeships, or college. As long as a veteran was accepted for admission to the institution or program and could perform well enough to meet the standards of the institution or program, the choice was left to the veteran.

The bill authorized payment of up to $500 per year to cover the costs of tuition and fees, books, supplies, and equipment. At the time, the average tuition for a four-year public college was $91 per year, and for a private college it was $273.[3] The bill's payments were thus sufficient to allow veterans to attend any college they were qualified to attend, public or private. Veterans could even choose to attend private religious schools, with federal monies transferred directly to these schools. The only costs not covered by this provision were travel and living expenses. For these costs, veterans received a monthly stipend or living allowance while they were in school. Those without spouses or children received $50 per month; those with dependents received $75 per month. These allowances were raised several times in subsequent years.

There were several motivations for the G.I. Bill. One was clearly a sense of responsibility on the part of the nation to the millions of veterans who had risked or were risking their lives to protect the country and its freedom. However, many historians believe that federal officials were even more motivated by fear. With the knowledge that the war had ended the mass unemployment of the Great Depression, there was fear of returning to this condition if veterans were not somehow smoothly reintegrated into society.[4] There was also fear of repeating the political turmoil associated with the returning World War I veterans. The lack of benefits for these veterans had bred resentments that led to years of social and political protest, ending with the violent suppression of the "bonus marchers" (World War I veterans demanding early payment of a promised bonus) in 1932. Capturing this sentiment, Congressman Hamilton Fish (R-NY) warned that veterans "would not come home and sell apples as they did after the last war. . . . I believe we would have chaotic and revolutionary conditions in America."[5] There was broad sentiment that steps needed to be taken to smooth the return of the veterans at the war's end.

To this end, President Franklin Roosevelt authorized the National Resources Planning Board (NRPB) to begin preliminary study of reintegration in mid-1942. The NRPB studied programs enacted by several of the states following World War I and Canadian legislation adopted in 1941. More concerned with prosecuting the war, Roosevelt showed little interest in this work. On November 13, 1942, however, he announced the formation of a new committee of education and War and Navy Department officials—known as the Osborn Committee after Brigadier General Frederick H. Osborn—to study ways to help veterans whose education was interrupted by military service. This was the same day he signed legislation lowering the draft age to 18, and the committee proposal was in part an effort to blunt opposition to this step.

While they differed in details, both the NRPB and the Osborn Committee proposed educational benefits for returning veterans. In a fireside chat to the nation in July 1943, Roosevelt called on Congress "to do its duty" and pass legislation providing comprehensive benefits to veterans. He then submitted the final recommendations of the Osborn Committee as a starting point for congressional action.[6]

Once the proposal was before Congress, various groups joined the battle. The most significant role was played by the American Legion, which lobbied both extensively and extremely effectively for the G.I. Bill. Some veterans' groups asserted that the bill was so large and comprehensive that it might not pass. They argued that a better strategy was to lobby for a series of smaller bills. The Legion, however, insisted on the full G.I. Bill throughout the debate and is given considerable credit for its passage.[7] Many educators also saw the potential of the bill, particularly the American Council on Education (ACE) and its president, Gregory F. Zook. The ACE invested considerable time and resources in lobbying for the bill.

Educators, though, were not unanimous in their support of the educational components of the G.I. Bill. While colleges of the day had been changed by the Morrill acts (see chapters 3 and 5), they still remained largely the province of the social elite and broad liberal training. Some feared that educational standards would tumble if a broader segment of society were admitted en masse to America's colleges and universities. Robert Hutchins, a renowned educator and president of the University of Chicago, published a magazine article entitled "The Threat to American Education" in which he argued that colleges and universities would move toward vocational training and would lower standards to attract veterans and the federal monies that would follow them. In the end, he argued, "Colleges and universities [would] find themselves converted into educational hobo jungles."[8] Mirroring Hutchins, Harvard University president James B. Conant also argued that the educational portions of the G.I. Bill would broaden access to higher education at the cost of lower quality.

In Congress, the House and the Senate passed different versions of the G.I. Bill in the spring of 1944. A joint committee of the two houses was appointed to try and work out the differences. Seven senators and seven representatives were appointed; any agreement required the support of a majority of the senators and a majority of the representatives. The committee set a deadline of 10:00 A.M. on June 10 to reach an agreement, or the bill would die.

A proposed compromise won the support of all seven senators, but the House members split three to three, with one member absent. The missing member, Congressman John Gibson of Georgia, had left a proxy vote in favor of the compromise with the chairman of the House delegation, John Rankin of Mississippi. Rankin, however, was opposed to the compromise and refused to exercise Gibson's proxy, break the tie, and move the bill forward. At 6:00 P.M. on June 9, the evening before the deadline, Gibson was still absent, and so the G.I. Bill appeared headed to a certain death.

The American Legion intervened, however, determined to find Congressman Gibson and get him to Washington in time to cast his favorable vote. The congressman was on the road somewhere in southern Georgia and could not be located. The *Atlanta Constitution*, which favored the bill, had an employee call Gibson's house every five minutes, and the Legion arranged radio broadcasts requesting information on Gibson's whereabouts. When Gibson was finally located at approximately 11:00 P.M., he was taken by police escort from his home to a nearby military base. From there, he was driven in a military vehicle to Jacksonville, Florida, where the American Legion had a plane waiting to get him to Washington. He arrived at a little past 6:30 A.M., less than three and a half hours before the deadline.[9] Once the G.I. Bill was out of committee, it was passed swiftly and unanimously (the opposition having evaporated when the issue became public) in both the House and the Senate and was signed into law by President Roosevelt on June 22, 1944. America and American education would never again be the same.

IMPACT

The most obvious impact of the G.I. Bill was on the returning veterans. The expectation was that only a small proportion of the veterans would use the education benefits, and fewer still would use them to attend college. In August 1945, The *Saturday Evening Post* ran an article entitled "G.I.'s Reject Education." Yet within a year of that publication, more than 1 million veterans were enrolled in education and training programs. The educational benefits proved enormously popular and effective.

Of the 15.4 million veterans eligible for educational benefits, 7.8 million took advantage of them. Of these, under 1 million pursued farm training, nearly 1.5 million apprenticeship programs, nearly 3.5 million secondary education, and 2.2 million college education.[10] The total cost of the G.I. Bill to the federal government was $14.5 billion. The veterans who pursued education did not flood the labor markets at the war's end, and when they did eventually enter the labor pool, they were far better trained and able to contribute to U.S. economic expansion.

With millions of new students almost overnight, the second major impact was on American colleges and universities. The fears earlier expressed by Hutchins and Conant proved misplaced. Indeed, the older, more disciplined, more focused veterans, as a class of stu-

dents, excelled. Their grades, attendance, work ethic, and graduation rates exceeded those of more traditional classes of students
who preceded them. President Conant repudiated his earlier "dis-
tress" over the veterans, remarking that the G.I. Bill classes at Harvard were the strongest in the university's history.

The basic administration of colleges and universities also
changed. The enrollment surge was fantastic—in 1939, total enrollment in all U.S. colleges and universities was approximately 1.4
million, but at the height of the G.I. Bill in 1947, it reached 2.3
million, an increase of nearly two-thirds over an eight-year period.
In 1947, very nearly half of all college and university students in
the United States were veterans. Colleges added facilities, faculty,
and staff. Hours of daily operation were extended, summer-school
sessions expanded, and the use of graduate students as teachers in
the classroom increased. Admission standards were changed to allow credit for relevant military training and experience. Curricula
were changed to reflect veterans' preferences for study in business
and engineering. Finally, and most noticeably, all kinds of housing
facilities were added, including tent cities, barracks, and Quonset
huts. Married students and students with children were an almost
entirely new phenomenon on most campuses.

Third, the G.I. Bill impacted veterans' affairs in the United States.
Official policies would never again treat veterans as poorly as they
had those who had returned from World War I. The G.I. Bill set
the standard, and so in 1952 the Korean G.I. Bill was passed to deal
with veterans of that war. It was patterned after the original, the
main substantive difference being that all monies were given directly to veterans, out of which they would pay the school tuition
and fees, rather than the government paying the school. This was
a response to the main criticism of the original bill, that it gave
colleges and universities an incentive to raise tuition and fees to
the maximum the federal government would reimburse and thus
fueled inflation in college costs.[11]

In 1966, in response to the escalating war in Vietnam, the Veterans Readjustment Act was passed. This served Vietnam veterans
and, retroactively, those who had served between the Korean and
Vietnam wars. Currently, the Montgomery G.I. Bill provides educational benefits to active-duty veterans. This, however, is a contrib-
utory program, with servicemen and women paying into an
educational fund, which is then matched at least two to one by the
federal government.

Finally, and most profoundly, the G.I. Bill impacted America socially. It provided access to higher education to more Americans than had ever been the case before. The opportunities it provided, the avenues to social and economic advancement, were unparalleled. It allowed millions of mostly working-class veterans, who would have otherwise remained working class, to move solidly into the middle class. On the 50th anniversary of the G.I. Bill, President Bill Clinton remarked that it was the wisest investment the United States had ever made in its people, that "it provided the undergirding for what has become the most successful middle class in all of history."[12]

Beyond this, the G.I. Bill prompted many colleges and universities that had previously denied admittance to women or blacks or Catholics or Jews to open their doors to these Americans too. The legislation provided benefits to all veterans, regardless of gender, race, or faith. To attract as many students and as much federal money as possible, many schools lifted admissions restrictions. Given this and the increased access to education, the G.I. Bill has been described as "one of the best pieces of legislation ever passed that has helped young Black males."[13] The same could be said with respect to women and other minorities.

The G.I. Bill was born of a sense of obligation and responsibility to the veterans and fear of mass unemployment and political turmoil. Regardless of the motivations for the bill, however, the result was legislation that affected the lives of millions of young men and women directly, and, by so doing, impacted the social and economic structure of the United States, the nature and shape of colleges and higher education, and the future course of veterans' relations in the country.

7. The Servicemen's Readjustment Act

AN ACT To provide Federal Government aid for the readjustment in civilian life of returning World War II veterans.[14]

Be it enacted by the Senate and House of Representatives of the United States of America in Congress assembled, That this Act may be cited as the "Servicemen's Readjustment Act of 1944." . . .

TITLE II

Chapter IV—Education of Veterans

Section 400. . . . Veterans Regulation Numbered 1(a), is hereby amended by adding a new part VIII as follows: . . .

Part VIII

"1. Any person who served in the active military or naval service on or after September 16, 1940, and prior to the termination of the present war, and who shall have been discharged or released therefrom under conditions other than dishonorable, and whose education or training was impeded, delayed, interrupted, or interfered with by reason of his entrance into the service, or who desires a refresher or retraining course . . . shall be eligible for and entitled to receive education or training under this part: Provided, That such course shall be initiated not later than two years after either the date of his discharge or the termination of the present war, whichever is the later: Provided further, That no such education or training shall be afforded beyond seven years after the termination of the present war: And provided further, That any such person who was not over 25 years of age at the time he entered the service shall be deemed to have had his education or training impeded, delayed, interrupted, or interfered with.

"2. Any such eligible person shall be entitled to education or training, or a refresher or retraining course, at an approved educational or training institution, for a period of one year. . . . Upon satisfactory completion of such course of education or training, according to the regularly prescribed standards and practices of the institutions . . . such person shall be entitled to an additional period or periods of education or training, not to exceed the time such person was in the active service on or after September 16, 1940, and before the termination of the war, . . . but in no event shall the total period of education or training exceed four years: Provided, That his work continues to be satisfactory throughout the period, according to the regularly prescribed standards and practices of the institution. . . .

"3. Such person shall be eligible for and entitled to such course of education or training as he may elect . . . and at any approved educational or training institution at which he chooses to enroll, which will accept or retain him as a student or trainee in any field or branch of knowledge which such institution finds him qualified to undertake or pursue. . . .

"4. From time to time the Administrator shall secure from the appropriate agency of each State a list of the educational and training institutions . . . which are qualified and equipped to furnish education or training. . . .

"5. The Administrator shall pay to the educational or training institution, for each person enrolled in full time or part time course of education or training, the customary cost of tuition, and such laboratory, health, infirmary, and other similar fees as are customarily charged, and may pay for books, supplies, equipment, and other necessary expenses, exclusive of board, lodging, other living expenses, and travel, as are generally required for the successful pursuit and completion of the course by other students in the institution: Provided, That in no event shall such payments, with respect to any person, exceed $500 for an ordinary school year. . . .

"6. While enrolled in and pursuing a course under this part, such person, upon application to the Administrator, shall be paid a subsistence allowance of $50 per month, if without a dependent or dependents, or $75 per month, if he has a dependent or dependents. . . .

"8. No department, agency, or officer of the United States, in carrying out the provisions of this part, shall exercise any supervision or control, whatsoever, over any State educational agency, or State apprenticeship agency, or any educational or training institution. . . .

"9. The Administrator of Veterans' Affairs is authorized and empowered to administer this title. . . .

"11. As used in this part, the term 'educational or training institutions' shall include all public and private elementary, secondary, and other schools furnishing education for adults, business schools and colleges, scientific and technical institutions, colleges, vocational schools, junior colleges, teachers colleges, normal schools, professional schools, universities, and other educational institutions, and shall also include business or other establishments providing apprentice or other training on the job. . . ."

Approved June 22, 1944.

NOTES

1. U.S. Senator Daniel Inouye, as quoted in "G.I. Bill," *West Legal Dictionary* (http://www.wld.com/conbus/weal/wgibill.htm, 2000).

2. Stephen E. Ambrose, as quoted in Sydney J. Freedburg, Jr., "Beyond the G.I. Bill," *National Journal*, August 21, 1999, p. 1.

3. Chester E. Finn, Jr., *Scholars, Dollars, and Bureaucrats* (Washington, DC: Brookings Institution, 1978), p. 62.

4. See, for instance, Harold M. Hyman, *American Singularity: The 1787 Northwest Ordinance, the 1862 Homestead and Morrill Acts, and the 1944 G.I. Bill* (Athens: University of Georgia Press, 1986), pp. 62–65.

5. Quoted in Reginald Wilson, "The G.I. Bill and the Transformation of America," *National Forum* 75, no. 4 (Fall 1995): p. 21.

6. For a full discussion of the thinking and actions within the Roosevelt administration, see Keith W. Olson, *The G.I. Bill, the Veterans, and the Colleges* (Lexington: University Press of Kentucky, 1974), pp. 3–24.

7. See, for instance, Edward Kiester, Jr., "The G.I. Bill May Be the Best Deal Ever Made by Uncle Sam," *Smithsonian* 25, no. 8 (November 1994): 130–135; and Olson, *The G.I. Bill, the Veterans, and the Colleges*, p. 18.

8. Robert M. Hutchins, "The Threat to American Education," *Collier's*, December 30, 1944, pp. 20–21.

9. Kiester, "The G.I. Bill May Be the Best Deal Ever Made by Uncle Sam," pp. 134–135.

10. "The G.I. Bill of Rights (1944)," Prentice Hall Documents Library (http://hcl.chass.ncsu.edu/garson/dye/docs/gibill.htm, 2000).

11. Alice M. Rivlin, *The Role of the Federal Government in Financing Higher Education* (Washington, DC: Brookings Institution, 1961), pp. 68–69; and Finn, *Scholars, Dollars, and Bureaucrats*, pp. 62–63.

12. Quoted in Ronald Roach, "From Combat to Campus: GI Bill Gave a Generation of African Americans an Opportunity to Pursue the American Dream," *Black Issues in Higher Education* 14, no. 13 (August 21, 1997): p. 26.

13. William Hytche, former president of the University of Maryland–Eastern Shore, quoted in Roach, "From Combat to Campus," p. 27.

14. *United States Statutes at Large*, vol. 58 (Washington, DC: U.S. Government Printing Office, 1945), pp. 284–301.

8

The National School Lunch Act

June 4, 1946

The adoption of the National School Lunch Act (NSLA) represented a significant step toward fuller federal participation in primary and secondary education. Previous federal efforts had
involved general financial support through land sales and support
for vocational programs and teacher training. With the NSLA, the
federal government involved itself in the broader social mission of
education. Schools would be the mechanism to ensure adequate
nutrition for poor children, and, in turn, healthier children would
learn more and better. The NSLA proved both successful and popular, undergoing repeated expansions. Today, it is an integral part
of day-to-day operations in most schools, both public and private,
affecting more than 26 million schoolchildren each year.

Politically, the adoption of the NSLA was not contentious in the
traditional sense—there were no intense floor debates or parliamentary maneuvers in Congress. Rather, the road to passage was
one of gradual acceptance across society of the need and propriety
of responding publicly to child hunger and malnourishment. The
movement began with private, voluntary efforts and continued with
a series of efforts on the part of state and city governments, then
temporary actions by the federal government, and, finally, a permanent response through the NSLA.

BACKGROUND

The School Lunch Program created by the NSLA was designed
to ensure that all students in primary and secondary education, in

both public and private schools, had reasonable access to a nutritionally sound lunch. The declared purpose was "to safeguard the health and well-being of the Nation's children and to encourage the domestic consumption of nutritious agricultural commodities and other food."[1] The intention was to serve both social and educational needs. Socially, at a time when many families could not adequately provide sound nutrition to their children, the National School Lunch Program would ensure that these children received at least one sound meal each day. Educationally, it was assumed that well-fed and nourished children learn better in school, a view that was later supported by research.[2]

The act provided a permanent appropriation in an amount sufficient to carry out the provisions of the legislation; there was thus an open-ended commitment by the federal government to the School Lunch Program. Administered by the Department of Agriculture, the School Lunch Program provided monies to purchase surplus commodities to be provided to schools, as well as funding for "nonfood assistance"—such things as transportation, storage, distribution, and handling of the foods.

Congress intended to focus the assistance on poor students, and therefore, funds were distributed to the states based on the number of school-age children and the per capita income in each state. Subsequent amendments in the 1960s further targeted aid to poor students and school districts. In the same vein, Section 9 of the act required that "no physical segregation of or other discrimination against any child shall be made by the school because of his inability to pay."[3] It mandated that any child identified by a school as unable to pay the full cost of a lunch receive lunches free or at reduced prices.

As with the Smith-Hughes Act before it, the NSLA required the states to match federal expenditures. In this instance, however, levels of state support were required to grow over time. From 1947 through 1950, the states had to match federal spending dollar for dollar; from 1951 through 1955, they needed to provide $1.50 for every dollar spent by the federal government; and from 1956 on, the ratio rose to three to one. For those states with a per capita income below the U.S. average, the matching requirement was reduced proportionally.

The NSLA required that lunches served under the act "meet minimum nutritional requirements prescribed by the Secretary [of Agriculture] on the basis of tested nutritional research."[4] New nutritional guidelines are released every five years, and much of the controversy over the School Lunch Program in the 1980s and 1990s centered on these nutritional standards.

The act was very clearly designed to meet the needs of all school-age children. To this end, as noted, both public and private schools were eligible to participate, including religious schools.[5] If state law prohibited the distribution of public funds to private schools, then a share of state funding proportional to the percentage of students in private schools was to be withheld from the state and distributed to the private schools directly by the secretary of agriculture.

Finally, the act took account of the segregated schools of the day. States with separate schools for white and black children were required to provide a plan for the "just and equitable" division of federal school-lunch funds. In the absence of such a plan, no funding could be distributed to the state.

These provisions of the NSLA came together quite easily and with little opposition in 1946, but they followed half a century of social activism and public experimentation. Private aid societies were active in a number of U.S. cities in the late 1800s, trying to provide adequate nutrition for school-age children. Broad public consciousness was not raised, however, until the publication of two polemics—Robert Hunter's *Poverty* in 1904, and John Spargo's *Bitter Cry of the Children* in 1906.[6] Both works cataloged the extent of the child-nutrition problem and argued forcefully for a public response. For example, Hunter wrote:

> The poverty of any family is likely to be most serious at the very time when the children most need nurture, when they are most dependent, and when they are obtaining the only education which they are ever to receive. . . . learning is difficult because hungry stomachs and languid bodies and thin blood are not able to feed the brain. The lack of learning among so many poor children is certainly due, to an important extent, to this cause. . . . If it is a matter of principle in democratic America that every child shall be given a certain amount of instruction, let us render it possible for them to receive it . . . by making full and adequate provision for the physical needs of the children who come from the homes of poverty.[7]

Following this publication, numerous private, city, and state programs were initiated to feed schoolchildren—in Boston, Milwaukee,

New York, and Cleveland, among other cities. They were largely of limited scope, and many were seen as experimental.

By the early 1920s, though, the boards of education in both New York and Chicago assumed responsibility for lunch programs in all of their schools. By the 1930s, a number of states, moreover, had authorized their public schools to provide school lunches, often at reduced costs to poor children. To this point, the federal government had remained uninvolved in the issue.[8]

What prompted the federal government to act were the basic realities of the Great Depression. Due to the depression, millions more Americans were in poverty and need; existing private, city, and state school-lunch efforts simply could not meet the financial need. In addition, amid the economic collapse, farmers lacked markets for their goods, and there were huge commodity surpluses. The federal government responded with a series of temporary measures to address these two problems.

Several New Deal organizations were involved with school lunches and the oversupply of farm commodities. In 1934, the Reconstruction Finance Corporation tested a loan program in Missouri to defray personnel costs associated with school-lunch programs. These efforts were expanded by both the Civil Works Administration and the Federal Emergency Relief Administration and ultimately reached most of the states. Both the Work Project's Administration and the National Youth Administration provided workers for school-lunch programs.

The most significant step, however, was passage of Public Law 320 in 1935, which dedicated 30 percent of all revenue from customs duties each year to promote the consumption of farm commodities. The thrust of this program was to purchase surplus foods and donate them to schools. By the early 1940s, it involved nearly 80,000 schools, more than 5 million children, and more than 450 million pounds of food each year. The success of these New Deal efforts, however, was largely undercut by changes brought by the onset of World War II. In a war environment, the oversupply of commodities quickly disappeared, and the military and war industries absorbed the labor pool that had largely filled out the New Deal institutions, especially the Work Projects Administration.[9]

The amount of food distributed to schools declined from 1942 to 1944 by 80 percent, negating progress that had been made in child nutrition. Congress responded with single-year appropriations of $50 million for each of the school years from 1943–1944 to 1945–

1946 to support school-lunch programs. These were straight cash transfers to help schools purchase needed foods. State and local governments still needed to provide space, equipment, and personnel to make use of these federal grants. With only single-year appropriations and no long-term commitment from the federal government, there was considerable reluctance on the part of state and local officials to underwrite these costs, and the program was largely ineffective.[10]

The collapse of the New Deal efforts and the inadequacy of the annual-appropriations approach prompted the federal government to address school lunches in a more comprehensive fashion. The NSLA was the result, increasing federal monies dedicated to school lunches and making appropriations permanent to reassure state and local partners. When it was passed by Congress on June 4, 1946, as noted, the NSLA itself was not controversial. It had taken half a century, however, to arrive at that point. There had been a slow, evolutionary process of acceptance that there was a need and a problem to be addressed through voluntary efforts, city and state efforts, temporary federal efforts, and, ultimately, a long-term federal response.

IMPACT

The immediate impact of the NSLA was dramatically to increase funding for and the number of children participating in lunch programs. Federal funding, which had hovered at $50 million a year in the mid-1940s, jumped to $81 million in the first year of the NSLA. More telling, the numbers of schoolchildren served school lunches rose very rapidly. Between 1947, when the program began, and 1958, student participation increased by more than 150 percent.[11] Access to nutritious school meals was thus expanded to millions of American schoolchildren.

Beyond this initial success, the basic program was expanded in successive steps. Several of the steps were particularly important. In 1954, the Special Milk Program was created, providing milk to primary and secondary schools. The Child Nutrition Act of 1966 created the School Breakfast Program, patterned directly on the NSLA. Finally, amendments to the NSLA in 1968 expanded eligibility to child-care centers.[12]

The NSLA, however, has had critics and controversies over its 50-plus years of existence. There have been concerns that federal appropriations fail to keep pace with inflation costs.[13] There were concerns, largely addressed by the changes made in 1966, that the program was insufficiently skewed toward schools with low-income students.[14] In the 1980s, the School Lunch Program faced significant budget cuts as the federal government struggled to deal with large budget deficits.[15] Proposed cuts in 1981 prompted the Department of Agriculture to label ketchup served with lunches as a serving of vegetables, which led to both criticism and ridicule, and the decision had to be reversed. In both the 1980s and 1990s, considerable criticism was directed at the nutritional standards of school lunches. Critics contend that despite changes, the required nutritional standards for school lunches have failed to keep pace with knowledge regarding sound nutrition for children.[16]

Overall, however, given the stated purpose of the act—to help "safeguard the health and well-being of the Nation's children and to encourage the domestic consumption of nutritious agricultural commodities"—the NSLA has clearly been successful. By the 50th anniversary of the program in 1996, more than 80 billion school lunches had been served. In 1999, nearly 27 million children were served by the program, with nearly three-fifths receiving lunches free or at reduced prices. Federal expenditures now exceed $5 billion a year and involve the purchase of over a billion pounds of commodities. The related programs, while smaller, have also thrived, with the School Breakfast Program serving 7.5 million children, the vast majority at reduced prices, and the Milk Program in 1999 was responsible for the distribution of nearly 127 million half-pint cartons of milk to schoolchildren.[17]

The adoption of the NSLA in 1946 followed years of social action and state and local efforts and a decade or more of federal experimentation. By 1946, the effort was motivated by the clear conviction that schools could not be effective without healthy children. The program has grown and expanded, and many of the criticisms of the program have been addressed over time. The NSLA affects the day-to-day lives of millions of schoolchildren each year, and it affects the finances and operation of nearly every school in the country.

8. The National School Lunch Act

AN ACT To provide assistance to the States in the
establishment, maintenance, operation, and expansion of
school-lunch programs, and for other purposes.[18]

Be it enacted by the Senate and the House of Representatives of the
United States of America in Congress assembled, That this Act may be
cited as the "National School Lunch Act."

Section 2. It is hereby declared to be the policy of Congress, as a measure
of national security, to safeguard the health and well-being of the Nation's
children and to encourage the domestic consumption of nutritious agricultural commodities and other food, by assisting the States, through
grants-in-aid and other means, in providing an adequate supply of foods
and other facilities for the establishment, maintenance, operation, and
expansion of nonprofit school-lunch programs.

Section 3. For each fiscal year, beginning with the fiscal year ending June
30, 1947, there is hereby authorized to be appropriated . . . such sums as
may be necessary to enable the Secretary of Agriculture (hereinafter referred to as "the Secretary") to carry out the provisions of this Act.

Section 4. The sums appropriated . . . shall be available to the Secretary
for supplying . . . agricultural commodities and other foods for the school-
lunch program. . . . Apportionment among the States shall be made on
the basis of two factors: (1) The number of school children in the State
and (2) the need for assistance in the State as indicated by the relation
of the per capita income in the United States to the per capita income in
the State. . . . For the purposes of this Act, "school" means any public or
nonprofit private school of high-school grade or under. . . .

Section 5. Of the sums appropriated for any fiscal year . . . $10,000,000
shall be available to the Secretary for the purpose of providing . . . nonfood assistance for the school-lunch program. . . .

Section 7. . . . Such payments to any State in any fiscal year during the
period 1947 to 1950, inclusive, shall be made upon condition that each
dollar thereof will be matched during such year by $1 from sources within
the State determined by the Secretary to have been expended in connection with the school-lunch program under this Act. Such payments in any
fiscal year during the period 1951 to 1955, inclusive, shall be made upon
the condition that each dollar thereof will be so matched by one and one-
half dollars; and for any fiscal year thereafter, such payments shall be
made upon condition that each dollar will be so matched by $3. In the
case of any State whose per capita income is less than the per capita

income of the United States, the matching required for any fiscal year shall be decreased by the percentage which the State per capita income is below the per capita income of the United States. . . .

Section 8. Funds paid to any State during any fiscal year pursuant to section 4 or 5 shall be disbursed . . . to those schools in the State which the State educational agency, taking into account need and attendance, determines are eligible to participate in the school-lunch program. Such disbursements to any school shall be made only for the purpose of reimbursing it for the cost of obtaining agricultural commodities and other foods for consumption by children in the school-lunch program and nonfood assistance in connection with such program. Such food costs may include, in addition to the purchase price of agricultural commodities and other foods, the cost of processing, distributing, transporting, storing, or handling thereof. . . .

Section 9. Lunches served by schools participating in the school-lunch program under this Act shall meet minimum nutritional requirements prescribed by the Secretary on the basis of tested nutritional research. Such meals shall be served without cost or at a reduced cost to children who are determined by local school authorities to be unable to pay the full cost of the lunch. No physical segregation of or other discrimination against any child shall be made by the school because of his inability to pay. School-lunch programs under this Act shall be operated on a nonprofit basis. . . .

Section 10. If, in any State, the State educational agency is not permitted by law to disburse the funds paid to it under this Act to nonprofit private schools in the State, or is not permitted by law to match Federal funds made available for use by such nonprofit private schools, the Secretary shall withhold from the funds apportioned to any such State under sections 4 and 5 of this Act the same portion of the funds as the number of children between the ages of five and seventeen, inclusive, attending nonprofit private schools within the State is of the total number of persons of those ages within the State attending school. The Secretary shall disburse the funds so withheld directly to the nonprofit private schools. . . .

Section 11. (a) States, State educational agencies, and schools participating in the school-lunch program under this Act shall keep such accounts and records as may be necessary for the Secretary to determine whether the provisions of this Act are being complied with. . . .

(c) In carrying out the provisions of this Act, neither the Secretary nor the State shall impose any requirement with respect to teaching personnel, curriculum, instruction, methods of instruction, and materials of instruction in any school. If a State maintains separate schools for minority and for majority races, no funds made available pursuant to this Act shall be paid or disbursed to it unless a just and equitable distribution is made within the State, for the benefit of such minority races, of funds paid to it under this Act . . .

Approved June 4, 1946.

NOTES

1. *United States Statutes at Large*, vol. 60 (Washington, DC: U.S. Government Printing Office, 1946), p. 230.

2. National School Public Relations Association, *School Lunch Breakthrough: Politics, Technology Spur Expansion of Food Programs* (Arlington, VA: National School Public Relations Association, 1972), pp. 13–15.

3. *United States Statutes at Large*, vol. 60, p. 233.

4. Ibid.

5. *Sidney W. Tiedt, The Role of the Federal Government in Education* (New York: Oxford University Press, 1966), p. 108; and R. Freeman Butts and Lawrence A. Cremin, *A History of Education in American Culture* (New York: Henry Holt and Company, 1953), p. 581.

6. On the role played by these two works, see Shirley R. Watkins, "Historical Perspective on the School Meals Programs: The Case for Strong Federal Programs," U.S. Department of Agriculture (http://fns1.usda.gov/fncs/shirley/speeches/support/sw971124.htm, 1997); and "The National School Lunch Program: Background and Development," U.S. Department of Agriculture (http://www.fns.usda.gov/cnd/INCLUDES/CONTENT/NSLPBackgroundandDevelopment.htm, 2000).

7. Quoted in "The National School Lunch Program," p. 7.

8. For a discussion of these early efforts, see "The National School Lunch Program," pp. 5–12.

9. For discussions of these New Deal efforts, see Marion Cronan, *The School Lunch* (Peoria, IL: Chas. A. Bennett Company, 1962), pp. 21–22, and "The National School Lunch Program," pp. 12–16.

10. Watkins, "Historical Perspective on the School Meals Programs," p. 2.

11. Cronan, *The School Lunch*, p. 24.

12. On these changes, see Irene Y. Ponti, *A Guide for Financing School Food and Nutrition Services* (Chicago: American School Food Service Association and the Research Corporation of the Association of School Business Officials, 1970), pp. 16–19.

13. Ponti, *A Guide for Financing School Food and Nutrition Services*, pp. 23–25.

14. National School Public Relations Association, *School Lunch Breakthrough*, p. 8.

15. Watkins, "Historical Perspective on the School Meals Programs," p. 4.

16. Charlene Price and Betsey Kuhn, "Public and Private Efforts for the National School Lunch Program," *Food Review*, May–August 1996, pp. 51–57.

17. All data are from "Child Nutrition Program Data, National Level Annual Summary Tables: Fiscal Years 1969–1999," U.S. Department of Agriculture (http://www.fns.usda.gov/pd/cnpmain.htm, 2000).

18. *United States Statutes at Large*, vol. 60, pp. 230–234.

9

The Impact Laws

September 23, 1950, and September 30, 1950

The term "impact laws" refers to two pieces of legislation adopted in tandem in 1950. Together, they were designed to compensate local school districts for the costs associated with federal lands and facilities. Federal purchase of land takes it off of local tax rolls, making it difficult for schools to be adequately financed. The placement of federal facilities in a school district can significantly and rapidly increase the number of schoolchildren to be served, thereby imposing a financial burden on the local community. During World War II, the federal government enacted temporary legislation to deal with these problems, but not a permanent response. In 1950, Congress attempted to fashion a lasting response to deal with the impact of federal activities on local schools.

The two pieces of legislation were constructed together and adopted a week apart. Public Law (P.L.) 815 provided funds for the construction of new school facilities needed due to federal activities, such as military bases and defense contractors. Public Law 874 provided funds for the ongoing maintenance and operational costs of schools needed due to federal activities. The laws created two of the very first programs whereby the federal government provided funding for general primary and secondary education. Since their adoption, the impact laws have been the focus of contentious debates over school desegregation and the equality of federal funding, but they are today politically sacrosanct. Impact aid now exceeds a billion dollars per year, spread across nearly all congressional districts, and the impact-aid coalitions in the House and Senate are large and influential. Despite early controversies, therefore, the impact laws are now fully integrated into the year-to-year workings of the public school system.

BACKGROUND

The intent of P.L. 815 and P.L. 874 was to defray the various costs that fall on local schools due to actions of the federal government. On the premise that small school districts would have more difficulty in handling federal impacts, both bills were structured to focus aid disproportionately on smaller schools. Because the legislation involved thousands of school districts and tens of thousands of schoolchildren connected to diverse federal activities—army bases, naval facilities, defense contractors, research laboratories, forest-service facilities, and so on—the impact laws were extraordinarily detailed. There were extensive definitions and rules and regulations specifying what federal activities counted and how many students had to be involved for a school district to qualify for various levels of aid.[1] Without getting into these details, the main thrusts of P.L. 815 and P.L. 874 can be summarized as follows.

P.L. 815 consisted of two main components. Title I of the act provided funds for the states to initiate surveys of school facilities and construction needs. These funds and surveys were not limited to construction needs related to federal impacts. Rather, this portion of the bill was sponsored by Senator Hubert Humphrey of Minnesota to collect data he felt would be useful for the design and passage of subsequent, broader legislation to provide general federal aid to all public schools.[2]

Title II, the larger portion of the act, focused specifically on construction aid related to federal impacts. Aid was provided to local school districts that needed to construct new school facilities—mainly classrooms, but also cafeterias, multipurpose rooms, gymnasiums, and so on—to educate children living on federal property, whose parents worked on federal property, or whose parents were connected to federal activities (primarily government contracts with private companies). The percentage of construction costs a school district was eligible to receive ranged from 45 to 95 percent, with smaller school districts receiving more. Recipient school districts were required to provide detailed annual reports, ensure that they would hold the title to any properties involved, and guarantee that all construction complied with Davis-Bacon Act requirement that workers on federal projects be paid no less than the wages prevailing in each region of the county.[3]

P.L. 874, by contrast, was intended to assist local school districts with recurring operational costs associated with federal impacts. While the details in terms of the number of students needed for a school to be eligible varied, four categories of schools were identified as eligible for assistance:

1. Schools whose local tax base was reduced by federal purchase and ownership of property

2. Schools that provided education to children who lived on federal property

3. Schools that provided education to children whose parents worked on federal property

4. Schools that experienced "sudden and substantial" increases in school attendance due to federal activities[4]

In both P.L. 815 and P.L. 874, the federal commitment of assistance was open ended. The federal government committed itself to compensate local schools fully for federal impacts, regardless of the total appropriations needed to achieve this goal. As enacted, the two laws provided aid for a three-year period, but they have been extended and expanded repeatedly since then. In 1965, the impact laws were folded into the Elementary and Secondary Education Act, and, today, their legal reference is P.L. 103–382, Title VIII.

The history and motivations that lay behind passage of these acts in 1950 are clear. The tax-exempt status of federal property and the sudden infusion of schoolchildren often associated with federal installations caused real and demonstrable financial burdens. In some instances, local schools simply refused to provide education for children of parents who lived on federal property. In 1931, the National Advisory Committee on Education raised concerns over the lack of any consistent policy to educate children associated with federal installations. Similarly, in 1938, the President's Advisory Committee on Education concluded that the chronic problems associated with federally impacted areas were one of several serious gaps in the nation's commitment to equitable educational opportunity for all children.

The tremendous expansion of defense-related activities associated with World War II exacerbated the problems. Congress responded by enacting the Lanham Act in 1941, which provided temporary financial assistance to affected schools. At the end of 1946, when it was due to expire, the Lanham Act was extended for an additional year. In 1948 and again in 1949, Congress adopted one-year stopgap measures patterned after the Lanham Act and began work on a permanent program.[5]

In 1949, the House Committee on Education and Labor and the Senate Committee on Labor and Public Welfare began to study approaches to resolve the problems of federally impacted areas. A series of House subcommittees released a joint report in early 1950 whose recommendations became the legislative basis for P.L. 815 and P.L. 874, adopted later the same year. While congressional passage was largely a response to the years spent struggling with the problems, it was aided by the increased federal impacts then being experienced by local schools due to the buildup associated with the Korean War.

IMPACT

P.L. 815, P.L. 874, and subsequent versions and reauthorizations of the laws have been very successful in putting resources into affected schools. School participation began immediately and grew very rapidly. In 1951–1952, for instance, P.L. 815 funding was used to build 13,699 classrooms for use by nearly 400,000 federally connected students. Under P.L. 874, nearly 1,200 school districts received operating funds in the first year of the program. This number grew significantly over the first decade of the program, with more than 4,000 participating school districts in the early 1960s. Between the two programs, total federal expenditures to local schools rose from approximately $30 million in 1950 to more than $177 million in 1959.[6]

Through congressional reauthorizations and integration into broader education legislation, the impact-aid programs have continued to grow. By the mid-1980s, despite efforts by the Reagan administration to cut impact aid as a deficit-reduction measure, annual expenditures totaled nearly $700 million. Aid currently flows to more than 3,000 separate school districts and affects the education of about two million federally connected schoolchildren.[7] Funding in 2000 exceeded one billion dollars and will do so again in 2001.

Many individuals who oppose federal funding for primary and

secondary education do so on principled ideological grounds. Political conservatives often view such aid as an intrusion on the part
of the federal government into an area best left to individual states
and local school districts. The impact laws have largely overcome
this traditional hurdle, however, and, indeed, enjoy remarkably
broad political support. Several factors have contributed to this political success.

First, the financial problems addressed by the impact laws are
real, and responsibility for them can be laid quite clearly on the
federal government. This alone overrides much of the traditional
opposition to federal school aid. Second, the impact laws have a
strong national defense component. While they respond to the effects of all schoolchildren connected to federal government activities, the bulk of these effects are tied to military installations and
defense contractors. It was not accidental that the temporary Lanham Act was enacted during the buildup to World War II, and, as
noted, the impact laws were passed during the buildup to the Korean War. Finally, the political success of the impact laws is also due
to effective political lobbying. The National Association of Federally
Impacted Schools (NAFIS) is nationally organized and is an effective proponent of impact aid.[8] Impact aid flows to nearly 90 percent
of all congressional districts. As a result, the House Impact Aid Coalition today has a membership of 129 representatives, and the Senate Impact Aid Coalition includes 46 senators. Impact aid was an
issue in the 2000 presidential campaign, with Republican nominee
George W. Bush proposing to increase impact aid for school construction by over $300 million (Democratic nominee Al Gore was
silent on the issue). The impact-aid laws have very broad political
support.

While the impact laws are politically secure, at times they have
been criticized; efforts have been made to tie other less popular
issues to them; and they were a point of serious contention as the
United States desegregated schools. Substantively, the major criticism of the laws was that they fostered inequality among schools.
As originally constituted, federal aid was tied strictly to the number
of federally connected students in a school district, regardless of
the size of the local tax base. As many (though clearly not all)
federal installations were located in relatively more affluent areas
within states, impact aid could have the effect of making relatively
rich school districts richer still. Congress addressed this problem in
1974, allowing the states to count federal impact aid when they

allocated their own monies to equalize education funding across school districts.[9]

Due to the political strength of the impact laws, efforts have been made to amend them to add less popular forms of educational assistance. In the early 1960s, for instance, proposals were made to tie public aid to parochial schools into the impact aid legislation.[10] Later in the 1960s, the Elementary and Secondary Education Act (see chapter 12) amended the impact laws to add aid to schools "impacted" by a large number of poor schoolchildren. While most of these efforts failed, clearly the intent was to leverage the support for impact aid to secure other forms of aid as well.

Finally, from the start, P.L. 815 and P.L. 874 were caught up in the political struggles surrounding the desegregation of schools. The issue was whether or not impact aid could or should be used to support segregated local schools. In 1951, the Department of Defense announced that racially segregated schools could not be operated on military property and set a deadline in 1955 to end all such facilities. Impact aid to some segregated schools off the bases, however, continued. In 1962, Secretary of Health, Education, and Welfare Abraham Ribicoff, noting that impact aid was intended to ensure that all children connected to federal activities received a "suitable free public education," announced that segregated schools did not meet this standard and would no longer be eligible for assistance (although *Brown* had legally ended segregation eight years earlier, it was still widespread in practice). Later in 1962, the Justice Department filed suit against Prince George County, Virginia, to prevent the use of impact aid to support segregated schools, and the impact-aid laws were quickly amended to prevent such aid.[11]

Despite the criticisms and controversial issues, the impact-aid laws clearly have been successful vis-à-vis their intended purpose. The financial burdens and educational disruptions associated with federal impacts, which had been chronic problems, have been largely addressed. The political success of the impact laws, moreover, is without question. Federal impact-aid expenditures have contributed to the education provided to millions of schoolchildren connected to federal activities, and they are now a regular and accepted part of school financial planning and administration.

9a. P.L. 815

An Act Relating to the construction of school facilities in areas affected by Federal activities, and for other purposes.[12]

Be it enacted by the Senate and House of Representatives of the United States in Congress assembled,

TITLE I—SURVEYS AND STATE PLANS FOR SCHOOL CONSTRUCTION

Section 101. In order to assist the several States to inventory existing school facilities, to survey the need for the construction of additional facilities in relation to the distribution of school population, to develop State plans for school construction programs, and to study the adequacy of State and local resources available to meet school facilities requirements, there is hereby authorized to be appropriated the sum of $3,000,000, to remain available until expended. . . .

TITLE II—SCHOOL CONSTRUCTION IN FEDERALLY AFFECTED AREAS

Section 201. In recognition of the impact which certain Federal activities have had on the school construction needs in the areas in which such Federal activities have been or are being carried on, the Congress hereby declares it to be the policy of the United States to bear the cost of constructing school facilities in such areas in the manner and to the extent provided in this title.

Section 202. (a) A local educational agency shall be eligible under this subsection for payment with respect to children who reside on Federal property with a parent employed on federal property, if the estimated number of such children who will be in average daily attendance at the schools of such agency during the current fiscal year . . . is at least fifteen and is at least 5 per centum of the estimated number of all children who will be in average daily attendance at the schools of such agency during the current fiscal year. Each such local educational agency shall be entitled to receive an amount not to exceed such estimated number of children with respect to whom it is eligible for payment under this subsection, multiplied by 95 per centum of the average per pupil cost of constructing complete school facilities in the State in which the school district of such agency is situated.

(b) A local educational agency shall be eligible under this subsection for payment with respect to children who reside on Federal property, or who reside with a parent employed on Federal property part or all of which is situated in such State, if the estimated number of such children who will be in average daily attendance at the schools of such agency during the current fiscal year is at least fifteen and is at least 5 per centum of the estimated number of all children who will be in average daily attendance at the schools of such agency during the current fiscal year. Each such local educational agency shall be entitled to receive an amount not to exceed such estimated number of children with respect to whom it is eligible for payment under this subsection, multiplied by 70 per centum of the average per pupil cost of constructing complete school facilities in the State in which the school district of such agency is situated.

(c) A local educational agency shall be eligible under this subsection for payment with respect to children whose attendance results from activities of the United States (carried on either directly or through a contractor) if, in the judgement of the Commissioner of Education—

(1) the estimated number of such children who will be in average daily attendance at the schools of such agency during the current fiscal year is at least twenty and is at least 10 per centum of the estimated number of all children who will be in average daily attendance at the schools of such agency during the current fiscal year; and

(2) the construction of additional school facilities to take care of the children whose attendance results from such activities of the United States has imposed or will impose an undue financial burden on the taxing and borrowing authority of the agency. . . .

Section 203. Notwithstanding the provisions of section 202, whenever the Commissioner determines that part or all of the attendance with respect to which any local educational agency is entitled to receive payment under such section will be of temporary duration only, such agency shall not be entitled to receive such payment. . . . Instead, the Commissioner shall make available to such agency such temporary school facilities as may be necessary to take care of such attendance. . . .

Section 204. In the case of children who reside on Federal property—

(1) if no tax revenues of the State or any political subdivision thereof may be expended for the free public education of such children; or

(2) if it is the judgement of the Commissioner . . . that no local educational agency is able to provide suitable free public education for such children,

the Commissioner shall make such arrangements for constructing or otherwise providing school facilities as may be necessary. . . .

Section 208. (a) In the administration of this Act, no department, agency, officer, or employee of the United States shall exercise any direction, supervision, or control over the personnel, curriculum, or program of instruction of any school or school system of any local or State educational agency. . . .

Approved September 23, 1950.

9b. P.L. 874

An Act To provide financial assistance for local educational agencies in areas affected by Federal activities, and for other purposes.[13]

Be it enacted by the Senate and House of Representatives of the United States in Congress assembled,

Section 1. In recognition of the responsibility of the United States for the impact which certain Federal activities have on the local educational agencies in which such activities are carried on, the Congress hereby declares it to be the policy of the United States to provide financial assistance . . . for those local educational agencies upon which the United States has placed financial burdens by reason of the fact that—

(1) the revenues available to such agencies from local sources have been reduced as a result of the acquisition of real property by the United States; or

(2) such agencies provide education for children residing on Federal property; or

(3) such agencies provide education for children whose parents are employed on Federal property; or

(4) there has been a sudden and substantial increase in school attendance as a result of Federal activities.

Section 2. (a) Where the Commissioner, after consultation with any local educational agency and with the appropriate State educational agency, determines . . .

(1) that the United States owns Federal property in the school district of such local educational agency, and that such property (A) has been acquired by the United States since 1938, (B) was not acquired by exchange for other Federal property in the school district which the United States owned before 1939, and (C) had an assessed value . . . aggregating 10 per centum or more of the assessed value of all real property in the school district . . . ; and

(2) that such acquisition has placed a substantial and continuing financial burden on such agency; and

(3) that such agency is not being substantially compensated for the loss in revenue resulting from such acquisition . . .

then the local educational agency shall be entitled to receive for such fiscal year such amount as, in the judgement of the Commissioner, is equal to the continuing Federal responsibility for the additional financial burden. . . .

Section 3. (a) For the fiscal year beginning July 1, 1950, and for each of the three succeeding fiscal years, each local educational agency which provides free public education during such year for children who reside on Federal property with a parent employed on Federal property shall be entitled to an amount equal to the number of such children in average daily attendance during such year at the schools of such agency, multiplied by the local contribution rate [a formula to determine the average expenditures made by the school per pupil]. . . .

(b) For the fiscal year beginning July 1, 1950, and for each of the three succeeding fiscal years, each local educational agency of a State which provides free public education during such year for children who reside on Federal property, or who reside with a parent employed on Federal property part or all of which is situated in such State, shall be entitled to an amount equal to the number of such children in average daily attendance during such year at the schools of such agency, multiplied by one-half the local contribution rate [a formula to determine the average expenditures made by the school per pupil]. . . .

Section 4. (a) If the Commissioner determines for the fiscal year beginning July 1, 1950, or for any of the three succeeding fiscal years—

(1) that, as the result of the activities of the United States (carried on either directly or through a contractor), an increase in the number of children in average daily attendance at the schools of any local educational agency has occurred in such fiscal year, which increase so resulting from activities of the United States is equal to at least 10 per centum of the number of all children in average daily attendance at the schools of such agency during the preceding three year period; and

(2) that such activities of the United States have placed on such agency a substantial and continuing financial burden; and

(3) that such agency is making a reasonable tax effort and is exercising due diligence in availing itself of State and other financial assistance but is unable to secure sufficient funds to meet the increased educational costs involved,

then such agency shall be entitled to receive for the fiscal year for which the determination is made, and for each of the two succeeding fiscal years . . . an amount equal to the product of—

(A) the number of children which the Commissioner determines to be the increase in average daily attendance, so resulting from activities of the United States . . . ; and

(B) the amount which the Commissioner determines to be the current expenditures per child necessary to provide free public education to such additional children. . . .

Section 6. In the case of children who reside on Federal property—

(1) if no tax revenues of the State or any political subdivision thereof may be expended for the free public education of such children; or

(2) if it is the judgment of the Commissioner . . . that no local educational agency is able to provide suitable free public education for such children,

the Commissioner shall make such arrangements . . . as may be necessary to provide free public education for such children. . . .

Section 7. (a) In the administration of this Act, no department, agency, officer, or employee of the United States shall exercise any direction, supervision, or control over the personnel, curriculum, or program of instruction of any school or school system of any local or State educational agency. . . .

Approved September 30, 1950.

NOTES

1. From their enactment in 1950 to the present, the impact laws have been reauthorized many times by Congress. With each consideration, changes have been made with respect to some of the details—how many schoolchildren connected to federal government activities are needed for a school district to qualify, levels of funding, and so on. As a rule, these gradual changes have almost always liberalized the process, providing more assistance to more schools.

2. I. M. Labovitz, *Aid for Federally Affected Public Schools* (Syracuse, NY: Syracuse University Press, 1963), p. 40.

3. For a detailed discussion of the provisions of P.L. 815, see Labovitz, *Aid for Federally Affected Public Schools*, pp. 40–45.

4. For a detailed discussion of the provisions of P.L. 874, see Labovitz, *Aid for Federally Affected Public Schools*, pp. 45–50.

5. For a discussion of the Lanham Act, see Gilbert E. Smith, *The Limits of Reform: Politics and Federal Aid to Education, 1937–1950* (New York: Garland Publishing, 1982), p. 89.

6. Advisory Commission on Intergovernmental Relations, *Intergovernmentalizing the Classroom: Federal Involvement in Elementary and Secondary Education* (Washington, DC: Advisory Commission on Intergovernmental Relations, 1981), pp. 21–22, and Labovitz, *Aid for Federally Affected Public Schools*, pp. 96–137.

7. For a discussion, see L. Dean Webb, Martha M. McCarthy, and Stephen B.

Thomas, *Financing Elementary and Secondary Education* (Columbus, OH: Merrill, 1988), p. 237.

8. For information on the NAFIS and its lobbying activities, see the NAFIS Web site at http://www.sso.org/nafis.

9. Webb, McCarthy, and Thomas, *Financing Elementary and Secondary Education*, pp. 236–237.

10. Hugh Davis Graham, *The Uncertain Triumph: Federal Education Policy in the Kennedy and Johnson Years* (Chapel Hill: University of North Carolina Press, 1984), p. 93.

11. For discussions of the desegregation fights vis-à-vis the impact laws, see Graham, *The Uncertain Triumph*, p. 32, and Labovitz, *Aid for Federally Affected Public Schools*, pp. 88–95.

12. *United States Statues at Large*, vol. 64 (Washington, DC: U.S. Government Printing Office, 1951), pp. 967–978.

13. *United States Statutes at Large*, vol. 64, pp. 1100–1109.

10

The National Defense Education Act

September 2, 1958

The National Defense Education Act (NDEA) represented a fundamental change and expansion in the role of the federal government in public education. It passed at the height of the Cold War amid immediate concerns, real or imagined, that the United States was unable to match the scientific and technical advances of the Soviet Union. The act provided comprehensive education assistance: student loans for higher education, fellowships for advanced graduate education, monies for science labs and equipment, monies for foreign-language labs and centers, and monies for research grants, vocational education, and new educational media. The NDEA affected the shape and curriculum of American education at the primary, secondary, and university levels and, in its size and breadth, set the precedent for a whole range of Great Society educational initiatives made by the administration of President Lyndon Johnson in the 1960s.

General educational assistance of the type inaugurated by the NDEA had been proposed on many occasions, from the various bills of Congressman George Hoar debated in the late 19th century[1] to repeated efforts made by the administration of President Harry Truman. The NDEA passed when all other efforts had failed because it was a bipartisan response to a perceived national-security emergency. The successful Soviet launch of *Sputnik I*, the first man-made satellite, galvanized growing concerns that U.S. long-term security was threatened by shortcomings in American education. The national-security component fundamentally changed the politics of federal education assistance and allowed for the quick and over-whelming passage of this path-breaking legislation.

BACKGROUND

The text of the NDEA begins with a long declaration of policy that reaffirms the traditional role of state and local governments in the area of education, but makes the case for expanded federal involvement. The language employed is sweeping:

> The security of the Nation requires the fullest development of the mental resources and technical skills of its young men and women. . . . The defense of the Nation depends upon the mastery of modern techniques developed from complex scientific principles. . . . We must increase our efforts to identify and educate more of the talent of our Nation. . . . no student of ability will be denied an opportunity for higher education because of financial need. . . . It is therefore the purpose of this Act to provide substantial assistance . . . in order to insure trained manpower of sufficient quality and quantity to meet the national defense needs of the United States.[2]

This represented a significant change in federal policy; from the inauguration of the NDEA forward, the federal government would play a far more substantial and active role in the form, content, and shape of American education. The G.I. Bill had moved the federal government in this direction in the area of higher education, but the NDEA was much broader, affecting all levels of the educational system.

The scope of the NDEA is very large, with substantial new federal assistance directed toward making college and university education affordable, improving primary and secondary education in the areas of science, mathematics, foreign languages, vocational education, guidance, and testing, and developing new and better ways to teach and share information in science, mathematics, and languages. The provisions of the NDEA were laid out in nine substantive titles.

Title II was the first substantive section of the act and provided loans to help students attend college. In the 1950s, many able students could not afford to attend college, and, therefore, the NDEA provided low-interest loans of up to a total of $5,000 for students to do so. Repayment of the loans did not begin until one year after a student left college. Loans were available for all potential students and areas of study, but preferences were given to those who intended to enter the teaching profession or who had particular aptitude in science, math, or languages.

Title III provided aid to the states to improve science, math, and language education in public elementary and secondary schools. This is the portion of the NDEA that was most visible to schoolchildren of the day, with monies provided to purchase classroom equipment and remodel laboratories. Monies were also made available to improve the supervision and administration of teaching in these areas and for the ongoing professional training of teachers of these subjects. Finally, a loan program was created to help nonprofit private schools improve their science, math, and language instruction.

Title IV provided for National Defense Graduate Fellowships. Up to 8,500 three-year fellowships were authorized over a six-year period. These were intended to make graduate education affordable for highly able students in areas of study deemed important to U.S. national defense.

Title V provided financial assistance to the states to improve and expand both testing and guidance programs. Improved testing systems were necessary to help identify students with strong abilities and aptitudes. Stronger guidance programs were needed to help these students choose careers that matched their abilities and to encourage them to pursue higher education generally.

Title VI provided assistance to expand and improve foreign-language instruction and related subjects. The main thrust was to encourage more and earlier study of foreign languages, but monies were also provided for instruction in fields related to an understanding of foreign cultures, such as history, geography, political science, sociology, and anthropology. Finally, monies were provided to establish language institutes at the university level to train more and better teachers in the languages and related fields.

Title VII provided a small appropriation for research into more effective use of media—films, television, and radio—in education, and for the dissemination of this research to teachers.

Title VIII provided increased financial aid for vocational education. Specifically, it aided "area" vocational programs, defined as those areas of vocational education requiring scientific training and related to, or necessary for, national defense. In practical terms, these were specialties needed by defense contractors.

Title IX provided for the establishment of the Science Information Service. The intent was to develop a means to disseminate more quickly and accurately new scientific research.

Finally, Title X provided funding to the states to assist them in improving their systems of educational statistics. The intent was to create systems of current, accurate, and reliable educational data with which to assess both national needs and progress.

While most of the NDEA titles provided a sliding scale of appropriations over the original five-year life span of the act, together they provided for more than $200 million in new federal education aid per year. The NDEA was also more ambitious than previous education legislation, expanding the federal role in elementary, secondary, and higher education.

The primary catalyst for the NDEA, as noted, was the successful Soviet launch of the *Sputnik I* communications satellite on October 4, 1957. This was at the height of the Cold War, roughly midway between the Berlin blockade and airlift of 1948–49 and the erection of the Berlin Wall in 1961. Tensions were very high, and when the Soviets beat the United States into space, it shook American confidence. There were immediate security concerns; many commentators at the time noted that a Soviet rocket capable of deploying a satellite was equally capable of delivering a nuclear warhead. There were also long-term security concerns, for example, whether the United States could successfully compete at the cutting edge of scientific and technological development.

Public concern over *Sputnik* was almost immediate. Scholarly publications such as *Foreign Affairs*, as well as popular publications such as *Time*, *Life*, and the *New York Times*, ran articles discussing the significance of, and security concerns raised by, the *Sputnik* challenge. Leading American scientists, including physicists Edward Teller, George Price, and Lloyd Berkner, publicly lamented the U.S. failure.[3] The political system needed to respond.

President Dwight Eisenhower grappled with how to react, and the White House considered organizing exhibitions of U.S. technological advances and a conference with business leaders to assure the public of American competitiveness. Such confidence-building measures were rejected, however, and the president commented on October 11, a week after *Sputnik*, that "we must have faith not to get hysterical, and we must not get complacent."[4] Eisenhower felt that the United States did need to respond, but he wanted to do so in a meaningful, lasting way that would improve American scientific competitiveness and security. The White House and Congress began to work together toward the creation and adoption of the NDEA.

Education was seen as the proper long-term, systemic response to the *Sputnik* challenge. For instance, Admiral Hyman Rickover, the father of U.S. nuclear submarine development, argued that *Sputnik* should "do in matters of intellect what Pearl Harbor did in matters industrial and military"[5] by spurring America into action and to new levels of achievement. While later developments demonstrated that the United States overreacted to *Sputnik*—while the United States lost the race for the first satellite, American scientific and technological skills were not falling woefully behind those of the Soviets—the clear sentiment at the time was that American scientific competitiveness would require generations of more, better-trained, and better-equipped scientists. The Eisenhower administration submitted a bill in January 1958, and, simultaneously, Senator Lester Hill (D-AL) and Congressman Carl Elliot (D-AL) drafted a congressional bill. Senator Hill had for years pushed for general federal education assistance, and *Sputnik* provided an opportunity to achieve the goal. He later noted that his fellow congressmen could never vote against both national defense and education when they were fused into one bill.

The two bills were quite similar—both provided assistance to primary and secondary education as well as colleges and universities, and both directed aid toward science, mathematics, and foreign languages. They differed over total funding, with the administration proposing less than Congress, but compromise was easily achieved. The only controversial issue that arose during congressional debate was a provision in the Hill-Elliot draft providing scholarships for undergraduate students. There was criticism that this would give students a "free ride," that there was a component that was almost welfare to it, and in the end the scholarship idea was replaced by the loan program in Title II.[6] The NDEA passed overwhelmingly and was signed into law by President Eisenhower on September 2, 1958, just eleven months after the *Sputnik* launch.

IMPACT

The size and scope of the National Defense Education Act were huge, and its impacts were wide-ranging. Then Senate Majority Leader Lyndon Johnson called it "an historic landmark" when it passed, and 10 years after passage it was labeled "the most important piece of national education legislation in a century."[7] Quite simply, it established an entirely new level of federal support for and involvement in education.

The NDEA was reauthorized and many of its provisions were expanded over the years. The data from just its first five-year authorization, however, speak volumes about its impact. By 1963, 500,000 students had taken advantage of the NDEA loan program to attend more than 1,500 colleges and universities, at a cost of approximately $330 million. The federal government had invested more than $100 million in improved guidance and testing programs and had lowered the counselor-to-student ratio across the country from 1/900 to 1/540. While there had been only 46 high-school language labs in the entire country in 1958, there were more than 6,000 in 1963. More than 30,000 students had received science-and technology-related vocational education, and more than 180,000 projects had been funded to purchase science, mathematics, and foreign-language equipment and instructional materials.[8] The impact of the NDEA, therefore, was both large and immediate.

Beyond this, the NDEA also impacted curriculum at all levels of the educational system, although its effect here is more difficult to quantify. The emphasis on science, math, and languages restructured the system. Primary and secondary schools put greater emphasis on, and dedicated more of the school day to, these areas of study. In higher education, these areas also received greater emphasis, as did all of the language-related fields identified in the act. Moreover, colleges of education and teacher-training programs were restructured to emphasize teaching in NDEA fields.[9]

It is important to note that in the interest of quick and consensual passage, the NDEA was crafted to sidestep the most controversial education issues of the day, religion and race. While the act explicitly called for aid to private schools to avoid the religion controversy, the act prohibited aid to parochial or other religious schools. More telling is the fact that although it was the first significant piece of federal education legislation after the *Brown v. Board of Education* desegregation ruling in 1954, the NDEA was entirely silent on the issue of race. None of this was by accident. Indeed, when Senator Hill was drafting the legislation, he directed his staff to "steer between the Scylla of race and the Charybdis of religion."[10] The perceived need at the time was to respond quickly to the Soviet challenge, and to deal with either race or religion would have been an impediment.

In the end, the most lasting effect of the NDEA was the new pattern of federal involvement in education it inaugurated. Prior to its enactment, while the federal government certainly had taken important steps with the land-grant colleges, vocational education, aid to veterans, and other programs, its role had remained quite limited by today's standards. The NDEA represented an entirely new level of federal participation, particularly at the primary-and secondary-school level; it has been described as "a quantum leap" in the accepted role of the national government.[11] While it passed under unique circumstances—a perceived national-security emergency—it established the precedent for future federal actions, especially President Lyndon Johnson's Elementary and Secondary Education Act in 1965. Before the NDEA, the federal government provided periodic aid to the states in narrow areas; since the NDEA, the federal government has been a regular, consistent partner with the states in shaping the education system.

10. The National Defense Education Act

An Act To strengthen the national defense and to encourage and assist in the expansion and improvement of educational programs to meet critical national needs; and for other purposes.[12]

Be it enacted by the Senate and House of Representatives of the United States of America in Congress assembled, That this Act . . . may be cited as the "National Defense Education Act of 1958."

TITLE I—GENERAL PROVISIONS

Section 101. The Congress hereby finds and declares that the security of the Nation requires the fullest development of the mental resources and technical skills of its young men and women. The present emergency demands that additional and more adequate educational opportunities be made available. The defense of the Nation depends upon the mastery of modern techniques developed from complex scientific principles. It depends as well upon the discovery and development of new principles, new techniques, and new knowledge.

We must increase our efforts to identify and educate more of the talent of our Nation. This requires programs that will give assurance that no student of ability will be denied an opportunity for higher education because of financial need; we will correct as rapidly as possible the existing imbalances in our educational programs which have led to an insufficient proportion of our population educated in science, mathematics, and modern foreign languages and trained in technology.

The Congress reaffirms the principle and declares that the States and local communities have and must retain control over and primary responsibility for public education. The national interest requires, however, that the Federal government give assistance to education for programs which are important to our defense.

To meet the present educational emergency requires additional effort at all levels of government. It is therefore the purpose of this Act to provide substantial assistance in various forms to individuals, and to States and their subdivisions, in order to insure trained manpower of sufficient quality and quantity to meet the national defense needs of the United States.

Section 102. Nothing contained in this Act shall be construed to authorize any department, agency, officer, or employee of the United States to exercise any direction, supervision, or control over the curriculum, program of instruction, administration, or personnel of any educational institution or school system. . . .

TITLE II—LOANS TO STUDENTS IN INSTITUTIONS OF HIGHER EDUCATION

Section 201. For the purpose of enabling the Commissioner [of Education] to stimulate and assist in the establishment at institutions of higher education of funds for the making of low-interest loans to students in need thereof to pursue their courses of study in such institutions, there are hereby authorized to be appropriated $47,500,000 for the fiscal year ending June 30, 1959, $75,000,000 for . . . 1960, $82,500,000 for . . . 1961, $90,000,000 for . . . 1962, and such sums for the fiscal year ending June 30, 1963, and each of the three succeeding fiscal years as may be necessary to enable students who have received a loan . . . to continue or complete their education. . . .

Section 205. (a) The total of the loans for any fiscal year to any student made by institutions of higher education from loan funds established pursuant to agreements under this title may not exceed $1,000, and the total for all years to any student from such funds may not exceed $5,000. . . .

TITLE III—FINANCIAL ASSISTANCE FOR STRENGTHENING SCIENCE, MATHEMATICS, AND MODERN FOREIGN LANGUAGE INSTRUCTION

Section 301. There are hereby authorized to be appropriated $70,000,000 for the fiscal year ending June 30, 1959, and for each of the three succeeding fiscal years, for (1) making payments to State educational agencies under this title for the acquisition of equipment (suitable for use in providing education in science, mathematics, or modern foreign language) and for minor remodeling described in paragraph (1) of section 303 (a), and (2) making loans authorized in section 305. There are also authorized to be appropriated $5,000,000 for the fiscal year ending June 30, 1959, and for each of the three succeeding fiscal years, for making payments to State educational agencies under this title to carry out the programs described in paragraph (5) of section 303 (a). . . .

Section 303. (a) Any State which desires to receive payments under this title shall submit to the Commissioner . . . a State plan which meets the requirements of section 1004 (a) and—

(1) sets forth a program under which funds paid to the State from its allotment under section 302 (a) [financial issues] will be expended solely for . . . (A) acquisition of laboratory and other special equipment, including audio-visual materials and equipment and printed material (other than textbooks), suitable for use in providing education in science, mathematics, or modern foreign language, in public elementary or secondary schools, or both, and (B) minor remodeling of laboratory or other space used for such materials or equipment . . .

(5) sets forth a program under which funds paid . . . under section 302 (b) [reserve funds] will be expended solely for (A) expansion or improvement of supervisory or related services in public elementary and secondary schools in the fields of science, mathematics, and modern foreign languages. . . .

TITLE IV—NATIONAL DEFENSE FELLOWSHIPS

Section 401. There are hereby authorized to be appropriated such sums as may be necessary to carry out the provisions of this title.

Section 402. During the fiscal year ending June 30, 1959, the Commissioner is authorized to award one thousand fellowships under the provisions of this title, and during each of the three succeeding fiscal years he is authorized to award one thousand five hundred such fellowships. Such fellowships shall be for periods of study not in excess of three academic years.

Section 403. (a) The Commissioner shall award fellowships under this title to individuals accepted for study in graduate programs approved by him under this section. . . .

TITLE V—GUIDANCE, COUNSELING, AND TESTING; IDENTIFICATION AND ENCOURAGEMENT OF ABLE STUDENTS

Section 501. There are hereby authorized to be appropriated $15,000,000 for the fiscal year ending June 30, 1959, and for each of three succeeding fiscal years, for making grants to State educational agencies under this part to assist them to establish and maintain programs of testing and guidance and counseling. . . .

Section 503. (a) Any State which desires to receive payments under this part shall submit to the Commissioner . . . a State plan which . . . sets forth—

(1) a program for testing students in the public secondary schools, and if authorized by law in other secondary schools, of such State to identify students with outstanding aptitudes and ability, and the means of testing which will be utilized in carrying out such program; and

(2) a program of guidance and counseling in the public secondary schools of such State (A) to advise students of courses of study best suited to their ability, aptitudes, and skills, and (B) to encourage students with outstanding aptitudes and ability to complete their secondary school education, take the necessary courses for admission to institutions of higher education, and to enter such institutions. . . .

TITLE VI—LANGUAGE DEVELOPMENT

Section 601. (a) The Commissioner is authorized to arrange through contracts with institutions of higher education for the establishment and operation by them . . . of centers for the teaching of any modern foreign language with respect to which the Commissioner determines (1) that individuals trained in such language are needed by the Federal government or by business, industry, or education in the United States, and (2) that adequate instruction in such language is not readily available in the United States. Any such contract may provide for instruction not only in such modern foreign language but also in other fields needed to provide a full understanding of the areas, regions, or countries in which such language is commonly used . . . including fields such as history, political science, linguistics, economics, sociology, geography, and anthropology. . . .

(b) The Commissioner is also authorized . . . to pay stipends to individuals undergoing advanced training in any modern foreign language . . . and other fields needed for a full understanding of the area, region, or country in which such language is commonly used. . . .

Section 611. There are hereby authorized to be appropriated $7,250,000 for the fiscal year ending June 30, 1959, and each of the three succeeding fiscal years, to enable the Commissioner to arrange, through contracts with institutions of higher education, for the operation by them of short-term or regular session institutes for advance training, particularly in the use of new teaching methods and instructional materials, for individuals who are engaged in or preparing to engage in the teaching, or supervising or training teachers, of any modern foreign language in elementary or secondary schools. . . .

TITLE VII—RESEARCH AND EXPERIMENTATION IN MORE EFFECTIVE UTILIZATION OF TELEVISION, RADIO, MOTION PICTURES, AND RELATED MEDIA FOR EDUCATIONAL PURPOSES

Section 701. In carrying out the provisions of this part the Commissioner, in cooperation with the Advisory Committee on New Educational Media . . . , shall (through grants and contracts) conduct, assist, and foster research and experimentation in the development and evaluation of projects involving television, radio, motion pictures, and related media of communication which may prove of value to State or local educational agencies in the operation of their public elementary or secondary schools, and to institutions of higher education, including the development of new and more effective techniques and methods—

(1) for utilizing and adapting motion pictures, video tapes and other audio-visual aids, film strips, slides and other visual aids, recordings (including magnetic tapes) and other auditory aids, and radio and television program scripts for such purposes;

(2) for training teachers to utilize such media with maximum effectiveness; and

(3) for presenting academic subject matters through such media.

TITLE VIII—AREA VOCATIONAL EDUCATION PROGRAMS

Section 801. The Congress hereby finds that the excellent programs of vocational education, which States have established and are carrying on with the assistance provided by the Federal Government under the Smith-Hughes Vocational Education Act and the Vocational Education Act of 1946 (the George-Barden Act), need extension to provide vocational education to residents of areas inadequately served and also to meet national defense requirements for personnel equipped to render skilled assistance in fields particularly affected by scientific and technological developments. It is therefore the purpose of this title to provide assistance to the States so that they may improve their vocational education programs through area vocational education programs approved by the State boards of vocational education as providing vocational and related technical training and retraining for youths, adults, and older persons, including related instruction for apprentices, designed to fit them for useful employment as technicians or skilled workers in scientific or technical fields.

Section 802. The Vocational Education Act of 1946 . . . is amended by adding after title II the following new title:

"Title III—Area Vocational Education Programs

"*Section 301.* There is authorized to be appropriated for the fiscal year ending June 30, 1959, and for each of the three succeeding fiscal years the sum of $15,000,000 for area vocational education programs. . . ."

TITLE IX—SCIENCE INFORMATION SERVICE

Section 901. The National Science Foundation shall establish a Science Information Service. The Foundation, through such Service, shall (1) provide, or arrange for the provision of, indexing, abstracting, translating, and other services leading to a more effective dissemination of scientific information, and (2) undertake programs to develop new or improved methods, including mechanized systems, for making scientific information available. . . .

Approved September 2, 1958.

NOTES

1. For a discussion, see chapter 5 on the Second Morrill Act, August 30, 1890.
2. For the complete text, see *United States Statutes at Large*, vol. 72 (Washington, DC: U.S. Government Printing Office, 1959), pp. 1580–1605.
3. On the public response to *Sputnik*, see Garrett Moritz, "From Sputnik to NDEA: The Changing Role of Science during the Cold War," (http://www.gtexts.com/college/papers/j3.html, 2000); and Robert A. Devine, *The Sputnik Challenge* (New York: Oxford University Press, 1993), pp. 15, 52–53.
4. Quoted in Devine, *The Sputnik Challenge*, p. 17.
5. Ibid., p. 53.
6. For a discussion of the legislative history of the NDEA, see Advisory Commission on Intergovernmental Relations, *The Evolution of a Problematic Partnership: The Feds and Higher Ed* (Washington, DC: Advisory Commission on Intergovernmental Relations, 1981), pp. 17–19.

7. James L. Sundquist, *Politics and Policy: The Eisenhower, Kennedy, and Johnson Years* (Washington, DC: Brookings Institution, 1968), p. 158.

8. On these data, see Sidney W. Tiedt, *The Role of the Federal Government in Education* (New York: Oxford University Press, 1966), pp. 30–31.

9. Gerald L. Gutek, *Education in the United States: An Historical Perspective* (Englewood Cliffs, NJ: Prentice-Hall, 1986), pp. 308–309.

10. Quoted in Advisory Commission on Intergovernmental Relations, *The Evolution of a Problematic Partnership*, p. 18.

11. See Lawrence E. Gladieux and R. Thomas Wolanin, *Congress and the Colleges* (Lexington, MA: Lexington Books, 1976), p. 9.

12. *United States Statutes at Large*, vol. 72, pp. 1580–1605.

11

The Economic Opportunity Act

August 20, 1964

The Economic Opportunity Act (EOA) was the centerpiece of President Lyndon Johnson's Great Society initiative. Johnson's comprehensive effort to eliminate poverty and expand opportunity in America represented a significant expansion of the role of the federal government in social policy. One of the central premises of the Great Society was that education was key to both reducing poverty and expanding opportunity—Johnson staffers believed that was the answer to most social problems. Over the 1960s, all told, there was a fivefold increase in federal spending on education. Educational initiatives were at the core of the EOA and the other legislative components of the Great Society (see, for instance, the Elementary and Secondary Education Act, 1965 [chapter 12], the Higher Education Act, 1965 [chapter 13], and the Bilingual Education Act, 1968 [chapter 14]). While the EOA had several educational components, its most lasting and influential educational effect was the creation of the Head Start program. Developed out of the EOA's Community Action Program provisions, Head Start provides early childhood education to hundreds of thousands of children from low-income families every year.

The politics surrounding the EOA were intense. President Johnson was personally committed to the act and deeply involved in all aspects of its formation and passage. It was proposed and pushed through Congress very quickly in order to be in place prior to the presidential election in the fall of 1964. One of the chief lobbyists for the act before Congress was then Attorney General Robert Kennedy, who argued that the move against poverty was fully in line with the intentions of his slain brother. The creation of Head Start under the EOA, by contrast, was largely unintended. There was no mention of Head Start or anything like it in the act itself. Rather, the EOA created the Community Action Program (CAP), which generated almost immediate opposition. Sargent Shriver, the first director of the Office of Economic Opportunity, wanted a CAP initiative that would be politically popular. From this motivation, ultimately, Head Start was created.

BACKGROUND

The purpose of the Economic Opportunity Act was to combat poverty in America—"to eliminate the paradox of poverty in the midst of plenty."[1] Johnson and his staff believed fundamentally that poverty resulted from a lack of opportunity. If doors could be opened, and opportunities could be provided for better, more prosperous, and more meaningful lives, people would seize these opportunities. Thus, in its declaration of purpose, the EOA calls for "opening to everyone the opportunity for education and training, the opportunity to work, and the opportunity to live in decency and dignity."[2] The act created a range of programs and services, several of which had an educational component, to provide these opportunities to low-income citizens.

Four sections of the EOA dealt explicitly with education. Title I, Part A, established the Job Corps, patterned after the Civilian Conservation Corps of the 1930s, which provided educational and work experience to young Americans. Targeted at unemployed or underemployed 16- to 21-year-olds, the Job Corps provided residential centers where enrollees would be provided the structure, training, and work experiences needed to help them succeed later in life. The centers were given an explicit mandate to provide necessary basic and vocational education to enrollees.

Title I, Part B, established work-training programs, intended to provide work experience or apprenticeship experiences to improve long-term employment prospects. The mandate was large, however, calling for programs that would see the education of enrollees "resumed or continued." Further, all such educational efforts were to be fully coordinated with local community schools.

Title I, Part C, established work-study programs for low-income students to pursue college education. The federal government was authorized to enter into contracts with individual colleges and universities to promote part-time employment for financially disadvantaged students who otherwise would be unable to attend these institutions.

Title II, Part A, established the Community Action Program. The intent was to provide funding for people in poor communities, at the grass-roots level, to determine what they needed to succeed. It was designed both to avoid top-down solutions to poverty from Washington and to empower and organize poor citizens. There was no explicit educational component to the CAP, but, as already noted and as will be detailed later, it became the mechanism for creating and organizing the Head Start program.

Title II, Part B, provided for programs of basic education for those 18 and older with limited English-language proficiency. The federal government paid for pilot or experimental programs to develop effective ways to improve the mastery of English and subsidized the costs incurred by local schools in teaching these adults.

After considerable debate and refinement within the administration, President Johnson submitted the War on Poverty bill—the EOA—to Congress on March 16, 1964. It was an opportune time to act against poverty: public consciousness had been raised through the publication of Michael Harrington's book *The Other America*, an expose of American poverty; the economy was very strong, and thus the means were available to act; and, so soon after President John F. Kennedy's assassination, support for President Johnson was extraordinarily high. The ultimate passage of the EOA was never seriously threatened, although there was an intense political fight.

President Johnson lobbied hard for the act, as did Robert Kennedy, Sargent Shriver, the brother-in-law of President Kennedy and then the director of the Peace Corps, Walter Heller, the respected chairman of the Council of Economic Advisors, the National Urban League, the AFL-CIO, and Walter Reuther, head of the United Auto Workers. Arguing against the EOA were the U.S. Chamber of Commerce, the National Association of Manufacturers, and the Farm Bureau Federation. In Congress, House and Senate opposition was led, respectively, by Peter Frelinghuysen (R-NJ) and John Tower (R-TX).[3]

The opponents of the bill mainly criticized the EOA as being far too expensive, promoting large, unwieldy government bureaucracy, and, in the end, likely to be ineffective in actually reducing poverty. Within Congress, however, Republican opponents also tried to undermine Southern Democratic support for the bill by emphasizing race. They argued that the bill was intended primarily to aid and help organize poor blacks. Johnson had foreseen this line of attack, however, and so had handpicked Congressman Phillip Landrum of Georgia to manage the bill in the House. Normally, the job would have fallen to Adam Clayton Powell, the flamboyant and controversial representative from Harlem in New York City, then the Chair of the Education and Labor Committee. As a Southern Democrat, Landrum argued forcefully that the EOA should be color blind.[4] In the end, while some Southern Democratic votes were lost, most stayed with Johnson. The EOA passed the Senate 62–33 and the House 228–190 and was signed into law by President Johnson on August 20, 1964. There had been tremendous pressure to pass the EOA before the fall presidential campaign, and, indeed, only six months elapsed between the submission of the bill and final passage.

The CAP almost immediately generated scrutiny and opposition. The CAP was intended to help poor communities help themselves; citizens in poor communities could organize themselves and play a central role in the design and administration of antipoverty measures. In practice, many city officials were uneasy about this level of citizen involvement and, especially, shared authority in the administration of programs.[5] As a result, relatively few cities applied for CAP funds for the first year of the EOA, and, consequently, an embarrassingly large surplus of unused CAP monies was projected. Such surpluses would have been used by critics to argue that the CAP was both unpopular and unneeded. Sargent Shriver, who had moved from the Peace Corps to head the War on Poverty, understood by the fall of 1964 that he needed to head off these two related problems.

Late in 1964, therefore, Shriver and his staff began thinking about a preschool educational program for poor children. Shriver had visited and been impressed by several small experimental programs around the country. In December, he asked Robert Cooke, the chair of the Department of Pediatrics at Johns Hopkins University, to head up an advisory council to design such a program— quickly, within just a couple of months. With the program still in the design stage, the administration pushed ahead.

In a message to Congress on the War on Poverty on January 12, 1965, just weeks after the Advisory Council was formed, President Johnson announced that there would be a new preschool program. The council then submitted a report and proposal in late January, and the administration immediately launched the initiative with a White House ceremony on February 19, 1965. It is unclear where the title "Head Start" came from, but it is known that Johnson's original preference was to call it the "Kiddy Corps." Regardless, no congressional action was needed, as the program fit under the CAP mandate to support services that "give promise of progress toward the elimination of poverty or a cause or causes of poverty."[6]

The Head Start program served several political purposes. By focusing on poor children, Shriver had a popular, nonthreatening initiative with which to promote the CAP. Shriver himself later said that he saw Head Start as a means to "overcome a lot of hostility in our society against the poor in general, and against black people who are poor in particular, by going at the children."[7] Beyond this, as an "off-the-shelf," predesigned program, Head Start made it easier for communities to get started in the CAP. Finally, in the short term, Head Start would use the CAP surplus for 1965. Given these advantages, in conjunction with the general action orientation of the entire War on Poverty, Head Start was implemented aggressively. The Advisory Council had recommended a small pilot program for 1965, involving several thousand children. The administration, however, was far more ambitious, announcing that 100,000 children would be in community Head Start programs during the summer of 1965. The result was the establishment of one of the largest and certainly one of the most popular of all federal education programs.

IMPACT

The educational impacts of the EOA largely derive from Head Start. The effects of Head Start have been studied extensively, and the results have been hotly debated. Politically, Head Start was heavily criticized by several presidential administrations but has enjoyed overwhelming popular and political support since the George Bush administration. Beyond Head Start, another, much smaller, but lasting educational component of the EOA has been the Job Corps. It has always been more controversial and far less popular than Head Start, but it has survived. Finally, the work-study program has become a regular, accepted part of higher education.

On both political and practical grounds, the mission of the Job Corps was difficult. First, from a political standpoint, unemployed, undereducated, frequently undisciplined 16- to 21-year-olds did not generate the same sympathy and care as the poor 4- and 5-year-old children in Head Start. Second, from a practical standpoint, the Job Corps was charged with dealing with problems after the fact, whereas Head Start was a preventive measure. Job Corps enrollees were already years behind in their schooling and/or a part of the hard-core unemployed in the country.

The residential centers established by the Job Corps were intended to provide discipline and structure, whatever educational help was needed, and job training and placement services. Studies done in the late 1960s hinted at some progress—higher educational attainment, higher rates of employment, increased earnings—but they were so unsystematic that no clear conclusions could be drawn.[8] Political opposition, however, became increasingly focused and vocal. Critics argued that the Job Corps was inefficient and wasteful and did little more than provide a resort atmosphere or coddle juvenile delinquents: "Why should juvenile virtue be rewarded with military service in the Vietnamese nightmare, while a record of delinquency exempts punks from the army and puts them in the line for Job Corps coddling?"[9] The administration of Richard Nixon was very hostile to the whole Job Corps idea. Authority for the program was transferred to the Labor Department, and President Nixon directed then Labor Secretary George Shultz to find a way to end the program.

The Job Corps endured, however, although as a much smaller-scale effort than was originally envisioned. Administrative responsibility for the Job Corps remains with the Labor Department today, and, all told, 1.7 million young adults have participated in the program since 1964. While the Job Corps retains an educational purpose, particularly emphasizing the need for enrollees to complete the general equivalency degree (GED), the greater focus is on job training and placement. The strictly educational benefits of the program, while real, have been minimal.

Head Start, as noted, was implemented on a fast track and on a large scale. The first summer, in 1965, 2,500 centers offered an eight-week Head Start program. On August 31, 1965, President Johnson announced that it would be expanded into a permanent, year-round program. During the four years from its inception to the end of the Johnson administration, Head Start received nearly $980 million, or approximately two-thirds of all CAP monies. By 1968, Head Start was being implemented in 1,300 summer programs and 1,100 year-round programs.

In 1966, Head Start encountered its first problem. The Coleman Report, a large study of educational opportunity in the United States mandated by the 1964 Civil Rights Act, was released and included an evaluation of the first summer programs. It focused strictly on educational gains associated with Head Start and concluded that they were quite minimal over time. Similar conclusions were then reached by the so-called Westinghouse Report in 1969.[10] These reports were themselves criticized for looking narrowly at test scores when Head Start was intended to be more holistic, promoting improvements in education, health, and parental involvement. Still, the fact that both studies found that Head Start produced educational gains that then faded out after a child entered traditional school had impacts.

When the "fade-out" issue was first raised by the Coleman Report, it prompted the Johnson administration to propose a new Follow Through program. Approved by Congress in 1967, Follow Through continues or extends Head Start services to children into the lower elementary grades.[11] The Westinghouse study, by contrast, led the Nixon administration to question the value of Head Start and prompted reductions in both funding and child enrollments.

Politically, Head Start experienced both administrative changes and varying levels of presidential support. In 1966, the EOA was amended explicitly to add the Head Start program. In 1969, administrative responsibility was transferred from the Office of Economic Opportunity to the Department of Health, Education, and Welfare. While the Nixon administration reduced funding, the administration of Jimmy Carter significantly increased funding and enrollees. Beyond this, however, President Carter also attempted to have Head Start transferred to the newly created Department of Education (see chapter 17). This proposal was successfully defeated by proponents of Head Start, who felt that under the Department of Education the noneducational purposes of the program would be diminished or lost entirely.

In 1982, the administration of Ronald Reagan proposed very significant funding cuts for Head Start, but these were rejected by Congress. Head Start has always enjoyed broad popular support and, since the Bush administration, tremendous political support as well. This is a reflection of public opinion and a series of large-scale longitudinal studies of the program. As a whole, these studies have concluded that Head Start produces modest, but real, meaningful, and lasting effects for the children involved.[12]

In 1990, the Human Services Reauthorization Act provided for a very significant increase in Head Start in terms of both funding and the number of children served. During the Bill Clinton administration, moreover, the expansion of Head Start was further accelerated, with funding more than doubled between 1992 and 1999. Annual funding for Head Start now exceeds $5 billion, and services are provided to more than 800,000 children.

In the end, these main educational initiatives of the Economic Opportunity Act have produced mixed results. The act was the core of the entire compilation of Great Society/War on Poverty legislation, and education, in turn, was at the core of much of the EOA. The work-study program, the Job Corps, and Head Start are all in place nearly 40 years later, with Head Start enjoying broad popularity and bipartisan political support. The educational benefits of the Job Corps, however—real improvements in learning and attainment—have been very limited. The educational benefits of Head Start are demonstrable and real, with the program clearly helping many children, but the benefits are more modest than what was hoped for in 1964 when the EOA was launched.

11. The Economic Opportunity Act

An Act To mobilize the human and financial resources of the Nation to combat poverty in the United States.[13]

Be it enacted by the Senate and House of Representatives of the United States of America in Congress assembled, That this Act may be cited as the "Economic Opportunity Act of 1964."

Section 2. Although the economic well-being and prosperity of the United States have progressed to a level surpassing any achieved in world history, and although these benefits are widely shared throughout the Nation, poverty continues to be the lot of a substantial number of our people. The United States can achieve its full economic and social potential as a nation only if every individual has the opportunity to contribute to the full extent of his capabilities and to participate in the workings of our society. It is, therefore, the policy of the United States to eliminate the paradox of poverty in the midst of plenty in this Nation by opening to everyone the opportunity for education and training, the opportunity to work, and the opportunity to live in decency and dignity. It is the purpose of this Act to strengthen, supplement, and coordinate efforts in furtherance of that policy.

TITLE I—YOUTH PROGRAMS

Part A—Job Corps

Section 101. The purpose of this part is to prepare for the responsibilities of citizenship and to increase the employability of young men and of young women aged sixteen through twenty-one by providing them in rural and urban residential centers with education, vocational training, useful work experience. . . .

Section 102. In order to carry out the purposes of this part, there is hereby established within the Office of Economic Opportunity . . . a Job Corps. . . .

Section 103. The Director of the Office . . . is authorized to . . .

(b) arrange for the provision of education and vocational training of enrollees in the Corps . . .

Part B—Work-Training Programs

Section 111. The purpose of this part is to provide useful work experience opportunities for unemployed young men and young women, through participation in State and community work-training programs, so that their employability may be increased or their education resumed or continued. . . .

Section 112. In order to carry out the purposes of this part, the Director shall assist and cooperate with State and local agencies and private non-profit organizations (other than political parties) in developing programs for the employment of young people in State and community activities hereinafter authorized, which, whenever appropriate, shall be coordinated with programs of training and education provided by local public educational agencies. . . .

Part C—Work-Study Programs

Section 121. The purpose of this part is to stimulate and promote the part-time employment of students in institutions of higher education who are from low-income families and are in need of the earnings of such employment to pursue courses of study at such institutions. . . .

Section 123. The Director is authorized to enter into agreements with institutions of higher education . . . to assist in the operation of work-study programs as hereinafter provided.

Section 124. An agreement entered into pursuant to section 123 shall—

(a) provide for the operation by the institution of a program for the part-time employment of its students in work—

(1) for the institution, or

(2) for a public or private nonprofit organization when the position is obtained through an arrangement between the institition and such an organization . . . and—

(A) the work is related to the student's educational objective . . .

TITLE II—URBAN AND RURAL COMMUNITY ACTION PROGRAMS

Part A—General Community Action Programs

Section 202. (a) The term "community action program" means a program—

(1) which mobilizes and utilizes resources, public or private, of any urban or rural, or combined urban and rural, geographical area . . . , including, but not limited to a State, metropolitan area, county, city, town, multicity unit, or multicounty unit in an attack on poverty;

(2) which provides services, assistance, and other activities of sufficient scope and size to give promise of progress toward elimination of poverty or a cause or causes of poverty . . .

(3) which is developed, conducted, and administered with the maximum feasible participation of residents of the areas and members of the groups served; and

(4) which is conducted, administered, or coordinated by a public or private nonprofit agency (other than a political party), or a combination thereof. . . .

Section 205. (a) The Director is authorized to make grants to, or to contract with, public or private nonprofit agencies . . . to pay part or all of the costs of community action programs . . . including the cost of carrying out programs which are components of a community action program and which are designed to achieve the purposes of this part. Such component parts shall be focused upon the needs of low-income individuals and families and shall provide expanded and improved services, assistance, and other activities, and facilities in connection therewith. Such programs shall be conducted in those fields which fall within the purposes of this part including employment, job training and counseling, health, vocational rehabilitation, housing, home management, welfare, and special remedial and other noncurricular educational assistance for the benefit of low-income individuals and families.

(b) No grant or contract authorized under this part may provide for general aid to elementary or secondary education in any school or school system. . . .

Part B—Adult Basic Education Program

Section 212. It is the purpose of this part to initiate programs of instruction for individuals who have attained age eighteen and whose inability to read and write the English language constitutes a substantial impairment of their ability to get or retain employment commensurate with their real ability, so as to help eliminate such inability and raise the level of education of such individuals. . . .

Approved August 20, 1964.

NOTES

1. *United States Statutes at Large*, vol. 78 (Washington, DC: U.S. Government Printing Office, 1965), p. 508.

2. Ibid.

3. For discussions of the political supporters and opponents of the EOA, see Irwin Unger, *The Best of Intentions: The Triumphs and Failures of the Great Society under Kennedy, Johnson, and Nixon* (New York: Doubleday, 1996); and James L. Sundquist, *Politics and Policy: The Eisenhower, Kennedy, and Johnson Years* (Washington, DC: Brookings Institution, 1968).

4. For a discussion of the roles of race and Congressman Landrum in the debate, see Unger, *The Best of Intentions*, pp. 91–99.

5. Sar A. Levitan, *The Great Society's Poor Law: A New Approach to Poverty* (Baltimore: Johns Hopkins Press, 1969), p. 111.

6. *United States Statutes at Large*, vol. 78, p. 516.

7. Quoted in Edward Zigler and Karen Anderson, "An Idea Whose Time Has Come: The Intellectual and Political Climate," in *Project Head Start: A Legacy of the War on Poverty*, ed. Edward Zigler and Jeanette Valentine (New York: Free Press, 1979), p. 12.

8. Ralph W. Tyler, "The Federal Role in Education," in *The Great Society: Lessons for the Future*, ed. Eli Ginzberg and Robert M. Solow (New York: Basic Books, 1974), pp. 164–187.

9. U.S. Congressman Paul A. Finno (R-NY), quoted in Shirley Scheibla, *Poverty Is Where the Money Is* (New Rochelle, NY: Arlington House, 1968), p. 102.

10. For a discussion of these reports, see Diane Ravitch, *The Troubled Crusade: American Education, 1945–1980* (New York: Basic Books, 1983), pp. 158–159, 238.

11. For a discussion of the Follow Through program, see Carol Doernberger and Edward Zigler, "Project Follow Through: Intent and Reality," in *Head Start and Beyond: A National Plan for Extended Childhood Intervention*, ed. Edward Zigler and Sally J. Styfco (New Haven: Yale University Press, 1993), pp. 43–72.

12. For an overview of these studies, see Francis H. Palmer and Lucille Woolis

Anderson, "Long-Term Gains from Early Intervention: Findings from Longitudinal Studies," in *Project Head Start: A Legacy of the War on Poverty*, ed. Edward Zigler and Jeanette Valentine (New York: Free Press, 1979), pp. 433–466.

   13. *United States Statutes at Large*, vol. 78, pp. 508–534.

12

The Elementary and Secondary Education Act

April 11, 1965

Immediately following passage of the Economic Opportunity Act (EOA) (see chapter 11), the Johnson administration moved ahead with plans to expand and deepen the War on Poverty. The central focus of these efforts, as with the EOA itself, was education. On January 12, 1965, President Lyndon Johnson made a major address and proposal to Congress on education. He called for passage of a wide-ranging set of educational reforms dealing with all levels of education, from preschool through graduate study. In considering the administration proposals, Congress quickly divided the initiatives into two legislative packages, one that became the Elementary and Secondary Education Act (ESEA), the other the Higher Education Act (HEA) (see chapter 13). In targeting primary and secondary education, the ESEA built upon the precedent of the 1958 National Defense Education Act (NDEA) (see chapter 10), but it went well beyond the NDEA in scope and reach. The ESEA extended federal financial assistance to 90 percent of all schools in the country. As a central part of the War on Poverty, the ESEA provided these monies to help improve the education and life opportunities of the most disadvantaged students.

Politically, the ESEA was unstoppable in 1965; the act passed Congress with little debate and virtually no amendments just 87 days after being introduced by the administration. This was no accident. President John F. Kennedy, Johnson's predecessor who was assassinated in 1963, had tried to follow up the NDEA with a broad education bill similar in scope to the ESEA, but he had been defeated due to intense conflicts over race and religion. The Johnson administration worked very diligently to line up votes and negotiate with groups Kennedy had fought before ever introducing the ESEA. While passage of the act looked easy, therefore, it was actually due to extensive planning done in 1964. Since its original passage, the ESEA has experienced a more troubled political life, at various times coming under both public and academic criticism. Today, however, it remains the single largest package of federal aid to and involvement in primary and secondary education.

BACKGROUND

The ESEA included five substantive titles. Far and away the largest and most important was Title I, representing five-sixths of all the monies appropriated by the act.[1] Title I amended P.L. 874, one of the two impact laws from the early 1950s (see chapter 9). Where the original purpose of P.L. 874 was to compensate local schools for the impact of federal employees and actions, Title I was to compensate them for the impact of large "concentrations of children from low-income families."[2] The explicit purpose of Title I was to fund programs that would meet "the special educational needs of educationally deprived children."[3] Then and now, Title I is the single largest federal program of aid to elementary and secondary schools.

An important provision of the act extended Title I benefits to private schools, including religious-affiliated schools. The ability to design legislative language to extend this federal aid to religious schools in a constitutionally sound manner, as discussed later, went a long way toward smoothing the road to passage for the entire act. Beyond this, Title I aid was provided without any requirement for matching funds from state or local governments. Taken together, the inclusion of private schools and the exclusion of a matching requirement ensured that Title I funding would reach the broadest possible segment of "educationally deprived" children.

While the other titles in the ESEA were by no means inconsequential, they were much smaller and less important than Title I. Title II provided federal funding for the purchase of library materials, including textbooks. As with Title I, these monies were fully extended to private and religious schools. There were concerns in some quarters that this would open the door for the federal government to involve itself in the actual selection of specific library materials and textbooks. As a result, a prohibition against such federal activities was added to the final "General Provisions" portion of the act.

Title III provided $100 million per year to fund "supplementary educational centers and services." The intent was to promote innovation in educational techniques to help reach children who are today labeled "at-risk" students. The mandate was very broad and provided for a great deal of flexibility. Title III enumerated a long list of eligible services and activities, including guidance programs, remedial instruction programs, the testing of model programs, and specialized educational programs.

Title IV provided funding for colleges and universities to carry out new educational research, and Title V provided resources to strengthen and improve state departments of education. The latter resulted from concerns that many state agencies were simply too weak or unprofessional successfully to plan and implement the varied educational programs needed to reach deprived children.

Passage of the ESEA has been described as a "piece of political artistry."[4] The earlier Kennedy education bill had foundered for several reasons. Conservatives in Congress were opposed to such a broad expansion of the federal role in education. Many Southern Democrats feared that federal education aid would be used as a stick to force the integration of schools. Finally, the deadlock between those supporting and opposing aid to parochial schools ensured congressional inaction. Due to a combination of circumstance and hard work, the Johnson proposal overcame all three problems and, as noted, was successfully rushed through Congress in under three months' time.

In Congress, conservative opposition and the race issue were largely resolved (if only temporarily) by political developments in 1964. The Johnson landslide over Barry Goldwater in the presidential election of November 1964 gave the president a strong mandate to act in 1965. Moreover, Johnson's election coattails generated huge Democratic congressional majorities—36 seats in the Senate and 155 in the House. Republican opponents criticized the ESEA and especially the speed with which it was moved through Congress (prompting some to suggest that the bill be renamed "the Railroad Act of 1965"), but they were simply overwhelmed by the new political realities of 1965.[5]

Similarly, the race issue had been largely addressed by the Civil Rights Act of 1964. Federal programs could not be administered on a discriminatory basis, and schools were going to be integrated regardless of any educational aid bill. As an impediment to passage of the ESEA, therefore, race did not have the same impact in 1965 that it had had on Kennedy's proposal in 1961.[6]

Religion, however, remained very much an issue. The administration worked on this issue, however, and effectively overcame the congressional parochial-school-aid logjam that had repeatedly blocked federal action in the past. Through planning and negotiation, the issue was largely settled before the ESEA was submitted to Congress. In 1964, the administration formed a White House task force on education, and this group worked with the National Education Association (historically opposed to parochial-school aid), the U.S. Catholic Conference (historically in favor of aid), and key members of Congress to find a workable solution to the impasse. This effort was aided immensely by casting the ESEA as a part of the War on Poverty, targeted at helping poor children. Politically, it was difficult for anyone to oppose such a goal, and, legally, this tactic allowed all parties to adopt the so-called child-benefit approach.

In 1947, in the *Everson v. Board of Education of the Township of Ewing* case, the U.S. Supreme Court had upheld the legality of public monies being spent to provide bus transportation for parochial-school students. The Court argued that the benefits in this instance went to the child, not the religious school. With the focus of the ESEA on uniquely disadvantaged children, the same argument was made. The act limited the use of federal funds to the support of nonreligious aspects of the school curriculum, and the child-benefit approach allowed for a truce in the "holy wars" over federal aid to elementary and secondary schools. Opponents of parochial-school aid were willing to accept this compromise.[7]

With the chronic impediments to broad federal education aid cleared away prior to submission, the path for the ESEA was clear: "These conditions produced a congressional debate that focused not on the hoary three R's of Race, Religion, and Reds, but on the formula for distributing Title I's proposed billion dollar aid."[8] With none of the contentiousness of prior education aid debates, the ESEA literally sailed through Congress. The only significant issue was raised by then Senator Robert Kennedy (D-NY), who wanted some system added to evaluate Title I programs and hold schools accountable, a notion that foreshadowed much of the debate over Title I in subsequent decades. At Kennedy's urging, the House added a provision for periodic evaluation of Title I program effectiveness.[9] Other than this, the House made virtually no amend-ments to the bill as proposed, and the Senate approved the House version in toto.

The final vote was overwhelming, 263–153 in the House and 73–18 in the Senate. President Johnson signed the ESEA into law in Stonewall, Texas, outside the one-room schoolhouse where he had begun his own elementary education. It was one of the high points of his administration, and he argued that all those who had worked for the act would "be remembered in history as men and women who began a new day of greatness in American society."[10]

IMPACT

That the ESEA has had a very large impact on American educa-tion is undeniable. Title I funding, originally authorized at $1 bil-lion for five years, now exceeds $8 billion per year. Then and now, about 90 percent of all schools in the country receive ESEA funding of some magnitude. Quite simply, the ESEA plays an important role in year-to-year school finance. While this funding flows to truly needy children and schools, there are real, persistent, and serious questions about the effectiveness of Title I. The evidence indicates that Title I has had only a marginal effect in terms of reducing educational disparities between advantaged and disadvantaged chil-dren.

The "minor" components of the ESEA largely achieved their ob-jectives. Title II has provided hundreds of millions of dollars for the purchase of library and related materials. Title III was intended to fund innovation and thereby loosen what was perceived to be an overly rigid, inflexible educational system. While there is debate today over the utility of such innovation, the funding did encourage many school districts to experiment with alternative schools of var-ious kinds, open classrooms, multiage classrooms, team teaching techniques, and teacher training in new methods.[11] Title IV pro-vided grants for educational research, although it is hard to derive a single evaluation of the impact and significance of the body of published work that resulted. Finally, Title V certainly strengthened state departments of education. At the time, many state education departments were viewed as tremendously understaffed and under-skilled; Title V provided funding that allowed the states to add more than 2,000 new staff members.

While Titles II, III, IV, and V succeeded in their intended purposes, these funds tended to flow disproportionately to middle-class and affluent school districts. To the extent that Title I was intended to redistribute educational resources from more affluent to less affluent communities, these subsidiary titles minimized the overall effect of the ESEA.[12]

Given the size of Title I within the ESEA, of course, its impact is central to any evaluation of the act as a whole. On the fundamental issue of Title I—improving the educational performance of disadvantaged students and thereby reducing the educational gap between these and more advantaged students—the evidence has always been very disappointing. The basic goal President Johnson had for the ESEA and Title I, for education to serve as "the vital factor in breaking the cycle of poverty,"[13] has simply not been realized.

From the start, empirical studies cast doubt on the effectiveness of Title I programs. As with Head Start before it (see chapter 11), the Coleman Report raised serious questions about the utility of all such compensatory education programs. Further studies initiated by the Department of Health, Education, and Welfare in the late 1960s reached similar conclusions. These early studies encouraged the Richard Nixon administration, already skeptical of all Great Society programs, to seek significant cuts in Title I funding. When Congress rejected these cuts, Nixon vetoed the appropriation, and his veto was then overridden by Congress. Further evaluations over the years, some commissioned by the federal government and some completed independently, have led to fairly consistent results: Title I programs produce some modest performance gains for disadvantaged students, but these gains fade after services are ended.[14]

The limited success of Title I in improving performance has several possible explanations. First, it has been argued that Title I expected educators to succeed in an area they knew very little about, to work in "what was essentially an uncharted area and to implement successful programs for the very group of children the schools historically had seemed least able to help."[15] Second, others argue that Title I is too unfocused to succeed. Services are to be provided to educationally deprived children, but such students are identified on a school-district-by-school-district basis. In districts with relatively few disadvantaged students, there may be sufficient funding to provide services to all students below the 50th percentile in performance. In communities where most students are objectively disadvantaged, however, funding may only cover services for those below the 25th or 30th percentile. Critics therefore argue that to see real, systematic improvements in performance, funding needs to be more tightly focused on the lowest-performing children.[16] Third, still others argue that performance gains have been minimal because funding has never been adequate to allow for success. While the total amount of Title I funding looks substantial, it is argued that on a per capita basis, it never amounted to much and therefore guaranteed failure.[17] Finally, following from the conclusions in the Coleman Report, it has been argued that school programs are less important vis-à-vis educational performance than family stability, support, and more. As Title I can do nothing about these latter issues, limited success is to be expected.

It is worth noting that some analysts, while acknowledging the minimal performance gains, believe that Title I and the ESEA generally have been successful in a number of nonquantifiable ways. A case can be made that the ESEA broke the congressional logjam preventing most forms of federal educational aid, and, indeed, that it helped create a "permanent coalition" in Congress supportive of education funding. In addition, Title I's emphasis on the poor helped raise the issue of equality and fairness in education and so contributed to later steps taken in the areas of bilingual education and education for children with handicaps or disabilities.[18]

In the end, the Elementary and Secondary Education Act has produced mixed results. It clearly set a legislative milestone; after many partial steps, with the ESEA the federal government became a full, if junior, partner with the states in primary and secondary education. The idea that the federal government ought to play an ongoing role in education at this level now enjoys very broad public and political support. In addition, it is equally clear that the ESEA has put needed monies into schools in very poor communities. The issue of effectiveness, however, is obviously a very serious problem; after 35 years of programming, the educational gap between advantaged and disadvantaged students remains stubbornly large. The issue of evaluation and accountability raised by Robert Kennedy at the start of the ESEA remains very much an issue and concern today.[19] The ESEA cannot be seen as a true success until far greater progress is made with respect to its central purpose of raising educational performance and extending opportunity.

12. The Elementary and Secondary Education Act

An Act To strengthen and improve educational quality and
educational opportunities in the Nation's elementary and
secondary schools.[20]

Be it enacted by the Senate and House of Representatives of the United
States of America in Congress assembled, That this Act may be cited as
the "Elementary and Secondary Education Act of 1965."

TITLE I—FINANCIAL ASSISTANCE TO LOCAL EDUCATIONAL AGENCIES FOR THE EDUCATION OF CHILDREN OF LOW-INCOME FAMILIES AND EXTENSION OF PUBLIC LAW 874, EIGHTY-FIRST CONGRESS

. . . .

Section 2. The Act of September 30, 1950, Public Law 874, . . . is
amended by . . . adding immediately after section 6 the following new title:

Title II—Financial Assistance to Local Educational Agencies for the Education of Children of Low-Income Families

"*Section 201.* In recognition of the special educational needs of children
of low-income families and the impact that concentrations of low-income
families have on the ability of local educational agencies to support adequate educational programs, the Congress hereby declares it to be the
policy of the United States to provide financial assistance . . . to local educational agencies serving areas with concentrations of children from low-
income families to expand and improve their educational programs by
various means (including preschool programs) which contribute particularly to meeting the special educational needs of educationally deprived
children.

"*Section 202.* The Commissioner [of Education] shall . . . make payments
to State educational agencies for basic grants to local educational agencies
. . . , and he shall make payments to State educational agencies for special
incentive grants to local educational agencies. . . .

"*Section 205.* (a) A local educational agency may receive a basic grant
or a special incentive grant . . . upon application therefor approved by the
appropriate State educational agency, upon its determination . . .

"(1) that payments under this title will be used for programs and
projects (including the acquisition of equipment and where necessary
the construction of school facilities) (A) which are designed to meet

the special educational needs of educationally deprived children in school attendance areas having high concentrations of children from low-income families and (B) which are of sufficient size, scope, and quality to give reasonable promise of substantial progress toward meeting those needs . . .

"(2) that, to the extent consistent with the number of educationally deprived children in the school district of the local educational agency who are enrolled in private elementary and secondary schools, such agency has made provision for including special educational services and arrangements (such as dual enrollment, educational radio and television, and mobile educational services and equipment) in which such children can participate; . . .

"(5) that effective procedures, including provisions for appropriate objective measurements of educational achievement, will be adopted for evaluating at least annually the effectiveness of the programs in meeting the special educational needs of educationally deprived children." . . .

TITLE II—SCHOOL LIBRARY RESOURCES, TEXTBOOKS, AND OTHER INSTRUCTIONAL MATERIALS

Section 201. (a) The Commissioner shall carry out during the fiscal year ending June 30, 1966, and each of the four succeeding fiscal years, a program for making grants for the acquisition of school library resources, textbooks, and other printed and published instructional materials for the use of children and teachers in public and private elementary and secondary schools. . . .

TITLE III—SUPPLEMENTARY EDUCATIONAL CENTERS AND SERVICES

Section 301. (a) The Commissioner shall carry out during the fiscal year ending June 30, 1966, and each of the four succeeding fiscal years, a program for making grants for supplementary educational centers and services, to stimulate and assist in the provision of vitally needed educational services not available in sufficient quantity or quality, and to stimulate and assist in the development and establishment of exemplary elementary and secondary school educational programs to serve as models for regular school programs. . . .

Section 303. Grants under this title may be used . . . for . . .

(b) the establishment, maintenance, and operation of programs, including the lease or construction of necessary facilities and acquisition of necessary equipment, designed to enrich the programs of elementary and secondary schools and to offer a diverse range of educational experience to persons of varying talents and needs by providing supplementary educational services and activities such as—

(1) comprehensive guidance and counseling, remedial instruction, and school health, physical education, recreation, psychological, and social work services designed to enable and encourage persons to enter, remain in, or reenter educational programs . . .

(2) comprehensive academic services . . .

(3) developing and conducting exemplary educational programs . . . for the purpose of stimulating the adoption of improved or new educational programs . . .

(4) specialized instruction and equipment for students interested in studying advanced scientific subjects, foreign languages, and other academic subjects which are not taught in the local schools . . .

(5) making available modern educational equipment and specially qualified personnel . . .

(6) developing, producing, and transmitting radio and television programs for classroom and other educational use;

(7) providing special educational and related services for persons who are in or from rural areas or who are or have been otherwise isolated from normal educational opportunities . . .

TITLE IV—EDUCATIONAL RESEARCH AND TRAINING

Section 401. The second section of the Act of July 26, 1954 . . . , entitled "An Act to authorize cooperative research in education", . . . is amended to read as follows: . . .

"*Section 2.* (a) (1) The Commissioner of Education . . . is authorized to make grants to universities and colleges and other public and private agencies, institutions, and organizations and to individuals, for research, surveys, and demonstrations in the field of education . . . , and for the dissemination of information derived from educational research (including but not limited to information concerning promising educational practices developed under programs carried out under the Elementary and Secondary Education Act of 1965). . . ."

TITLE V—GRANTS TO STRENGTHEN STATE DEPARTMENTS OF EDUCATION

Section 501. (a) The Commissioner shall carry out during the fiscal year ending June 30, 1966, and each of the four succeeding fiscal years, a program for making grants to stimulate and assist States in strengthening the leadership resources of their State educational agencies, and to assist those agencies in the establishment and improvement of programs to identify and meet the educational needs of States. . . .

TITLE VI—GENERAL PROVISIONS

. . .

Section 604. Nothing contained in this Act shall be construed to authorize any department, agency, officer, or employee of the United States to exercise any direction, supervision, or control over the curriculum, program of instruction, administration, or personnel of any educational institution or school system, or over the selection of any library resources, textbooks, or other printed or published instructional materials by any educational institution or school system.

Section 605. Nothing contained in this Act shall be construed to authorize the making of any payment under this Act . . . for religious worship or instruction.

Approved April 11, 1965.

NOTES

1. In 1981, Title I was formally changed to Chapter 1 of the Education Consolidation Improvement Act. In public discussions, it is still routinely referred to as Title I, however, and this convention will be used throughout.

2. *United States Statutes at Large,* vol. 79 (Washington, DC: U.S. Government Printing Office, 1965), p. 27.

3. *United States Statutes at Large,* vol. 79, p. 27.

4. Hugh Davis Graham, *The Uncertain Triumph: Federal Education Policy in the Kennedy and Johnson Years* (Chapel Hill: University of North Carolina Press, 1984), p. 68.

5. Diane Ravitch, *The Troubled Crusade: American Education, 1945–1980* (New York: Basic Books, 1983), pp. 148–149; and Hugh Davis Graham, "The Transformation of Federal Education Policy," in *The Johnson Years,* vol. 1, *Foreign Policy, the Great Society, and the White House,* ed. Robert A. Divine (Lawrence: University Press of Kansas, 1987), pp. 161–163.

6. Ravitch, *The Troubled Crusade,* p. 148.

7. On the whole religious-school-aid debate and compromise, see Sar A. Levitan, *The Great Society's Poor Law: A New Approach to Poverty* (Baltimore: Johns Hopkins Press, 1969), pp. 21–22; and Stephan K. Bailey and Edith K. Mosher, *ESEA: The Office of Education Administers a Law* (Syracuse, NY: Syracuse University Press, 1968), pp. 9–10, 33–34, 51.

8. Graham, "The Transformation of Federal Education Policy," p. 163. "Reds" refers to the heated rhetoric then sometimes used by conservative critics in discussing federal aid to education, associating it with socialism or communism.

9. On Kennedy's concerns and why the House chose to act first, see Graham, *The Uncertain Triumph,* pp. 78–79; and Bailey and Mosher, *ESEA,* p. 51.

10. Quoted in *Federal Role in Education* (Washington, DC: Congressional Quarterly Service, 1965), p. 45.

11. Ravitch, *The Troubled Crusade*, p. 256.

12. Graham, *The Uncertain Triumph*, p. 210.

13. Remarks made at the signing ceremony for the ESEA, quoted in Carmen G. Arroyo and Edward Zigler, "Title 1/Chapter 1 Programs: Why the Promise Has Not Been Met," in *Head Start and Beyond: A National Plan for Extended Childhood Intervention*, ed. Edward Zigler and Sally J. Styfco (New Haven: Yale University Press, 1993), p. 73.

14. See, for example, Stephen P. Mullins and Anita A. Summers, "Is More Better? The Effectiveness of Spending on Compensatory Education," *Phi Delta Kappan* 64, no. 5 (January 1983): 339–347; and Virginia R.L. Plunkett, "From Title 1 to Chapter 1: The Evolution of Compensatory Education," *Phi Delta Kappan*, 66, no. 8 (April 1985): 533–537.

15. Milbrey Wallin McLaughlin, "Implementation of ESEA Title I: A Problem of Compliance," *Teachers College Record* 77 (February 1976): 404; Ravitch, *The Troubled Crusade*, pp. 159–60; and Ralph W. Tyler, "The Federal Role in Education," in *The Great Society: Lessons for the Future*, ed. Eli Ginzberg and Robert M. Solow, (New York: Basic Books, 1974), pp. 168–69.

16. Arroyo and Zigler, "Title 1/Chapter 1 Programs," p. 82.

17. Irwin Unger, *The Best of Intentions: The Triumphs and Failures of the Great Society under Kennedy, Johnson, and Nixon* (New York: Doubleday, 1996), p. 358; James L. Sundquist, *Politics and Policy: The Eisenhower, Kennedy, and Johnson Years* (Washington, DC: Brookings Institution, 1968), p. 536; and Tyler, "The Federal Role in Education," pp. 168–69.

18. See, for instance, Graham, *The Uncertain Triumph*, pp. 209–210.

19. It was an issue, for instance, in the 2000 presidential race, with Republican nominee George W. Bush proposing changes in Title I. He argued that in schools where Title I programs were deemed ineffective for three straight years, federal funds should be transferred to the parents of disadvantaged students for use as vouchers. Democratic nominee Vice-President Al Gore argued against using Title I monies for vouchers, suggesting instead that the administrative and teaching staff in failing school, be removed or otherwise held accountable.

20. *United States Statutes at Large*, vol. 79, pp. 27–58.

13

The Higher Education Act

November 8, 1965

The Higher Education Act (HEA) was the last of the major Great Society education bills initiated by President Lyndon Johnson. In 1965, it was seen as the smaller, less controversial partner to the Elementary and Secondary Education Act (ESEA) (see chapter 12). President Johnson's single package of comprehensive educational initiatives had been divided into these two bills for consideration by Congress. Because various forms of aid to colleges and universities had been passed previously, whereas general aid to primary and secondary schools was new, the HEA was a far less controversial proposal than the ESEA. Considered independently, however, it was a very large and significant act, helping consolidate prior federal higher-education provisions and putting in place new programs that today represent the largest commitment of federal resources to higher education. The act provided assistance to strengthen institutions that served poor and underrepresented student populations and to make higher education affordable for such students. At root, therefore, the intent of the HEA was significantly to broaden access to college and university education.

The politics of the ESEA in the spring of 1965 had been quite unusual, for the bill had been rushed through Congress with little debate and virtually no amendments in under three months' time (see chapter 12). The politics surrounding the HEA, by contrast, were far more normal, with the bill moving through Congress on a typical schedule and being subject to debate, amendment, and competing group interests. While the ESEA was passed almost exactly as submitted by the White House, the HEA reflected far more political compromise. Still, given all of the political advantages enjoyed by the Johnson administration and congressional Democrats in 1965, the ultimate passage of the act was always secure.

BACKGROUND

In broadening access to higher education, the HEA had two related emphases, to provide resources to strengthen colleges and universities as institutions, and to provide direct financial assistance to students. Of the six substantive titles in the act, Title IV focused on the latter goal, while the other titles focused on the former. Throughout, the act incorporated aspects of prior legislation—the student loan program from the National Defense Education Act (see chapter 10) and the work-study program from the Economic Opportunity Act (see chapter 11), for instance—while also creating a series of new initiatives. The result was a single, comprehensive statement of federal activities to improve and broaden access to higher education.

Title I of the HEA was, in many ways, a logical extension of the Community Action Program of Johnson's War on Poverty (see chapter 11 on the Economic Opportunity Act). It was based on the idea of an "urban land-grant extension," something President Johnson had discussed in several speeches. The concern was that the land-grant colleges and universities supported by the federal government, given their agricultural roots, tended to direct federal resources toward smaller, rural communities. The intent of Title I, therefore, was to provide resources to encourage colleges and universities to establish extension programs and services in urban areas. For 1966, $25 million was provided for grants to institutions to create or expand community-service programs to help alleviate urban problems.[1]

Title II provided federal funds for grants to individual colleges and universities to purchase library materials and improve library training and research. The provision was the result of significant lobbying by both the American Library Association and the Association of Research Libraries.[2] Because benefits flowed to institutions all across the country, congressional support was substantial.

Title III provided monies for so-called developing institutions, defined, roughly, as institutions of higher education whose growth and/or quality were seriously impeded by a lack of financial resources. The central motive for Title III was to provide needed resources to historically black colleges. These institutions had been systematically underfunded for generations and, as a rule, struggled financially. If the opportunity for higher education were expanded to significantly greater numbers of African Americans, many students would choose to attend these institutions, and they would need to be strengthened, enlarged, and improved. Rather than single out institutions on the basis of race, however, the notion of "developing institutions" was employed.[3] As will be discussed later, the vagueness of the term allowed Title III to expand well beyond aid to the historically black colleges and universities and to become one of the single largest programs of federal aid to higher education.

Title IV dealt with student financial assistance and created the most significant of the new HEA programs. The goal was to create greater opportunities for middle- and lower-class students, especially the latter, to attend college. To achieve this, the act established a four-part system of assistance, incorporating two new and two existing programs. The first of the new programs was a $70-million annual appropriation for "Educational Opportunity Grants," which are still in use today and which became the organizational basis for the later creation of Pell Grants. These were grants (originally to the colleges and universities, later amended to flow directly to the students) for scholarships to students "of exceptional financial need." The other new student aid program created by the HEA was the guaranteed student loan (GSL) program. As opposed to the Educational Opportunity Grants, the GSL program was aimed at the middle class. No financial-needs test was attached to GSLs; middle-class students could secure school loans from private commercial institutions, with the federal government subsidizing a below-market interest rate, and the loan was payable over a 10-year period after schooling was complete. In addition to these new programs, Title IV also incorporated the work-study program created a year earlier in the Economic Opportunity Act and the narrower student loan program created in 1958 in the National Defense Education Act.[4]

Title V was quite small, but was easily the most controversial part of the act. Sponsored by Senator Edward Kennedy (D-MA), it established a national Teacher Corps, patterned after President John Kennedy's Peace Corps. The idea was to create a corps of dedicated young teachers to work in the most distressed urban school systems around the country. As a Kennedy rather than an administration proposal, it received only lukewarm support from President Johnson. As a form of direct federal involvement in local classrooms, it drew intense opposition from conservatives in Congress. Further, given its implicit criticism of the existing teachers in, and teacher training for, urban schools, the proposal drew the opposition of many teachers and the teachers' colleges. Kennedy originally tried to add the Teacher Corps as an amendment to the ESEA, where it logically belonged, but due to the opposition and the administration's imperative to push the ESEA through Congress quickly, it was dropped. Kennedy then successfully attached the Teacher Corps proposal to the HEA. Highlighting the controversy around the proposal, however, was the fact that while Senator Kennedy secured the creation of the corps on paper, it received no appropriation actually to begin functioning. Monies for the Teacher Corps had to be fought for and were just barely secured in 1966.[5]

Finally, Title VI provided funding for grants to individual colleges and universities to purchase and upgrade classroom equipment. Support was given particularly for the purchase of laboratory, audiovisual, and other specialized classroom equipment.

Congress had repeatedly passed bills related to higher education—the Northwest Ordinance (chapter 2), the two Morrill Acts (chapters 3 and 5), the G.I. Bill (chapter 7), and much of the NDEA (chapter 10)—and so consideration of the HEA followed a normal legislative path. There were months of hearings, and amendments were made to the administration proposal. Again, this separated the HEA from the more controversial ESEA. Politically, however, the most difficult part of the HEA was Title IV, dealing with financial aid for college and university students. Democrats wanted a college scholarship program, while Republicans wanted tuition tax credits. The former would largely focus benefits on lower- and working-class families, a largely Democratic constituency. The latter would focus benefits on middle-class families, a largely Republican constituency. Democrats had originally tried to provide scholarships in the NDEA in 1958, but had been defeated by critics who felt that scholarships provided "something for nothing" and would be open to abuse by some students. In 1965, however, with a very different political makeup in Congress, Democrats were able to create scholarships through $70 million per year in funding for the Educational Opportunity Grants program.

Congressional Republicans, by contrast, had long advocated tuition tax credits, whereby families could effectively deduct college tuition costs from their federal taxes. The Johnson administration saw such credits as far too expensive, putting a serious drain on federal revenues. The political appeal of helping middle-class families was very real, however, and the compromise was found in the guaranteed student loan program. The GSL program was clearly aimed at the middle class, but provided aid at a much smaller cost to the U.S. Treasury.[6]

All of the political advantages enjoyed by the White House and congressional Democrats in passing the ESEA were still operative with the HEA. The 1964 Johnson landslide election victory gave the administration tremendous legislative momentum, and Democrats enjoyed huge majorities in both the House and the Senate. The final bill easily passed, and President Johnson held the signing ceremony at his own alma mater, Southwest Texas State. With the EOA and ESEA already in place, the HEA was the last major piece of the administration's education agenda. President Johnson, never shy in his use of rhetoric, in reflecting on the passage of both the ESEA and the HEA in one year, stated that in 1965 Congress "did more for the wonderful cause of education in America than all the previous 176 regular sessions of Congress, put together."[7]

IMPACT

The HEA has had a significant impact on the role of the federal government in higher education. The act consolidated the existing components of a higher-education policy from the NDEA and the EOA into one place and added to and filled out the overall policy. The HEA has been reauthorized repeatedly since 1965 and continues to provide the framework for federal higher-education policy. In addition, the HEA represented a tremendous expansion of the federal resources dedicated to higher education, and appropriations have increased still further with each reauthorization.

The biggest effects of the HEA derive from Titles III and IV, but, as in the debate over passage, the most controversial and difficult part of the act involved Title V, the Teacher Corps. As noted, the Teacher Corps was created, but no monies were provided for 1966. Senator Kennedy and the White House spent 1966 fighting for an appropriation for 1967 and only barely succeeded. At one point, after the House deleted all funding, it was restored by the Senate on a narrow 46–45 vote. The funding achieved, moreover, was quite limited; the administration had requested $31 million for 6,000 teachers, but received only $9.5 million for 1,600 teachers. The Teacher Corps always remained small and contentious, with limited political support, and was ultimately abolished in 1981.[8]

Title III, dealing with "developing institutions," achieved its immediate goals and then grew and expanded into a much larger program. The goal of aiding historically black colleges and thereby allowing for increased minority enrollments was achieved. From 1966 to 1971, 56 percent of all Title III monies flowed to historically black colleges, and enrollments at these institutions increased by 25 percent. Overall, the percentage of African Americans aged 18 to 24 attending institutions of higher education increased from 10 to 16 percent in the five years following passage of the HEA.[9]

In subsequent years, Title III was continually and very significantly expanded. Begun with a $5-million annual appropriation in 1966, Title III totaled $110 million 10 years later and $408 million in 1999. Institutions with largely majority, white student enrollments quickly received the bulk of Title III funds. This change led to some tensions between institutions, especially in the 1970s and 1980s. Further, some congressional critics have complained that "developing institutions" never cease to be "developing," that once an institution becomes eligible for Title III monies, it never ceases to receive aid. A performance audit of Title III completed in 2000, however, was very positive. It concluded that a significant share of funding continues to flow to largely minority institutions, and that monies are primarily employed to strengthen academic programs, curricular development, and new technology.[10]

Title IV, dealing with college affordability and access, has had a huge impact, one that is widely viewed as positive and productive. In 1966 alone, 200,000 low-income students received Educational Opportunity Grants to attend college. By 1970, the four component parts of Title IV had provided financial assistance to more than 2 million students. The programs involved have been expanded even more since then.[11]

The Nixon administration proposed consolidating the work-study program, the NDEA loan program, and Educational Opportunity Grants into one new Basic Educational Opportunity Grant. Congress rejected the consolidation proposal, but did create a new grant, quickly labeled Pell Grants (after Senate sponsor Claiborne Pell). Thus Pell Grants were not created by the HEA, but were an expansion of the HEA system of student aid.[12] The GSL program grew very rapidly and by the 1980s was heavily criticized for high default rates as growing numbers of students defaulted on loans guaranteed by the federal government. The entire GSL system was thus reformed in the early 1990s, with the program changed to the Federal Family Education Loan system with much more stringent oversight, and default rates have declined dramatically. Altogether, 1999 federal funding for student aid—Educational Opportunity Grants, Pell Grants, Federal Family Education Loans, and work-study—totaled more than $15.6 billion dollars, a dramatic increase since 1965.

In 1965, the HEA was cast as the junior partner to the ESEA, but its impact was, and continues to be, significant. The federal government now plays a large, ongoing role in the financing of higher education. It does so directly, through hundreds of millions of dollars in appropriations for institution building under Title III, and indirectly, through the funding of millions of college students. Since 1965, enrollments in institutions of higher education have increased more than twofold, from 6 million to more than 15 million. College enrollments have grown at a much faster rate than the total U.S. population. Many factors have contributed to this tremendous expansion of higher education and all it means for opportunity in American society, but the HEA is certainly one of these factors.

13. The Higher Education Act

An Act To strengthen the educational resources of our colleges and universities and to provide financial assistance for students in postsecondary and higher education.[13]

Be it enacted by the Senate and House of Representatives of the United States of America in Congress assembled, That this Act may be cited as the "Higher Education Act of 1965."

TITLE I—COMMUNITY SERVICE AND CONTINUING EDUCATION PROGRAMS

For the purpose of assisting the people of the United States in the solution of community problems such as housing, poverty, government, recreation, employment, youth opportunities, transportation, health, and land use by enabling the Commissioner [of Education] to make grants under this title to strengthen community service programs of colleges and universities, there are authorized to be appropriated $25,000,000 for the fiscal year ending June 30, 1966, and $50,000,000 for . . . 1967, and for the succeeding fiscal year . . .

Section 102. For the purposes of this title, the term "community service program" means an educational program, activity, or service, including a research program and a university extension or continuing education offering, which is designed to assist in the solution of community problems. . . .

TITLE II—COLLEGE LIBRARY ASSISTANCE AND LIBRARY TRAINING AND RESEARCH

Part A—College Library Resources

Section 201. There are authorized to be appropriated $50,000,000 for the fiscal year ending June 30, 1966, and for each of the two succeeding fiscal years, to enable the Commissioner to make grants under this part to institutions of higher education to assist and encourage such institutions in the acquisition for library purposes of books, periodicals, documents, magnetic tapes, phonograph records, audiovisual materials, and other related library materials (including necessary binding). . . .

Part B—Library Training and Research

Section 221. There are authorized to be appropriated $15,000,000 for the fiscal year ending June 30, 1966, and for each of the two succeeding fiscal years, for the purpose of carrying out this part. . . .

Section 223. The Commissioner is authorized to make grants to institutions of higher education to assist them in training persons in librarianship. . . .

Section 224. (a) The Commissioner is authorized to make grants to institutions of higher education, and other public and private agencies, institutions, and organizations, for research and demonstration projects relating to the improvement of libraries or the improvement of training in librarianship. . . .

Part C—Strengthening College and Research Library Resources

Section 231. There are hereby authorized to be appropriated $5,000,000 for the fiscal year ending June 30, 1966, $6,315,000 for . . . 1967, and $7,770,000 for . . . 1968, to enable the Commissioner to transfer funds to the Librarian of Congress for the purpose of—

(1) acquiring, so far as possible, all library materials currently published throughout the world which are of value to scholarship; and

(2) providing catalog information for these materials promptly after receipt. . . .

TITLE III—STRENGTHENING DEVELOPING INSTITUTIONS

Section 301. (a) The purpose of this title is to assist in raising the academic quality of colleges which have the desire and potential to make a substantial contribution to the higher education resources of our Nation but which for financial and other reasons are struggling for survival and are isolated from the main currents of academic life, and to do so by enabling the Commissioner to establish a national teaching fellow program and to encourage and assist in the establishment of cooperative arrangements under which these colleges may draw on the talent and experience of our finest colleges and universities, and on the educational resources of business and industry, in their effort to improve their academic quality. . . .

Section 304. (a) The Commissioner is authorized to make grants to developing institutions and other colleges and universities to pay part of the cost of planning, developing, and carrying out cooperative arrangements which show promise as effective measures for strengthening the academic programs and the administration of developing institutions. . . . Grants under this section may be used for projects and activities such as—

(1) exchange of faculty or students . . .

(2) faculty and administration improvement programs . . .

(3) introduction of new curriculums and curricular materials;

(4) development and operation of cooperative education programs . . .

(5) joint use of facilities. . . .

TITLE IV—STUDENT ASSISTANCE

Part A—Educational Opportunity Grants

Section 401. (a) It is the purpose of this part to provide, through institutions of higher education, educational opportunity grants to assist in making available the benefits of higher education to qualified high school graduates of exceptional financial need, who for lack of financial means of their own or of their families would be unable to obtain such benefits without such aid.

(b) There are hereby authorized to be appropriated $70,000,000 for the fiscal year ending June 30, 1966, and for each of the two succeeding fiscal years, to enable the Commissioner to make payments to institutions of higher education . . . for payments to undergraduate students for . . . educational opportunity grants . . .

Part B—Federal, State, and Private Programs of Low-Interest Insured Loans to Students in Institutions of Higher Education

Section 421. (a) The purpose of this part is to enable the Commissioner (1) to encourage States and nonprofit private institutions and organizations to establish adequate loan insurance programs for students . . . , (2) to provide a Federal program of student loan insurance for students who do not have reasonable access to a State or private nonprofit program of student loan insurance . . . , and (3) to pay a portion of the interest on loans to qualified students. . . .

Part C—College Work-Study Program Extension and Amendments

Section 441. Parts C and D of the title I of the Economic Opportunity Act of 1964 . . . are amended as follows . . .

(3) By striking out section 123 and inserting in lieu thereof the following:

"*Section 123.* (a) The Commissioner is authorized to enter into agreements with institutions of higher education under which the Commissioner will make grants to such institutions to assist in the operation of work-study programs. . . ."

Section 442. There are authorized to be appropriated $129,000,000 for the fiscal year ending June 30, 1966, $165,000,000 for . . . 1967, and $200,000,000 for . . . 1968, to carry out the purposes of part C of title I of the Economic Opportunity Act of 1964. . . .

TITLE V—TEACHER PROGRAMS

Part A—General Provisions

Section 501. (a) The Commissioner shall establish in the Office of Education an Advisory Council on Quality Teacher Preparation. . . .

Section 502. Nothing contained in this title shall be construed to authorize the making of any payment under this title for religious worship or instruction.

Part B—National Teacher Corps

Section 511. (a) The purpose of this part is to strengthen the educational opportunities available to children in areas having concentrations of low-income families and to encourage colleges and universities to broaden their programs of teacher preparation by—

(1) attracting and training qualified teachers who will be made available to local educational agencies for teaching in such areas; and

(2) attracting and training inexperienced teacher-interns who will be

made available for teaching and inservice training to local educational agencies in such areas in teams led by an experienced teacher.

(b) For the purpose of carrying out this part, there are authorized to be appropriated $36,000,000 for the fiscal year ending June 30, 1966, and $64,715,000 for . . . 1967. . . .

Section 516. Members of the Teacher Corps shall be under the direct supervision of the appropriate officials of the local educational agencies. . . .

Part C—Fellowships for Teachers

Section 521. The Congress hereby declares it to be the policy of the United States to improve the quality of education offered by the elementary and secondary schools of the Nation by improving the quality of the education of persons who are pursuing or who plan to pursue a career in elementary or secondary education. The purpose of this part is to carry out this policy by awarding fellowships for graduate study at institutions of higher education and by developing or strengthening teacher education programs in institutions of higher education. . . .

Section 528. There are hereby authorized to be appropriated to carry out this part $40,000,000 for the fiscal year ending June 30, 1966, $160,000,000 for . . . 1967, $275,000,000 for . . . 1968. . . .

TITLE VI—FINANCIAL ASSISTANCE FOR THE IMPROVEMENT OF UNDERGRADUATE INSTRUCTION

Part A—Equipment

Section 601. (a) The purpose of this part is to improve the quality of classroom instruction in selected subject areas in institutions of higher education.

(b) There are hereby authorized to be appropriated $35,000,000 for the fiscal year ending June 30, 1966, $50,000,000 for . . . 1967, and $60,000,000 for . . . 1968, to enable the Commissioner to make grants to institutions of higher education pursuant to this part for the acquisition of equipment . . . described in section 603 (2) (A).

(c) There are hereby authorized to be appropriated $2,500,000 for the fiscal year ending June 30, 1966, $10,000,000 for . . . 1967, and for the succeeding fiscal year, to enable the Commissioner to make grants to institutions of higher education pursuant to this part for the acquisition of television equipment . . . described in section 603 (2) (B). . . .

Section 603. Any State desiring to participate in the program under this part shall . . . submit to the Commissioner . . . a State plan. . . . The Commissioner shall approve any such plan which . . .

(2) sets forth . . . objective standards and methods (A) for determining the relative priorities of eligible projects for the acquisition of laboratory and other special equipment . . . for classrooms or libraries, suitable for providing education in science, mathematics, foreign languages, history, geography, government, English, other humanities, the arts . . . ; (B) for determining relative priorities of eligible projects for (i) the acquisition of television equipment for closed circuit direct instruction in such fields . . . [and] (ii) the acquisition of necessary instructional materials for use in such television instruction. . . .

TITLE VIII—GENERAL PROVISIONS . . .

. . .

Section 804. (a) Nothing contained in this Act shall be construed to authorize any department, agency, officer, or employee of the United States to exercise any direction, supervision, or control over the curriculum, program of instruction, administration, or personnel of any educational institution, or over the selection of library resources by any educational institution. . . .

Approved November 8, 1965.

NOTES

1. For a discussion of the urban land-grant idea, see Hugh Davis Graham, *The Uncertain Triumph: Federal Education Policy in the Kennedy and Johnson Years* (Chapel Hill: University of North Carolina Press, 1984), pp. 80–81.

2. See Graham, *The Uncertain Triumph,* p. 81.

3. For a discussion of the motivation and origins of Title III, see Henry E. Cobb, *Report on an Examination of the Developing Institutions Program* (Washington, DC: U.S. Office of Education, 1977), pp. 15–42.

4. On the development of the various components of Title IV, see Advisory Commission on Intergovernmental Relations, *The Evolution of a Problematic Partnership: The Feds and Higher Ed* (Washington, DC: Advisory Commission on Intergovernmental Relations, 1981), p. 23; and Graham, *The Uncertain Triumph,* pp. 80–82.

5. On the fight and controversy over the Teachers Corps, see Irwin Unger, *The Best of Intentions: The Triumphs and Failures of the Great Society under Kennedy, Johnson, and Nixon* (New York: Doubleday, 1996), pp. 127–128.

6. On the development of the Title IV provisions, see James L. Sundquist, *Politics and Policy: The Eisenhower, Kennedy, and Johnson Years* (Washington, DC: Brookings Institution, 1968), pp. 215–216; and Advisory Commission on Intergovernmental Relations, *The Evolution of a Problematic Partnership,* p. 23.

7. Quoted in Sundquist, *Politics and Policy,* p. 216.

8. On the appropriations fight for the Teachers Corps, see Unger, *The Best of Intentions,* pp. 209–212.

9. Eli Ginzberg and Robert M. Solow, eds., *The Great Society: Lessons for the Future* (New York: Basic Books, 1974), pp. 176–177.

10. On the impact of Title III, see Cobb, *Report on an Examination of the Developing Institutions Program*, pp. 15–42; and U.S. Department of Education, *The Performance Measurement Study of the Title III Institutional Aid Program: Highlights of Findings* (http://www.ed.gov/offices/OUS/PES/higher/title3.html, 2000).

11. Ginzberg and Solow, *The Great Society*, pp. 176–177.

12. Lawrence E. Gladieux and Arthur M. Hauptman, *The College Aid Quandary: Access, Quality, and the Federal Role* (Washington, DC: Brookings Institution and the College Board, 1995), pp. 16–17.

13. *United States Statutes at Large*, vol. 79 (Washington, DC: U.S. Government Printing Office, 1966), pp. 1219–1220.

14

The Bilingual Education Act

January 2, 1968

The Bilingual Education Act (BEA) was the first piece of federal legislation to deal specifically with language and culture in the schools. Prior to passage of the act, language-related programs— like those encouraging innovative teaching techniques and anti-poverty measures—were possible under broader federal programs such as NDEA and EOA grants, but these measures did not deal exclusively with language and culture. The BEA raised questions and issues regarding diversity and assimilation, cultural pride, and national unity that are still intensely debated today. The act and all of the issues it highlighted are very controversial, and consequently, the act has been substantially amended several times since 1968. The act has endured, however, and has provided significant federal funding for bilingual and other language-related programs in the schools, adult-education programs, vocational-education programs, efforts to reduce dropout rates among targeted populations, and efforts to promote cultural knowledge and appreciation.

The BEA is often cast as a part of President Lyndon Johnson's Great Society/War on Poverty package of education legislation, but it was actually initiated by Congress. The administration at first opposed the act, and, when passage became clear, only reluctantly and tepidly endorsed the effort. Senator Ralph Yarborough (D–TX) actually led the push for the BEA in an effort to mobilize Hispanic voters for what he expected to be a very tough reelection bid in 1970. That Yarborough saw the bill through to passage is testament to real political skill. The more important politics, however, involve the debate since passage. The language/culture issue raises strong emotions on all sides, and political debate from the 1970s to the present has usually been intense and sometimes inflammatory.

BACKGROUND

The Bilingual Education Act was incorporated as a part of amendments to the Elementary and Secondary Education Act (ESEA) of 1965 (see chapter 12) creating a new Title VII within the ESEA. In constructing the BEA, Congress made the intention of the act very clear: "The Congress hereby finds that one of the most acute educational problems in the United States is that which involves millions of children of limited English-speaking ability . . . [therefore,] Congress hereby declares it to be the policy of the United States to provide financial assistance to local educational agencies to develop and carry out new and imaginative elementary and secondary school programs designed to meet these special educational needs."[1] To meet this objective, $15 million was appropriated for 1968, with funding rising to $40 million by 1970. These monies were originally targeted at students from poor families, although this provision was later changed.

The act was designed to fund two basic activities, programs to train teachers and staff who worked with students with English deficiencies, and programs that provided direct services to such students. It is important to note that despite the title of the act, it did not mandate or even define bilingual education programs. Under the act as passed, grants could be provided to support bilingual programs, but other eligible activities included programs to increase the contact and cooperation between families and schools, programs to promote knowledge of the history and cultures associated with particular languages, adult and vocational education, and efforts designed to reduce the number of students who dropped out of school. All of these latter programs were to be targeted at students, adults, and families who had an English-language deficiency.

The enactment of the BEA owed everything to Senator Yarborough. Yarborough entered the Senate from Texas in 1957, winning a simple plurality in a special election with a field of 22 candidates. He was reelected to a full term in 1958, but his very liberal voting record was expected to lead to a difficult reelection campaign in 1964. The assassination of President John F. Kennedy and the subsequent Johnson landslide in the presidential election of 1964, however, helped sweep him back into the Senate for another term. Such a Democratic landslide was unlikely to be repeated, and Senator Yarborough anticipated a serious challenge for renomination in 1970 from the conservative wing of his own party.[2] Yarborough's coalition consisted of poor whites, African Americans, and Hispanic Americans. Yarborough pushed the BEA in an effort to shore up an essential part of his political base prior to the 1970 election.

Senator Yarborough managed to be appointed as the sole member of a special subcommittee on bilingual education of the Senate Committee on Labor and Public Works. In this capacity, he organized hearings in Texas, California, and New York—states that accounted for approximately three-quarters of all Hispanic Americans. The hearings focused on the disparities in educational attainment between majority and Hispanic students and the commensurate poverty levels among Hispanics. From these hearings, Yarborough developed a legislative proposal drawn narrowly to aid Hispanic students—the proposed bill explicitly called for programs to help students whose native language was Spanish, and students who spoke other languages were not included. As one scholar has stated, "Senator Yarborough was not primarily interested in the [small] bloc vote of Korean Texans."[3]

Yarborough sought and won cosponsorship for his bill from the other five senators from Texas, California, and New York, including conservatives John Tower (R-TX) and George Murphy (R-CA) and liberals Robert Kennedy (D-NY) and Jacob Javits (R-NY). The united, bipartisan, nonideological support of the Senate delegations from three of the largest states in the country gave the bill tremendous political momentum.

The Johnson administration came out against the bill. It argued that all of the language/culture-related programs to be funded by the BEA were or could be funded through existing grant programs under the Elementary and Secondary Education Act, the Higher Education Act, and the National Defense Education Act. Beyond this, the administration expressed concern over the creation of a program aimed at one particular ethnicity. When it became clear that the bill was likely to pass, however, and under pressure from congressional Democrats, the administration formally though unenthusiastically endorsed the idea. In return for the endorsement, the administration won several concessions: the explicit mention of, and limitation of the program to, Spanish-speaking students was changed to the more inclusive focus on all students of "limited

English-speaking ability," and an explicit mandate for bilingual programs was made more flexible, allowing funding for a broad range of language-related programs. With these changes in place, Congress easily passed the BEA.

Part of the reason for successful passage of the bill was its vagueness; the term "bilingual education," for instance, was never actually defined. Senator Yarborough himself noted that "every time people ask me, 'what does bilingual education mean?' I reply that it means different things to different people."[4] Some clearly interpreted it to mean long-term instruction in the student's native language, while others just as clearly saw it as a short-term program of support en route to full English instruction and mastery. Such vagueness helped build a broad coalition to pass the BEA, but it contributed tremendously to the contention and debate that have surrounded the act since its passage.

IMPACT

Since 1968, the BEA has provided federal financial assistance—first to the states, later directly to local school districts—for teacher and staff training, bilingual and English-as-a-second-language programs, a variety of language-immersion and experimental programs, and the underwriting of academic research. These programs are aimed at the now 3.4 million primary- and secondary-school-age children classified as "limited English proficient" (LEP). Funding for the BEA has fluctuated from year to year, depending on the level of support of each presidential administration, with funding falling furthest during the Ronald Reagan administration. In the 1990s, with the number of LEP students increasing rapidly around the country, funding increased, and current BEA appropriations are approaching $300 million a year.[5]

Almost since its inception, the BEA has generated debate and some uncertainty. Given the vagueness and flexibility of the act as adopted, much of this was to be expected: "Bilingual-bicultural education is like an impressionist painting—very attractive from a distance, but unclear and confusing when one gets close to it."[6] Several related issues have been at the heart of debate over the BEA—should the BEA be voluntary or mandatory, should the focus be on extended instruction in the native language or a rapid transition to instruction in English, and should the focus be narrowly on language acquisition or also involve awareness and appreciation of native cultures? Political fights over these issues have been interwoven and began almost immediately after the act became law.

In 1970, a class-action lawsuit was filed on behalf of Chinese-speaking students in San Francisco, arguing that their inability to understand English-language instruction meant that they were denied "education on equal terms."[7] The school district argued that while the students certainly did struggle due to the language barrier, this was not due to any discrimination on the part of the government, which treated all students the same. The U.S. Supreme Court resolved the issue in its 1974 decision of *Lau v. Nichols.* The Court ruled that under Title VI of the 1964 Civil Rights Act, non-English-speaking students were entitled to special assistance in school: "There is no equality of treatment merely by providing students with the same facilities, textbooks, teachers, and curriculum; for students who do not understand English are effectively foreclosed from any meaningful education."[8] While the *Lau* decision rested on the Civil Rights Act, it had a major impact on the implementation of, and debates over, the BEA.

In *Lau,* the Supreme Court did not identify the form of special assistance schools were required to provide to LEP students. Indeed, it explicitly suggested that there was a range of possible ways to meet the requirement.[9] The Department of Health, Education, and Welfare's Office of Civil Rights (OCR), however, subsequently issued very specific guidelines for compliance with *Lau*—known as the "*Lau* Remedies"—for school districts receiving BEA monies to follow. The Lau Remedies called for very specific programs, namely, bilingual education with instruction in the native language, with an emphasis on the maintenance of culture and heritage. English-as-a-second-language (ESL) programs, in which students received intensive instruction in English, were deemed "inappropriate." School districts that failed to comply were subject to OCR enforcement actions and the loss of federal funding.

Also in 1974, the BEA was up for reauthorization by Congress. Funding was increased, and Congress added a number of important amendments to the act. The original act limited federal aid to LEP students who were poor; the 1974 amendments removed the poverty criterion. The amendments also required schools to provide instruction in an LEP student's native language "to the extent necessary to allow a child to progress effectively through the educational system." Finally, the amendments put greater emphasis on language maintenance (as opposed to a transition to English) in order to help preserve individual diversity and cultural traditions.[10]

The new emphasis on language maintenance has been described as bilingual education's "Achilles' heel." When the BEA was next considered for reauthorization in 1978, this was the main point of contention. A four-year study of bilingual education programs, sponsored by the U.S. Office of Education and conducted by the American Institute of Research (AIR), raised serious concerns in Congress. The report found that many students in programs funded by the BEA were not actually limited English proficient, but were in the classes to improve or maintain speaking ability in their native, non-English language. Many members of Congress, most of whom viewed bilingual education as a bridge to English, were upset by the report. President Jimmy Carter, who had been very supportive of bilingual education, told his cabinet, "I want English taught, not ethnic culture."[11] The act was reauthorized, but was amended to emphasize English-language acquisition rather than native-language maintenance. In contrast to the 1974 language, the 1978 amendments provided for instruction in the LEP student's native language only "to the extent necessary to allow a child to achieve competence in the English language,"[12] and schools were required individually to evaluate any student who remained in a bilingual education program for more than two years.

The *Lau* Remedies had never been established as formal OCR rules, a classification that would have required public comment and review. In a settlement of a 1978 lawsuit in Alaska, however, the federal government agreed to go through the formal rule-making process. The rules were officially announced and opened to public comment in 1980, just prior to the presidential election. They generated intense opposition, especially from local school districts, and the newly elected Ronald Reagan administration withdrew the rules. The irony was that Terrel Bell, who had been in charge of the old Office of Education in the Gerald Ford administration that had developed and issued the *Lau* Remedies, was then the secretary of education in the Reagan administration that withdrew them, calling them "harsh, inflexible, burdensome, unworkable, and incredibly costly."[13]

The Reagan administration, throughout Ronald Reagan's terms in office, was quite hostile to the idea of bilingual education and the BEA. The fight was led by William Bennett after he was named secretary of education in 1985. He declared bilingual education "a failed path" and spoke out on the issue on many occasions. In 1983, the administration had secured an amendment to the BEA allowing use of up to 4 percent of funding for "special alternative instructional programs" (SAIPs), that is, alternatives to traditional bilingual programs. Led by Bennett, an intensive lobbying effort in 1988 increased available funds for SAIPs from 4 to 25 percent of available BEA monies.

In the 1990s, the fight over the BEA and related issues calmed somewhat in Washington. Compared to the previous two decades, the BEA provided far greater flexibility to local schools in designing programs, and the focus was much more clearly on a transition to English. There was little support for using bilingual funds to promote or maintain a students native language. Rather, BEA funding flowed primarily to ESL programs. With rapidly growing numbers of LEP students, there was a rough consensus over funding, and monies steadily increased over the decade.

Outside of Washington, however, debate over these issues remained very intense. The fringe of the debate involves the "English First" movement, those lobbying to make English the official and sanctioned language in the United States, but far more central has been a serious disagreement over the practical effectiveness of bilingual education programs. The utility of various types of language programs has been studied extensively, using different cases, time periods, and methodologies, which have produced widely divergent results.[14] Given this, both critics and proponents of bilingual education publicly argue their cases, citing the studies they prefer. Finally, the 1990s also saw the divide over language move into the ballot-initiative arena. Most prominently, voters in California passed initiative 227 in 1998, replacing most bilingual programs with English-immersion programs, a change that is still being implemented and that has generated often-bitter conflict.

Overall, the practical impact of the Bilingual Education Act has been substantial. With approximately 3.4 million LEP students now in American schools each year, many millions of students have received specialized services since passage of the BEA in 1968. Debate continues, however, over the proper shape, focus, and effectiveness of bilingual and other language programs. Although Senator Yarborough still lost his reelection bid in 1970, the BEA began as a political exercise, and it has had a large impact in the political arena. The BEA has been at the heart of serious political conflict over federal mandates, local flexibility, and language transition and maintenance. These fights have raised serious issues of government reach and influence and cultural heritage and diversity, some of the issues at the center of American politics over the last quarter of a century.

14. The Bilingual Education Act

An Act To strengthen, improve, and extend programs of assistance for elementary and secondary education, and for other purposes.[15]

Be it enacted by the Senate and House of Representatives of the United States of America in Congress assembled, That this Act may be cited as the "Elementary and Secondary Education Amendments of 1967."

TITLE VII—BILINGUAL EDUCATION PROGRAMS

Section 701. The Congress hereby finds that one of the most acute educational problems in the United States is that which involves millions of children of limited English-speaking ability because they come from environments where the dominant language is other than English; that additional efforts should be made to supplement present attempts to find adequate and constructive solutions to this unique and perplexing educational situation; and that the urgent need is for comprehensive and cooperative action now on the local, State, and Federal levels to develop forward-looking approaches to meet the serious learning difficulties faced by this substantial segment of the Nation's school-aged population.

Section 702. The Elementary and Secondary Education Act of 1965 is amended by . . . inserting after title VI the following new title:

"Title VII—Bilingual Education Programs

"*Section 701.* This title may be cited as the 'Bilingual Education Act.'

"*Section 702.* In recognition of the special educational needs of the large numbers of children of limited English-speaking ability in the United States, Congress hereby declares it to be the policy of the United States to provide financial assistance to local educational agencies to develop and carry out new and imaginative elementary and secondary school programs designed to meet these special educational needs. For the purposes of this title, 'children of limited English-speaking ability' means children who come from environments where the dominant language is other than English.

"*Section 703.* (a) For the purposes of making grants under this title, there is authorized to be appropriated the sum of $15,000,000 for the fiscal year ending June 30, 1968, $30,000,000 for ... 1969, and $40,000,000 for ... 1970. ...

"*Section 704.* Grants under this title may be used ... for—

"(a) planning for and taking other steps leading to the development of programs designed to meet the special educational needs of children of limited English-speaking ability in schools having a high concentration of such children from families (A) with incomes below $3,000 per year, or (B) receiving payments under a program of aid to families with dependent children [AFDC—the central welfare program from 1935 to 1997] ...

"(b) providing preservice training designed to prepare persons to participate in bilingual education programs as teachers, teacher-aides, or other ancillary education personnel such as counselors, and inservice training and development programs designed to enable such persons to continue to improve their qualifications while participating in such programs; and

"(c) the establishment, maintenance, and operation of programs, including acquisition of necessary teaching materials and equipment, designed to meet the special educational needs of children of limited English-speaking ability ... through activities such as—

"(1) bilingual education programs;

"(2) programs designed to impart to students a knowledge of the history and culture associated with their languages;

"(3) efforts to establish closer cooperation between the school and the home;

"(4) early childhood educational programs related to the purposes of this title, particularly for parents of children participating in bilingual programs;

"(5) adult education programs related to the purposes of this title, particularly for parents of children participating in bilingual programs;

"(6) programs designed for dropouts or potential dropouts having need of bilingual programs;

"(7) programs conducted by accredited trade, vocational, or technical schools; and

"(8) other activities which meet the purposes of this title ...

"*Section 707.* The Commissioner [of Education] shall establish in the Office of Education an Advisory Committee on the Education of Bilingual Children. ..."

Approved January 2, 1968.

NOTES

1. *United States Statutes at Large*, vol. 81 (Washington, DC: U.S. Government Printing Office, 1968), p. 816.

2. This proved to be a well-founded concern. In 1970, Senator Yarborough was in fact defeated for renomination by conservative Democrat Lloyd Bentsen.

3. Hugh Davis Graham, *The Uncertain Triumph: Federal Education Policy in the Kennedy and Johnson Years* (Chapel Hill: University of North Carolina Press, 1984), p. 157.

4. Quoted in Diane Ravitch, *The Troubled Crusade: American Education, 1945–1980* (New York: Basic Books, 1983), p. 273.

5. Although $30 million was authorized in 1969, $7.5 million was actually appropriated.

6. Civil rights consultant Gary Orfield, quoted in James Crawford, *Bilingual Education: History, Politics, Theory, and Practice* (Trenton, NJ: Crane, 1989), p. 31.

7. This specific language was used by bilingual advocates because it mirrored the language used in the 1954 *Brown v. Board of Education of Topeka* desegregation case.

8. Ravitch, *The Troubled Crusade*, p. 274.

9. Kathleen Escamilla, *A Brief History of Bilingual Education in Spanish* (Charleston, WV: ERIC Clearinghouse on Rural Education and Small Schools, 1989), p. 2.

10. Crawford, *Bilingual Education*, pp. 37–39.

11. Quoted in Crawford, *Bilingual Education*, p. 40.

12. *United States Statutes at Large*, vol. 92 (Washington, DC: U.S. Government Printing Office, 1980), p. 2270.

13. Ravitch, *The Troubled Crusade*, p. 278.

14. See, for example, Peter Duignan, "Bilingual Education: A Critique" (http://www-hoover.stanford.edu/publications/he/22/22a.html, 2000); Richard Rothstein, "Bilingual Education: The Controversy" (http://www.pdkintl.org/kappan/krot9805.htm, 2000); and James Crawford, *Best Evidence: Research Foundations of the Bilingual Education Act* (Washington, DC: National Clearinghouse for Bilingual Education, 2000), pp. 1–39.

15. *United States Statutes at Large*, vol. 81, pp. 816–820.

15

Title IX

June 23, 1972

Title IX of the 1972 Education Amendments represented the first federal legislative treatment of gender discrimination in education. Gender discrimination in employment had been prohibited by the Civil Rights Act of 1964, but discrimination with respect to students was not covered, and there was growing evidence of and social concern over such discrimination throughout the 1960s. The federal government took several initiatives against gender discrimination in the 1960s—the Equal Pay Act of 1863, the Civil Rights Act of 1964, and Executive Order 11246 in 1967 requiring affirmative action to address employment discrimination—but these did not focus on education. Title IX addressed the issue comprehensively. With only a few exceptions, it prohibits any form of gender discrimination in all educational programs receiving federal funds, whether at the primary, secondary, or postsecondary level. It covers the treatment of all women in education, whether they are students, teachers, or support staff. Title IX has played a key, perhaps essential, role in protecting the rights of female students and personnel in schools and expanding educational programming and opportunity to women.

Politically, a series of competing proposals in Congress dealt with gender discrimination in 1971 and 1972, but Title IX was not a major factor in the larger debate over the Education Amendments. Following some parliamentary maneuvers, the final version of Title IX passed rather uneventfully. Significant political conflict followed passage, however, particularly over the impact of Title IX on collegiate athletics and the extent to which Title IX allowed the federal government to control or affect school administration. This latter issue ultimately resulted in significant action by both the U.S. Supreme Court and Congress in the 1980s. Finally, there has been recurring criticism of the federal government's lax enforcement of Title IX.

BACKGROUND

Because it is intended as a general, comprehensive statement against gender discrimination, the language and content of Title IX are quite simple and straightforward. Title IX states that "no person in the United States shall, on the basis of sex, be excluded from participation in, be denied the benefits of, or be subjected to discrimination under any educational program or activity receiving Federal assistance."[1] The title included five exceptions to this basic rule. First, it was not applied to admissions at private institutions below the level of graduate education. Second, again with respect to admissions only, it was not applied to schools making a transition from single-sex to coeducational status for a six-year period. Third, it was not applied to religious schools in cases where compliance would conflict with religious tenets. Fourth, it was not applied to the military academies. Fifth, it was not applied to admissions in traditionally single-sex public colleges and universities. These exceptions were quite narrowly drawn, and thus Title IX was applied to nearly all educational institutions receiving federal aid under nearly all circumstances.

With respect to gender issues in education, some limited steps had been taken by the federal government prior to passage of Title IX. The Equal Pay Act was passed in 1963, requiring that men and women receive equal pay for equal work, and this certainly included schools. In 1968, President Lyndon Johnson signed Executive Order 11375, prohibiting gender discrimination in employment in the administration of any federal contract, and this applied to educational institutions—primarily in higher education—exercising federal contracts. These were piecemeal approaches to the issue, with no single, general statement against gender discrimination in education. These partial steps, for instance, only covered employment practices and said nothing about the treatment or inclusion of female students. The inadequacy of these steps was highlighted when the Women's Equity Action League filed a class-action lawsuit in 1970 charging hundreds of colleges and universities with violating

Executive Order 11375. It was increasingly clear that some legislative approach was necessary.

The first explicit effort to deal with gender discrimination in education was made by Congresswoman Edith Green (D-OR), who, as chair of the House Special Subcommittee on Education, held hearings on a legislative proposal in 1971. The seven days of hearings were the first ever held on gender discrimination in education, with the focus mainly on higher education. Green's proposal had several points, the heart of which was to amend the Civil Rights Act of 1964 to add a prohibition against gender discrimination. Her proposal, however, was never acted on after the hearings.

With several pieces of education legislation due for reauthorization in 1972, however, it was clear that an educational bill of some kind would be fashioned in 1971. The starting point was a bill sponsored by Senator Claiborne Pell (D-RI), chair of the Senate Subcommittee on Education. The Pell bill had no provision or language dealing with gender discrimination, but an alternative bill supported by the Richard Nixon administration did include some relevant language. Later in the year, both Senator Birch Bayh (D-IN) and Senator George McGovern (D-SD) proposed separate amendments to the Pell bill prohibiting gender discrimination.

In the House, in addition to the administration proposal, Congresswoman Green introduced a bill patterned on her proposal of the previous year. In addition, Congressman John Brademas (D-IN) also introduced a bill, but it was substantially similar to the Green proposal. All of this activity speaks to the fact that there was considerable interest in Congress in taking action. In 1971, therefore, five different proposals were introduced in the House and Senate intended to deal with gender discrimination in education.

These proposals varied considerably in the mechanism employed and their reach. Several of the proposals called for amending the Civil Rights Act, while others called for separate statutory language. Several of the proposals covered most educational institutions and activities, while others included many exemptions and were quite limited in scope. All possibilities and permutations were being discussed, but the omnibus education bill reported out of committee to the full Senate actually mirrored Senator Pell's original bill—it included no gender-discrimination language at all.

In the Senate, McGovern agreed to drop his own proposal and support Senator Bayh's anti-gender-discrimination amendment instead, and Bayh's proposal was debated by the full Senate. Before a final vote, however, the amendment was challenged and ultimately voted nongermane (unrelated) to the education bill under consideration, and so it died. In the House, Green modified her proposal, dropping the amendment to the Civil Rights Act and substituting a separate legislative provision on gender discrimination.[2] The House subcommittee was generally supportive, but there was opposition to covering admissions policies. Congressman Albert Quie (R-MN) successfully pushed an amendment to the Green proposal exempting all undergraduate admissions policies. Once her bill was before the full Education and Labor Committee, however, Green fought back. She compromised, adding an exemption for admissions at traditionally single-sex institutions, but otherwise successfully reinstated coverage for all other admissions. On the floor of the House, Congressman John Erlenborn (R-IL) introduced an amendment effectively reinstating the Quie exemption, which passed in a tight 194–189 vote. The House thus passed a bill with a substantive anti-gender-discrimination provision, but one that, after considerable political give and take, exempted all undergraduate college admissions policies.

The Senate did not complete work on the education bill in 1971, and in February 1972, as deliberation continued, Senator Bayh convinced his colleagues to consider a reworked proposal. While his first amendment had been deemed nongermane, the real opposition, as in the House, centered on admissions policies. In his revised proposal, therefore, Bayh added several exemptions regarding admissions, and, so amended, it was added to the education bill.

A conference committee was charged with reconciling the differences between the Bayh language from the Senate and the modified Green language from the House. In nearly every respect, the Senate version was approved by the committee, producing the final version of Title IX with the exceptions for admissions at private undergraduate colleges, schools in transition to coeducational status, and public colleges and universities that were traditionally single sex. The conference language was quickly and easily approved as a part of the broader Education Amendments, and President Richard Nixon signed the entire legislative package on June 23, 1972.[3]

IMPACT

The immediate impact of Title IX was a flurry of legislative proposals, lobbying, and public pressure designed to affect its implementation. In Congress, a series of efforts sought to limit or dilute the impact of Title IX, especially in the area of athletics. In 1974, Senator John Tower (R-TX) introduced an amendment exempting all revenue-producing collegiate sports from Title IX requirements. The measure passed in the Senate, but was later deleted by a conference committee. Also in 1974, the House passed an amendment by Congresswoman Marjorie Hold (R-MD) preventing the Department of Health, Education, and Welfare (HEW) from collecting any information on gender discrimination in educational institutions, thereby making enforcement of Title IX impossible. Like the Tower amendment, this was also dropped in conference. In 1975 and again in 1977, Senator Jesse Helms (R-NC) introduced legislation severely restricting the application of Title IX in athletics, with both efforts dying in committee. Finally, in 1976, Senators Tower, Dewey Bartlett (R-OK), and Roman Hruska (R-NB) introduced legislation similar to Tower's 1974 effort exempting revenue-producing college athletics, but this effort also died in committee.

Beyond this series of legislative measures introduced by critics, there was also extensive debate over the establishment of administrative rules for the implementation of Title IX. The Title IX language, as noted earlier, was general and comprehensive. It was left to HEW to develop specific rules governing implementation and enforcement for schools actually to follow. This process took the department several years and was the object of intense lobbying by groups on all sides of the issues. Draft rules were opened for public comment in 1974, and HEW received more than 10,000 written comments, a record at the time. While this demonstrated the degree of feeling over Title IX, there was no clear consensus in the public comments, and, as a result, HEW personnel largely proceeded based on their own judgments.[4] President Gerald Ford approved the final rules in July 1975. There were immediate efforts in Congress to pass legislation overturning the rules, but these were uniformly defeated.

Much of the opposition to Title IX, both in Congress and in the rule-making stage, dealt with collegiate athletics. Concerns have been expressed over schools being forced to allow women to play traditionally male sports. The more serious criticisms, however, revolved around the potential for "defunding" large, popular male-dominated sports, particularly football, in order to equalize athletic funding across genders. Women's athletics do receive far more resources today than prior to Title IX, and some second- and third-tier male sports programs have been cut or eliminated here and there, but male collegiate athletics have remained very well funded.[5]

In the 1980s, the critical focus on Title IX changed to the question of how much authority the title gives the federal government to reach into and regulate educational institutions. The rules adopted in the 1970s called for compliance with Title IX throughout an entire educational institution if any part of the institution received federal financial assistance, even indirectly. In the 1984 *Grove City College v. Bell* decision, the U.S. Supreme Court ruled that under Title IX the federal government could only regulate those educational programs and activities that directly received financial assistance. This led to a response from Congress, which passed the Civil Rights Restoration Act over President Ronald Reagan's veto in 1988. The act largely reversed the *Grove City* decision, explicitly mandating that educational institutions receiving any federal financial assistance—directly or indirectly—must be in compliance with Title IX.

Title IX is administered and enforced by the Office of Civil Rights within the Department of Education and currently covers some 16,000 school districts, more than 3,000 colleges and universities, and approximately 5,000 libraries, museums, and for-profit schools. The effect of Title IX on these institutions and all of the female students, teachers, and staff affiliated with them has been enormous. It is a comprehensive prohibition against gender discrimination in schools. Other than the handful of exceptions detailed earlier, it covers nearly all schools and nearly all school activites.[6] Title IX has been implemented over a period of time that has seen a general societal shift toward gender equality. It is difficult, therefore, to sort out which changes in educational institutions vis-à-vis gender are due specifically to Title IX, and which are due to other social changes. It is clear, however, that women in America today are afforded far greater educational opportunities than prior to passage of Title IX, and Title IX certainly played a substantive and constructive role in expanding these opportunities.

In 1997, in celebrating the first 25 years of Title IX, the U.S. Department of Education published "indicators of progress" toward gender equality in education, changes to which Title IX contributed. These indicators included the following:

- While 8 percent more men than women had attended at least four years of college in 1971, an equal percentage of men and women held bachelor's degrees by 1994.

- The percentage of women between the ages of 16 and 24 having graduated from high school rose from 43 percent in 1973 to 63 percent in 1994.
- The percentage of all doctoral degrees awarded to women rose from 25 percent in 1977 to 44 percent in 1994.
- The percentage of all law degrees awarded to women rose from 7 percent in 1972 to 43 percent in 1994.
- The percentage of all medical degrees awarded to women rose from 9 percent in 1972 to 38 percent in 1994.
- The number of high-school girls participating in organized school athletics increased from 300,000 in 1971 to 2.4 million in 1996—rising from 7.5 to 39 percent of all high-school athletes.
- The number of women in college athletics increased from approximately 25,000 in 1971 to more than 100,000 in the 1990s—rising from 15 to 37 percent of all college athletes.[7]

While Title IX is not solely responsible for these changes, it substantially contributed to them and to a general expansion of educational opportunities for women.

While the progress made is real, Title IX remains subject to substantive criticism, particularly over what is seen by some as weak federal enforcement and problem areas where the impact has been limited. A number of issues are raised: continuing problems of sexual harassment in schools, for both students and staff, the fact that schools could not be held liable for monetary damages for failing to comply with Title IX until the early 1990s, the limited numbers of women in positions of educational leadership (fewer than 10 percent of all school superintendents are women), and continuing disparities in both the resources and attention given to male dominated school sports programs.[8]

In the end, while it is important to recognize these criticisms and acknowledge that additional progress is needed in many areas, the overall impact of Title IX has been significant. It was passed amid growing awareness of profound gender inequalities in education and in recognition of what that meant in terms of life opportunities. It was the first federal effort to address gender issues in the schools and represented a statement of national principle—a statement about the direction in which the country wished to move. The fights over the scope, reach, and implementation of Title IX have been contentious at times, but Title IX has had lasting impact on the operation of schools and the lives and opportunities of women.

15. The Education Amendments of 1972

An Act To amend the Higher Education Act of 1965, the
Vocational Education Act of 1963, the General Education
Provisions Act . . . , the Elementary and Secondary Education
Act of 1965, Public Law 874, . . . and for other purposes.[9]

Be it enacted by the Senate and House of Representatives of the United
States of America in Congress assembled, That this Act may be cited as
the "Education Amendments of 1972. . . ."

Section 901. (a) No person in the United States shall, on the basis of
sex, be excluded from participation in, be denied the benefits of, or be
subjected to discrimination under any educational program or activity receiving Federal assistance, except that:

(1) in regard to admissions to educational institutions, this section
shall apply only to institutions of vocational education, professional education, and to graduate higher education, and to public institutions
of undergraduate higher education;

(2) in regard to admissions to educational institutions, this section
shall not apply (A) for one year from the date of enactment . . . , nor
for six years . . . in the case of an educational institution which has begun the process of changing from being an institution which admits
only students of one sex to being an institution which admits students
of both sexes . . . or (B) for seven years from the date an educational
institution begins the process of changing . . . , whichever is the later;

(3) this section shall not apply to any educational institution which
is controlled by a religious organization if the application of this subsection would not be consistent with the religious tenets of such organization;

(4) this section shall not apply to an educational institution whose
primary purpose is the training of individuals for the military services
of the United States, or the merchant marine; and

(5) in regard to admissions this section shall not apply to any public
institution of higher education which is an institution that traditionally
and continually from its establishment has had a policy of admitting
only students of one sex.

(b) Nothing contained in subsection (a) of this section shall be interpreted to require any educational institution to grant preferential or dis-
parate treatment to the members of one sex on account of an imbalance
which may exist with respect to the total number or percentage of persons
of that sex participating in or receiving the benefits of any federally sup-

ported program or activity, in comparison with the total number or percentage of persons of that sex in any community, State, section, or other area. . . .

Section 902. Each Federal department or agency which is empowered to extend Federal financial assistance to any educational program or activity . . . is authorized and directed to effectuate the provisions of section 901. . . . Compliance . . . may be effected (1) by the termination of or refusal to grant or to continue assistance under such program or activity to any recipient as to whom there has been an express finding on the record . . . of a failure to comply. . . .

Section 907. Notwithstanding anything to the contrary contained in this title, nothing contained herein shall be construed to prohibit any educational institution receiving funds under this Act, from maintaining separate living facilities for the different sexes. . . .

Approved June 23, 1972.

NOTES

1. *United States Statutes at Large*, vol. 86 (Washington, DC: U.S. Government Printing Office, 1972), p. 273.

2. Green was apparently concerned about setting a precedent for amending the Civil Rights Act that might be used in weakening provisions in the future.

3. On this legislative history, see Andrew Fishel and Janice Pottker, *National Politics and Sex Discrimination in Education* (Lexington, MA: Lexington Books, 1977), pp. 95–105; and Hugh Davis Graham, *Civil Rights and the Presidency: Race and Gender in American Politics, 1960–1972* (New York: Oxford University Press, 1992), pp. 204–206.

4. Andrew Fishel, "Organizational Positions on Title IX: Conflicting Perspectives on Sex Discrimination in Education," *Journal of Higher Education* 47 (January–February 1976): 93–105.

5. On the general issue of Title IX rules and school athletics, see Steven C. Wade and Robert D. Hay, *Sports Law for Educational Institutions* (New York: Quorum Books, 1988), pp. 40–46.

6. Debate over Title IX has often concentrated on collegiate athletics, and, as a result, the focus tends to be on higher education. Title IX applies equally to primary and secondary education as well, however, and for one discussion of the comprehensive impact of Title IX at these levels of education, see Andrew Fishel and Janice Pottker, "Sex Bias in Secondary Schools: The Impact of Title IX," in *Sex Bias in the Schools: The Research Evidence*, ed. Janice Pottker and Andrew Fishel (Rutherford, NJ: Fairleigh Dickinson University Press, 1977), pp. 92–104.

7. U.S. Department of Education, *Title IX: 25 Years of Progress* (http://www.ed.gov/pubs/TitleIX/title.html, 1997).

8. For discussions of these criticisms, see Catherine Marshall, "Undomesticated Gender Policy," in *Gender, Equity, and Schooling: Policy and Practice*, ed. Barbara J. Bank and Peter M. Hall (New York: Garland Publishing, 1997), pp. 65–96; Marilyn

Tallerico, "Gender and School Administration," in *Gender, Equity, and Schooling: Policy and Practice*, ed. Barbara J. Bank and Peter M. Hall, pp. 205–206; and Council of Chief State School Officers, Resource Center on Education Equity, "The Continuing Struggle for Female Leadership in Education: Partial Analysis and Recommendations," *Concern*, November 1993, pp. 1–8.

9. *United States Statutes at Large*, vol. 86, pp. 235–381.

16

Education for All Handicapped Children Act

November 29, 1975

The Education for All Handicapped Children Act, often referred to as P.L. 94–142, fundamentally changed how disabled students are treated in American schools.[1] It established, as a matter of national principle, that every child—including those with disabilities or handicaps—is guaranteed a free and appropriate public education: "The passage of [P.L. 94–142] was about getting the doors open and acknowledging that kids were supposed to be in school."[2] Beyond this, the act required that disabled students be educated in "the least restrictive environment"; that is, they could no longer automatically be segregated from the general school population. Finally, P.L. 94–142 empowered parents of disabled students, investing them with due-process rights to help ensure that their children's unique needs are met. The Education for All Handicapped Children Act significantly changed the operation of all public schools, and, more important, dramatically changed the school experience for millions of disabled children.

The federal government had taken some modest steps to address the needs of disabled children prior to P.L. 94–142—P.L. 85–926 in 1958 provided source funding to train teachers dealing with children with mental retardation, and amendments to the Elementary and Secondary Education Act allowed Title I monies to be used for special education, but responsibility overwhelmingly remained with the states and local school districts. The inadequacy of state and local efforts was made clear by the advocacy work of several groups and by two landmark legal cases, as will be detailed below. It was clear in the early 1970s that far greater action was needed on behalf of disabled students, and that many or most state and local governments were simply not up to the task. This was the political environment that led to the nearly unanimous vote in Congress for the act. Since passage, political debates surrounding P.L. 94–142 have centered on the proper degree of federal control, limited federal funding, and the workability of mainstreaming disabled students in traditional classrooms.

BACKGROUND

P.L. 94–142 went further than any previous federal legislation in mandating actions by local schools, and, consequently, it began with a long series of findings by Congress justifying the act. The findings list the problems then extant in the education of handicapped children: the large number of handicapped children, the inadequacy of existing educational approaches and programs, the number of children excluded from public schools entirely, and the problems state and local governments had in adequately meeting the needs of these children. Following this extensive justification, three purposes for the act are detailed: (1) to ensure that all children with disabilities are provided "a free appropriate public education which emphasizes special education . . . to meet their unique needs,"[3] (2) to protect the legal rights of parents of disabled children, and (3) to help state and local governments meet the educational needs of all handicapped children.

The act was built around six basic principles:[4]

1. Zero rejection: Every handicapped child has an affirmative right to a free and appropriate public school education. Schools do not have the option of excluding children.

2. Nondiscriminatory evaluation: Schools must actively work to identify children with disabilities, on a nondiscriminatory basis, and appropriately evaluate their unique needs.

3. Individualized education plans (IEPs). An IEP must be written for each handicapped child and agreed to by both school officials and parents. An IEP must outline the child's current level of performance, both short-term and long-term goals, and a method for evaluating outcomes.

4. Least restrictive environment: Disabled children must be educated

as much as possible in a regular classroom, integrated with children who are not disabled.

5. Due process: Parents have due-process rights if they do not agree with school decisions to either provide or deny particular educational services.

6. Parental participation: The act anticipates active parental involvement. Parents can trigger IEP meetings, must agree to and sign all IEPs, can demand due process, and are guaranteed access to all student records.

This was a precedent-setting legislative formula for the federal government; never before had the federal government mandated with such specificity the actions of local schools vis-à-vis individual parents and children. The unmet needs of disabled children and the inadequacy of state and local efforts were viewed as justifying far-reaching federal action.

States that submit approved plans for the education of all handicapped children are eligible for federal financial assistance. It was never anticipated that this federal aid would fully cover state and local costs to educate disabled students; rather, this aid was intended to facilitate the effort. Under the act as designed, it was expected that the federal government would assume approximately 40 percent of the costs of special education; critics often note that this goal has never been met.

Several factors led to the enactment of P.L. 94–142. The civil rights movement and President Lyndon Johnson's War on Poverty program created an environment where there was a heightened awareness and concern for both legal rights and society's treatment of powerless groups. The drive for special education was an extension of the social ideals of equal treatment and expanded opportunities.[5]

Beyond this, there was a growing awareness of the way many handicapped children were actually treated: "As a general rule, the nation's public schools were highly ingenious and very successful in denying educational opportunities, equal or otherwise, to handicapped children."[6] States had begun to create special classes in the 1800s, and by the 1950s, nearly all schools offered such classes. They almost always segregated handicapped children from the general student population, however, and many were taught by untrained or undertrained teachers. Moreover, most of these classes were geared to students who were only moderately handicapped, with many states labeling more severely handicapped children as "uneducable" and excluding them from the schools. When P.L. 94–142 was being debated, Congress was well aware that more than a million children were then wholly excluded from the nation's schools.

In the 1950s, the federal government initiated modest steps to improve the education of disabled children. P.L. 85–926 was passed in 1958 and provided financial assistance to train education faculty to help prepare teachers of the handicapped. P.L. 88–164, in 1963, provided additional financing for teacher training and for demonstration projects. The Elementary and Secondary Education Act of 1965 included some monies for state-run residential schools. In 1968, P.L. 90–247 established resource centers to improve the education of handicapped children. The Handicapped Children's Early Education Assistance Act was also passed in 1968, providing for experimental programs for disabled children from birth to age six. In 1969, these various programs were consolidated into the Education of the Handicapped Act, which, as amended in 1974, required states to set as a goal the full education of all handicapped children. The federal government clearly had an established interest in improving special education, but none of these steps involved the detail and comprehensiveness of P.L. 94–142.[7]

The final push for the act came from parents, professionals in special education, and the courts. The "parents' movement" began in the 1950s to advocate improved treatment of disabled children. Numerous parent and related professional groups were organized, particularly the National Association for Retarded Children,[8] the Association for Children with Learning Disabilities, and the Council for Exceptional Children. Their advocacy quickly moved into the courts, where two crucial decisions were handed down in 1972.

The first was a class-action lawsuit brought by the Pennsylvania Association for Retarded Children (PARC) against the state of Pennsylvania in 1971. Many disabled children in Pennsylvania were excluded from the public schools, and PARC fought for the principle of education for all children. *Pennsylvania Association for Retarded Children v. The Commonwealth of Pennsylvania* was settled by means of a consent agreement in 1972, with the state of Pennsylvania agreeing to recognize and respect the right of all disabled children to receive a free appropriate public education.[9]

The second important case was *Mills v. Board of Education of the District of Columbia*, also decided in 1972. The U.S. District Court for the District of Columbia ruled, based on the equal-protection clause of the Fourteenth Amendment, that schools could not deny educational services and opportunities to disabled children due to a lack of funds. The PARC case sent a clear signal to all states, but *Mills*, resting on a constitutional ruling, clearly mandated action on the part of all schools.[10]

P.L. 94–142 was a response to this series of factors—the civil rights movement and President Johnson's War on Poverty, the growing experience of the federal government in the area of special education, increasing parental and professional advocacy, and crucial court rulings. The need for fundamental action in the early 1970s was manifest, and there was a clear sense that many of the states were not up to the job. The Education for All Handicapped Children Act therefore moved through Congress essentially unopposed. It enjoyed nearly unanimous support, with only 14 members of the House and Senate voting against final passage. President Gerald Ford signed P.L. 94–142 into law on November 29, 1975, with the provisions going into effect on October 1, 1977.

IMPACT

Once described as "blockbuster legislation,"[11] P.L. 94–142 has unquestionably had a major impact on American schools and schoolchildren. Its most important effects are those related to the actual treatment of disabled students. The act, however, has also changed teacher-training programs, classroom structure and teaching, and school administration and funding. Further, it has ushered in a wholly new degree of federal involvement in local schools, a role hailed in some quarters and deeply criticized in others.

As a result of P.L. 94–142, the day-to-day treatment of disabled children in schools has improved markedly. Nearly six million children a year now receive special education or related services called for by the act. Services are now determined on an individual basis—with the unique needs of each student considered—with parental participation and consent, and with full public funding. Disabled students are educated in the least restrictive environment, or "mainstreamed," with more than two-thirds receiving some or all of their instruction in classes with the general student population. Unlike the findings reached by Congress regarding the treatment of disabled students in 1975, students are no longer systematically segregated from the larger population, they are not typically taught by untrained teachers, and they are rarely excluded from the schools entirely.

While the treatment of disabled children has certainly improved, the educational value of P.L. 94–142 is currently debated. On the positive side, increased numbers of disabled students are graduating from high school, as well as going on to various forms of postsecondary education. On the negative side, some studies have found only minimal performance gains, and the dropout rate for disabled students remains twice that of the general school population. Fundamentally, however, there are simply too few large, methodologically sound studies of academic performance among disabled students to reach any firm conclusion.[12]

The act has been amended and expanded on several occasions since it was originally passed. In 1983, Congress reaffirmed its commitment to P.L. 94–142 and provided for additional research in special education and some additional funding. In 1986, as a part of the Education of the Handicapped Amendments, Congress required every state to provide needed services to all disabled children of preschool age. In 1990, again as part of the Education of the Handicapped Amendments, Congress added autism as a covered disability, changed the name to the Individuals with Disabilities Education Act (IDEA), and required schools to provide "transition services." The latter are services to help disabled students make a smooth and successful transition from school to postschool life and may include further education and training, employment, and independent living.[13]

Solid cost and funding data for P.L. 94–142 specifically, and special education generally, are difficult to determine. Each state and school district dedicates its own monies to special education, in addition to what the federal government contributes, and the total effort is unclear. The federal component alone, however, amounted to nearly five billion dollars in 1999. The federal funding is augmented by some additional funding, of indeterminate size, from Medicare, Medicaid, and related programs for a variety of in-school special-education-related services. From all of this, several conclusions can be drawn: for the nation as a whole, special education is very expensive; the federal government invests considerable monies in the effort; and state and local governments nevertheless assume the majority of the financial costs. State and local officials often characterize P.L. 94–142 as a large unfunded federal mandate, but, given the *Mills* case discussed earlier, these governments would be responsible for most or all special-education costs even without the federal legislation.

The act has also had a major impact on teaching and school administration. Special education is now a major part of every college of education's teacher-training program. Every school has had to respond—recruiting specialized teachers, providing ongoing in-service training for nearly all teachers, adding staff to identify and evaluate disabled students, changing funding priorities within districts, and, administratively, managing IEPs for each disabled student. These impacts often generate criticism from teachers and school administrators. These concerns include the difficulty of recruiting adequate numbers of special-education teachers, costs, and too much paperwork and record keeping. Beyond this, many regular classroom teachers feel unprepared properly to educate disabled students who are "mainstreamed" in their classes, a concern that the American Federation of Teachers has championed.[14]

Finally, P.L. 94–142 is subject to criticism from political conservatives opposed to the significant federal role or the intrusion it represents in local school operations. They have described the program as "an incredible case of . . . micromanaging local school districts" and have lambasted it for involving "onerous, unfunded mandates; extra benefits and rights for government designated populations; opportunities for activists and lawyers to hustle more taxpayer-financed largesse; and, most of all, the smug assumption that Washington knows best how to run the nation's schools."[15] This ideological opposition, while intense and occasionally vitriolic, has had little effect. The federal government acted only after many states and local schools proved themselves unable or unwilling adequately to address the pressing needs of disabled students. There is today an overwhelming consensus, including most members of both parties in Congress, to continue federal action in this area.

Overall, the Education for All Handicapped Children Act—or, today, the Individuals with Disabilities Education Act—must be seen as a success. Disabled children receive far better treatment and opportunities in nearly every school across the United States. While there is little hard data on educational performance, and certainly more can be achieved, there is some evidence that the act has raised performance levels as well. Criticisms remain, of course, but they are largely technical or administrative in nature—issues of funding, paperwork, and training. There is no serious opposition to the central tenets of the legislation. There is a nearly universal consensus in support of the underlying principle of P.L. 94–142, that every child in America has a right to a free, appropriate public education.

16. Education for All Handicapped Children Act

An Act To amend the Education of the Handicapped Act to provide educational assistance to all handicapped children, and for other purposes.[16]

Be it enacted by the Senate and House of Representatives of the United States of America in Congress assembled, That this Act may be cited as the "Education for All Handicapped Children Act of 1975." . . .

Section 3. . . .

"(b) The Congress finds that—

"(1) there are more than eight million handicapped children in the United States today;

"(2) the special educational needs of such children are not being fully met;

"(3) more than half of the handicapped children in the United States do not receive appropriate educational services which would enable them to have full equality of opportunity;

"(4) one million of the handicapped children in the United States are excluded entirely from the public school system and will not go through the educational process with their peers;

"(5) there are many handicapped children throughout the United States participating in regular school programs whose handicaps prevent them from having a successful educational experience because their handicaps are undetected;

"(6) because of the lack of adequate services within the public school system, families are often forced to find services outside the public school system, often at great distance from their residence and at their own expense;

"(7) developments in the training of teachers and in diagnostic and instructional procedures and methods have advanced to the point that, given appropriate funding, State and local educational agencies can and will provide effective special education and related services to meet the needs of handicapped children;

"(8) State and local educational agencies have a responsibility to provide education for all handicapped children, but present financial resources are inadequate to meet the special educational needs of handicapped children; and

"(9) it is in the national interest that the Federal Government assist State and local efforts to provide programs to meet the educational needs of handicapped children in order to assure equal protection of the law.

"(c) It is the purpose of this Act to assure that all handicapped children have available to them . . . a free appropriate public education which emphasizes special education and related services designed to meet their unique needs, to assure that the right of handicapped children and their parents or guardians are protected, to assist States and localities to provide for the education of all handicapped children, and to assess and assure the effectiveness of efforts to educate handicapped children." . . .

Section 4. . . .

"(16) The term 'special education' means specially designed instruction, at no cost to parents or guardians, to meet the unique needs of a handicapped child, including classroom instruction, instruction in physical education, home instruction, and instruction in hospitals and institutions.

"(17) The term 'related services' means transportation, and such developmental, corrective, and other supportive services (including speech pathology and audiology, psychological services, physical and occupational therapy, recreation, and medical and counseling services, except that such medical services shall be for diagnostic and evaluation purposes only) as may be required to assist a handicapped child to benefit from special education, and includes the early identification and assessment of handicapping conditions in children. . . .

"(19) The term 'individualized education program' means a written statement for each handicapped child developed in any meeting by a representative of the local educational agency . . . who shall be qualified to provide . . . specially designed instruction to meet the unique needs of handicapped children, the teacher, the parents or guardian of such child, and, whenever appropriate, such child, which statement shall include (A) a statement of the present levels of educational performance of such child, (B) a statement of annual goals, including short-term instructional objectives, (C) a statement of the specific educational services to be provided to such child, and the extent to which such child will be able to participate in regular educational programs, (D) the projected date for initiation and anticipated duration of such services, and (E) appropriate objective criteria and evaluation procedures and schedules for determining, on at least an annual basis, whether instructional objectives are being achieved. . . .

"*Section 612.* In order to qualify for assistance under this part in any fiscal year, a State shall demonstrate to the Commissioner [of Education] that the following conditions are met:

"(1) The State has in effect a policy that assures all handicapped children the right to a free appropriate public education.

"(2) The State has developed a plan . . . [that] shall set forth in detail the policies and procedures which the State will undertake or has undertaken in order to assure that—

"(A) there is established (i) a goal of providing full educational opportunity to all handicapped children, (ii) a detailed timetable for accomplishing such a goal, and (iii) a description of the kind and number of facilities, personnel, and services necessary throughout the State to meet such a goal;

"(B) a free appropriate public education will be available for all handicapped children between the ages of three and eighteen within the State not later than September 1, 1978, and for all handicapped children between the ages of three and twenty-one . . . not later than September 1, 1980 . . .

"(C) all children residing in the State who are handicapped, regardless of the severity of their handicap, and who are in need of special education and related services are identified, located, and evaluated . . .

"(4) Each local educational agency in the State will maintain records of the individualized education program for each handicapped child . . .

"(5) The State has established . . . (B) procedures to assure that, to the maximum extent appropriate, handicapped children, including children in public or private institutions or other care facilities, are educated with children who are not handicapped, and that special classes, separate schooling, or other removal of handicapped children from the regular educational environment occurs only when the nature or severity of the handicap is such that education in regular classes with the use of supplementary aids and services cannot be achieved satisfactorily, and (C) procedures to assure that testing and evaluation materials and procedures used for the purpose of the evaluation and placement of handicapped children will be selected and administered so as not to be racially or culturally discriminatory. . . .

"*Section 615.* (a) Any State educational agency, any local educational agency, and any intermediate educational unit which receives assistance under this part shall establish and maintain procedures . . . to assure that handicapped children and their parents or guardians are guaranteed procedural safeguards with respect to the provision of free appropriate education by such agencies and units.

"(b) (1) The procedures required by this section shall include . . .

"(A) an opportunity for the parents or guardian of a handicapped child to examine all relevant records with respect to the identification, evaluation, and educational placement of the child . . .

"(C) written prior notice to the parents or guardian's of the child whenever such agency or unit—

"(i) proposes to initiate or change, or

"(ii) refuses to initiate or change,

the identification, evaluation, or educational placement of the child or the provision of a free appropriate public education to the child; . . .

"(E) an opportunity to present complaints with respect to any matter relating to the identification, evaluation, or educational placement of the child, or the provision of a free appropriate public education.

"(2) Whenever a complaint has been received . . . , the parents or guardian shall have an opportunity for an impartial due process hearing. . . .

"*Section 618.* (a) The Commissioner shall measure and evaluate the impact of the program authorized under this part and the effectiveness of State efforts to assure the free appropriate public education of all handicapped children.

"(b) The Commissioner shall conduct, directly or by grant or contract, such studies, investigations, and evaluations as are necessary to assure effective implementation. . . ."

Approved November 29, 1975.

NOTES

1. In 1990, the official name of the act was changed to the Individuals with Disabilities Education Act.

2. Judith E. Heumann, former assistant secretary of the U.S. Department of Education, as quoted in Joetta Sack, "Bringing Special Education Students into the Classroom," *Education Week on the Web* (http://www.edweek.com/ew/vol-18/20inclus.h118, 2000).

3. *United States Statutes at Large,* vol. 89, (Washington, DC: U.S. Government Printing Office, 1975), p. 775.

4. These categories come from Samuel A. Kirk and James J. Gallagher, *Educating Exceptional Children,* 6th ed. (Boston: Houghton Mifflin, 1989), pp. 50–51.

5. For a discussion of this point, see David Neal and David L. Kirp, "The Allure

of Legalization Reconsidered: The Case of Special Education," in *School Days, Rule Days: The Legislation and Regulation of Education*, ed. David L. Kirp and Donald N. Jensen (Philadelphia: Falmer Press, 1985), pp. 345–346.

6. H. Rutherford Turnbull and Ann Turnbull, *Free Appropriate Public Education: Law and Implementation* (Denver: Love Publishing Company, 1978), p. 19.

7. On these various federal efforts, see Bill R. Gearheart, *Special Education for the '80s* (St. Louis: C. V. Mosby Company, 1980), pp. 12–16, and Kirk and Gallagher, *Educating Exceptional Children*, p. 49.

8. The name was later changed to the National Association for Retarded Citizens.

9. On the PARC case, see Edwin W. Martin, Reed Martin, and Donna L. Terman, "The Legislative and Litigation History of Special Education," *The Future of Children: Special Education for Children with Disabilities* 6, no. 1 (Spring 1996): 28–29; and Kirk and Gallagher, *Educating Exceptional Children*, p. 49.

10. On the *Mills* case, see Martin, Martin, and Terman, "The Legislative and Litigation History of Special Education," pp. 28–29, and Laura F. Rothstein, *Special Education Law* (New York: Longman, 2000), pp. 2–3.

11. L. V. Goodman, "A Bill of Rights for the Handicapped," *American Education*, 12, no. 6 (1976): 6–8.

12. For summaries of these points, pro and con, see U.S. Department of Education, "IDEA '97, General Information" (http://www.ed.gov/offices/OSERS/IDEA/overview.html, 2000); and Chester E. Finn, "Corrupted Intentions: Reforming Special Education," *National Review* 48, no. 4 (March 11, 1996): pp. 46–48.

13. On these changes, see William L. Heward and Michael D. Orlansky, *Exceptional Children: An Introductory Survey of Special Education* 4th ed. (New York: Merrill, 1992), pp. 45–47.

14. On these practical concerns or criticisms, see Heward and Orlansky, *Exceptional Children*, pp. 76–77.

15. For both quotes, see Finn, "Corrupted Intentions," p. 46.

16. *United States Statutes at Large*, vol. 89, pp. 773–796.

17

Department of Education Organization Act

October 17, 1979

The Department of Education Organization Act created the modern U.S. Department of Education. The best way to administer federal education programs had been a chronic source of debate both in and out of government. Those who wished to protect the traditional role and prerogatives of state and local governments in education fought to keep the federal administrative structure small and weak. Those who wished to see the federal government play a more active role in setting the country's educational agenda pushed for a more pronounced and influential administrative structure. A department of education was first created in 1867, but it was quickly downgraded to a "bureau" and then to an "office." During the administration of Franklin Roosevelt in the 1930s, the Office of Education was folded into the new Federal Security Agency, which would become the Department of Health, Education, and Welfare (HEW). When the federal government expanded its role in education during the 1960s, there was growing concern that the existing Office of Education within HEW was both inadequate to the expanded administrative task and unable forcefully to advocate on behalf of education. In the 1976 presidential campaign, Democratic nominee Jimmy Carter formally endorsed the idea of a new separate department of education, and his victory initiated the process that culminated in the Organization Act in 1979.

During the fight for passage, the politics over the Department of Education were hard fought. The effort to pass the act failed in 1978, when it was killed by a unique coalition of the most conservative and most liberal members of the House of Representatives.

The congressional debate engaged dozens of interest groups, both for and against. The political fights continued even after final passage in 1979, with candidate Ronald Reagan calling for the abolition of the new department in the 1980 presidential campaign. There were repeated proposals made by Republican platforms, presidential candidates, and members of Congress to abolish the department well into the 1990s. The politics have moderated more recently, with public opinion polls showing significant support for the existence of the department, and George W. Bush—far from calling for elimination—advocated an expanded role for the Department of Education in the 2000 election.

BACKGROUND

The Organization Act itself is quite brief and straightforward. Congress declares that "there is established an executive department to be known as the Department of Education," to be administered by a cabinet-level secretary "appointed by the President, by and with the advice and consent of the Senate."[1] Much of the act consists of laying out the organizational structure and administrative titles of the new department and of formally transferring legal responsibility for federal education programs from existing departments to the new department.

The most telling parts of the act are Sections 101 and 103. In the former, Congress lays out an extensive listing of findings to justify elevating the federal presence in education. The need for a federal department is justified on several grounds: education is the right of all citizens, regardless of the state in which they live; all U.S. citizens are guaranteed equal access to education, regardless of their state; increasing technology and complexity demand management techniques that some states lack; and new and expanded federal education programs have been disorganized and fragmented across multiple administrative departments. In Section 103, Congress lays out guarantees to protect the roles of state and local governments in education. The traditional and predominant roles of these governments are reaffirmed, and the act explicitly states that it will in no way increase the authority of the federal government in education or provide for federal control of state or local educational activities. The detail and extent of these sections are a reflection of the significant concerns many people then had over the creation of the department.

Education advocates had long sought the establishment of a separate department of education. In the first half of the twentieth century, more than 50 bills were introduced in Congress to create such a department. Significant political pressure began to build in the 1960s as the federal government did more and more in the area of education. President Lyndon Johnson's Task Force on Government Reorganization recommended the creation of an education department in 1964. His Task Force on Education subsequently recommended either a department or a stand-alone office of education answerable directly to the president. In Congress, the leading role was taken by Senator Abraham Ribicoff (D-CT), a former secretary of HEW, who argued that education was mismanaged and shortchanged within the larger structure. From 1964, when the first Johnson education initiative was enacted, until 1970, 48 separate bills were introduced in Congress to create a department of education. Clearly, there was growing and considerable interest in the idea.[2]

The Richard Nixon administration, however, was far more interested in consolidating departments than in creating new entities. This administration's proposals on government reorganization were ultimately marginalized by the Watergate events and Nixon's forced resignation. The idea of a department of education became an issue in the 1976 presidential campaign when Jimmy Carter committed himself to the idea before a convention of the National Education Association (NEA), the country's largest teachers' union. Carter became the first presidential candidate ever endorsed by the NEA, and critics have long maintained that his commitment to the department was a political deal for the endorsement.[3] The NEA endorsement would have been most important during the Democratic primaries, however, and Carter did not make his commitment to a department of education until well after he had the nomination secured.[4]

Carter's interest in separating education from HEW was one of several reorganization goals he had for the federal government. It took his administration some time to sort through these goals, set priorities, and, especially, craft legislative language. The planning within the administration was complicated by the fact that Carter's secretary of HEW, Joseph Califano, was intensely opposed to creating the new department. At least part of his opposition was rooted in a desire to protect his bureaucratic turf, but he made a substantive argument that education would have a stronger voice in government as a part of HEW. HEW was the largest domestic policy department in the federal government, and as a result, the secretary carried considerable political weight. Califano argued that a secretary for a department of education would represent a much smaller organization, carry less political weight, and be unable to focus much attention on educational goals. Califano's opposition was tolerated until it became apparent that he was actively lobbying Congress against the president's proposal; it became the main reason he was fired.[5]

The legislative push for the Organization Act came in 1978 and 1979. While critics labeled the proposal a political deal with the NEA—Senator Dan Quayle (R-IN) called it a "political payoff in every sense of the word"[6]—Carter outlined five rationales for the act in a message to Congress:

> Establishing a separate Department will create . . . a Cabinet-level advocate for education with direct access to the President, the Congress, and the public.
>
> Second, it will give Federal education programs . . . full-time, high-level leadership and management. . . .
>
> Third, it will provide greater accountability. . . .
>
> Fourth, it will provide simpler, more reliable, and more responsive support to states, localities, and public and private institutions. . . .
>
> Fifth, the new Department will allow better coordination of educational programs.[7]

The proposed department, Carter explained, would have more than 16,000 employees, be responsible for more than 150 separate programs, and have a first-year budget in excess of $13 billion— from the start it would be larger than each of the existing Departments of State, Justice, Energy, Commerce, and Interior.

The Senate considered the bill first in 1978, and the fight there was over "transfer issues," that is, which existing programs would be transferred to the new department. Existing departments and interest groups, especially the Children's Defense Fund, largely fought the administration to prevent several transfers—particularly Head Start from HEW, nutrition programs from the Department of Agriculture, and Indian schools from the Interior Department. There was a fight to include one program—vocational rehabilitation from HEW—that the administration did not want in the new department. The Carter administration lost every one of these transfer fights.[8] The biggest fight was over Head Start, where there was a very large and effective lobbying effort mounted by Marian Wright Edelman, director of the Children's Defense Fund. The concern from opponents was that the health and parental-participation components of Head Start would be lost or minimized if it were transferred to an education department. Head Start was quickly removed from the proposed department and remains in DHHS today. With all of the transfer issues decided, the Senate approved the Organization Act by a lopsided vote of 72 to 11.

The intense political fight that followed in the House was unexpected. Opposition from many Republicans was expected; opposition from more liberal members of the House and interest groups was not. For instance, the American Federation of Teachers (AFT), the second-largest teachers' union, lobbied strongly against the creation of the department. In part, this was simply a reflection of ongoing AFT-NEA competition. Beyond this, however, the AFT was an affiliate of the AFL-CIO, which had allies on and worked very effectively through the existing House Education and Labor Committee. There was a concern that with a new department, committee assignments, staff, and responsibilities would be reorganized, undercutting a union stronghold in the House. The result of AFT opposition was to pull liberal supporters of education in two directions.

Further, an ad hoc coalition of civil rights and education groups—including both the National Association for the Advancement of Colored People (NAACP) Legal Defense Fund and the Children's Defense Fund—argued that civil rights enforcement in education would be weakened. While the administration proposal called for an office of civil rights in the new department of education, it was structured in such a way that civil rights enforcement would be less effective in comparison to existing procedures within HEW. The coalition lobbied for either very significant amendment of the proposal or outright rejection. Again, liberal members of the House were pulled in different directions.[9]

What emerged in the House was thus an unusual coalition of the most conservative and the most liberal members to oppose the creation of the department. It was late in the fall, and these opponents tied the bill up with scores of amendments, hoping to prevent a vote before the legislative session ended. This was done first in committee and again later on the floor of the House. Most of the amendments were substantive and intentionally contentious, but at one point Congressman John Erlenborn (R-IL) offered an amendment to name the new entity the Department of Public Education and Youth—to create the acronym DOPEY. Given the time limits, the House leadership was unable to overcome this strategy of "filibuster by amendment," and the session ended without a vote.

In 1979, the NEA took a lower profile in pushing the bill, and the administration effectively persuaded many higher-education groups to lobby for the bill. Support in the Senate declined from the previous year, but the bill still passed with a very comfortable margin of 72 to 21. The major fight was again in the House, where the administration hoped to break the liberal-conservative coalition. The bill barely made it out of committee, surviving by only one vote. Republicans then successfully added a series of contentious amendments—against school busing, affirmative action, and abortion and for school prayer—with the goal of making the bill unacceptable to many Democrats. In this form, the bill squeaked through the House by a 210–206 vote.[10]

In the conference committee, while the issues were hotly debated, all of the "killer amendments" contained in the House version were stripped from the bill. Proponents knew that this would serve to increase conservative opposition, but hoped that by casting it as an ideological fight over civil rights, abortion, and other such issues, they would pick up more votes among liberals. The gamble paid off, with the conference report being approved in the House— with fewer Republicans but more Democrats—by a slightly more comfortable margin of 215 to 201.[11] The bill was again easily approved in the Senate, and President Carter signed the legislation into law on October 17, 1979, ending a long and divisive political fight and creating the 13th cabinet department.

IMPACT

The creation of the U.S. Department of Education had several impacts, some quite clear, others less so. The department has grown substantially and has become an accepted part of the federal administrative system. Through its actions, it has raised national awareness of educational problems and reforms. It has sponsored and helped disseminate research on educational best practices. Finally, it continued to affect politics and provoke political debate well into the 1990s.

In 1980, the first year of its existence, the Department of Education had a budget of $13.1 billion. By 1999, the budget had risen substantially, to $34.5 billion. When the department was established, it formally had about 17,000 employees, but 11,000 of these worked in the Overseas Schools program transferred from the Department of Defense. The actual bureaucratic or administrative staff of the department therefore stood at about 6,000. These numbers were cut in the 1990s, largely as a result of Vice President Al Gore's "Reinventing Government" initiative, with the current administrative staff totaling about 4,900, an 18 percent reduction. When the department was established, it took responsibility for approximately 150 programs, a figure that has risen to 175 today.

At the signing ceremony, President Carter said that the creation of the Department of Education would "profoundly transform . . . the quality of education in our nation."[12] This has clearly not occurred, but some or all of the rationales Carter gave Congress for creating the department, quoted earlier, have materialized. Carter argued that the department would create a national advocate for education and provide real national leadership in education, and these goals have been achieved. Simply by existing, the Department of Education became an advocate and provided at least some symbolic leadership. More tangibly, however, the department has clearly led in the area of education reform, advocating improved educational performance. Under the direction of Ronald Reagan's secretary of education Terrel Bell, the department sponsored the work of the National Commission on Excellence in Education, which resulted in the landmark report *A Nation at Risk: The Imperative for Educational Reform*. It made a compelling case for comprehensive reforms to improve educational quality and played a major role in motivating the states to enact far-reaching reforms.

Later in the 1980s, under Secretary William Bennett, the department produced a series of research-based reports on educational best practices. It manages the Educational Resource Information Center (ERIC) to catalog and disseminate educational research. During both the George Bush and Bill Clinton administrations, the Department of Education participated in national education summits in cooperation with the states, out of which emerged the Goals 2000 approach to national educational standards (see chapter 18). On the whole, it is clear that the department has achieved its advocacy and leadership goals.

Success with respect to the remaining rationales laid out by President Carter—greater accountability, increased responsiveness to state and local governments, and better coordination of federal programs—is more ambiguous. Education-related programs formerly administered by a wide range of federal departments are now under one administrative umbrella, and so a case can be made that this increases coordination and accountability. The fact that the department now administers a budget that has more than doubled with a staff that has been reduced by nearly a fifth may be cited as further evidence of accountability. Still, there are no measurable data, and critics argue that the department is both inefficient and wasteful.[13] With regard to responsiveness to state and local governments, there is a similarly mixed evaluation. In some areas, with Goals 2000 being an excellent example, local, state, and federal officials work together very cooperatively. There are many generalized complaints, however, that the department provides too little flexibility to and demands too much paperwork from state and local agencies.

Politically, as noted, the fight over the department continued long after the vote for passage of the act. Ronald Reagan campaigned for president in 1980 with a call to reverse the decision and abolish the department. His administration repeatedly made budget requests substantially to cut funding for the department, which were routinely rejected by Democrats in Congress. The Republican Party platforms drafted for presidential elections through the 1996 election called for the abolition of the Department of Education. The "Contract with America" manifesto used by Republicans in successfully recapturing control of the House in 1994 also called for eliminating the department.

The case for abolition has always rested on several related criticisms. As recently summarized by Diane Ravitch, who served as an assistant secretary of education in the George Bush administration, the Department of Education is wasteful and inefficient, tends to serve educational lobbyists rather than the interests of schoolchildren, has personnel with little real knowledge of education, continues funding for failed programs, provides too little flexibility to local schools, and is too distant to understand or appreciate local needs.[14] The various efforts and proposals to abolish the department have failed because of concerted Democratic defense of the department in Congress and public opinion polls that consistently show broad public support for maintaining the department. As a result, the politics surrounding the Department of Education have moderated, with the 2000 Republican platform calling for a slimmer, more efficient department rather than no department. Indeed, a number of the educational proposals made by George W. Bush in his presidential campaign called for increasing the role and oversight responsibilities of the department.

In the end, the Department of Education was a response to changing circumstances. As the federal government became more and more actively involved in education—with the National Defense Education Act, the Economic Opportunity Act, the Elementary and Secondary Education Act, the Higher Education Act, and the Bilingual Education Act—there were inevitable calls for a single department to coordinate and manage these activities. The fight for passage and then repeal reflected the continuing divisions in the United States over the proper role of the federal government in education. It reflected the division between those who view education as a national issue and priority and those who view it as a central power and responsibility of state and local governments. Since it was created, the Department of Education has increased the nation's focus on education and has provided real, ongoing leadership in the area of educational reform.

17. Department of Education Organization Act

An Act To establish a Department of Education, and for other purposes.[15]

Be it enacted by the Senate and House of Representatives of the United States of America in Congress assembled,

Section 1. This Act may be cited as the "Department of Education Organization Act." . . .

Section 101. The Congress finds that—

(1) education is fundamental to the development of individual citizens and the progress of the Nation;

(2) there is a continuing need to ensure equal access for all Americans to educational opportunities of a high quality, and such educational opportunities should not be denied because of race, creed, color, national origin, or sex;

(3) parents have the primary responsibility for the education of their children, and States, localities, and private institutions have the primary responsibility for supporting that parental role;

(4) in our Federal system, the primary public responsibility for ed-

ucation is reserved respectively to the States and the local school systems and other instrumentalities of the States;

(5) the American people benefit from a diversity of educational settings, including public and private schools, libraries, museums and other institutions, the workplace, the community, and the home;

(6) the importance of education is increasing as new technologies and alternative approaches to traditional education are considered, as society becomes more complex, and as equal opportunities in education and employment are promoted;

(7) there is need for improvement in the management and coordination of Federal education programs to support more effectively State, local, and private institutions, students, and parents in carrying out their educational responsibilities;

(8) the dispersion of educational programs across a large number of Federal agencies has led to fragmented, duplicative, and often inconsistent Federal policies relating to education;

(9) Presidential and public consideration of issues relating to Federal education programs is hindered by the present organizational position of education programs in the executive branch of the Government; and

(10) there is no single, full-time, Federal education official directly accountable to the President, the Congress, and the people.

Section 102. The Congress declares that the establishment of a Department of Education is in the public interest, will promote the general welfare of the United States, will help ensure that education issues receive proper treatment at the Federal level, and will enable the Federal Government to coordinate its education activities more effectively. Therefore, the purposes of this Act are—

(1) to strengthen the Federal commitment to ensuring access to equal educational opportunity for every individual;

(2) to supplement and complement the efforts of the States, the local school systems and other instrumentalities of the States, the private sector, public and private educational institutions, public and private non-profit educational research institutions, community-based organizations, parents, and students to improve the quality of education;

(3) to encourage the increased involvement of the public, parents, and students in Federal education programs;

(4) to promote improvements in the quality and usefulness of education through federally supported research, evaluation, and sharing of information;

(5) to improve the coordination of Federal education programs;

(6) to improve the management and efficiency of Federal education activities . . . ; and

(7) to increase the accountability of Federal education programs to the President, the Congress, and the public.

Section 103. (a) It is the intention of the Congress in the establishment of the Department to protect the rights of State and local governments and public and private educational institutions. . . . The establishment of the Department of Education shall not increase the authority of the Federal Government over education or diminish the responsibility for education which is reserved to the States and the local school systems and other instrumentalities of the States.

(b) No provision of the program administered by the Secretary or by any other officer of the Department shall be construed to authorize the Secretary or any such officer to exercise any direction, supervision, or control over the curriculum, program of instruction, administration, or personnel of any educational institution, school, or school system, over any accrediting agency or association, or over the selection or content of library resources, textbooks, or other instructional materials by any educational institution, school, or school system, except to the extent authorized by law. . . .

Section 201. There is established an executive department to be known as the Department of Education. The Department shall be administered . . . under the supervision and direction of a Secretary of Education. The Secretary shall be appointed by the President, by and with the advice and consent of the Senate. . . .

Section 301. (a) There are transferred to the Secretary—

(1) all functions of the Assistant Secretary for Education and of the Commissioner of Education of the Department of Health, Education, and Welfare . . .

(2) all functions of the Secretary of Health, Education, and Welfare and of the Department of Health, Education, and Welfare under—

(A) the General Education Provisions Act;

(B) the Elementary and Secondary Education Act of 1965;

(C) the Higher Education Act of 1965; . . .

(F) the National Defense Education Act of 1958;

(G) the International Education Act of 1966;

(H) the Education of the Handicapped Act; . . .

(K) the Vocational Education Act of 1963; . . .

Approved October 17, 1979.

NOTES

1. *United States Statutes at Large*, vol. 93 (Washington, DC: U.S. Government Printing Office, 1979), p. 671.

2. For a discussion of these developments, see Beryl A. Radin and Willis D. Hawley, *The Politics of Federal Reorganization: Creating the U.S. Department of Education* (New York: Pergamon Press, 1988), pp. 12–36.

3. See, for instance, Donald K. Sharpes, *Education and the US Government* (New York: St. Martin's Press, 1987), pp. 173–175.

4. For a discussion of the politics, see Erwin C. Hargrove, *Jimmy Carter as President: Leadership and the Politics of the Public Good* (Baton Rouge: Louisiana State University Press, 1988), pp. 60–61.

5. On Califano's opposition and firing, see Charles O. Jones, *The Trusteeship Presidency: Jimmy Carter and the United States Congress* (Baton Rouge: Louisiana State University Press, 1988), p. 185; and Hargrove, *Jimmy Carter as President*, pp. 61–65.

6. Quoted in Radin and Hawley, *The Politics of Federal Reorganization*, p. 124.

7. From the message of President Carter to Congress on February 13, 1979, as reprinted in Congressional Quarterly, *President Carter, 1979* (Washington, DC: Congressional Quarterly Press, 1980), p. 11-A.

8. On these transfer fights and interest-group lobbying, see Radin and Hawley, *The Politics of Federal Reorganization*, pp. 96–120.

9. On these divisions in the House, see Radin and Hawley, *The Politics of Federal Reorganization*, pp. 126–128.

10. On this amendment strategy, see Congressional Digest, *Action in the 95th Congress: Proposed U.S. Department of Education* (Washington, DC: Congressional Digest Corp., 1978), p. 268; and Jones, *The Trusteeship Presidency*, pp. 186–187.

11. On the coalition of supporters and the winning strategy, see Congressional Quarterly, *President Carter, 1979*, p. 78.

12. Quoted in Radin and Hawley, *The Politics of Federal Reorganization*, p. 149.

13. See, for instance, Diane Ravitch, "Euthanasia," *Forbes* 155, no. 11, (1995): p. 130.

14. Ravitch, "Euthanasia," p. 130.

15. *United States Statutes at Large*, vol. 93, pp. 668–696.

18

Goals 2000: Educate America Act

March 31, 1994

The Goals 2000: Educate America Act formalized and added structure to education-reform efforts begun in the late 1980s. It established education reform—improving the quality and performance of American primary and secondary schools—as a national concern and priority. It commits the country to a shared set of specific educational goals and to national curricular and student-performance standards to measure progress toward these goals. The act provides for a uniquely cooperative effort among the federal government and the states. It provides resources, a framework, and tremendous flexibility to states and schools; it has been described as offering "a structure, not a prescription," for what should be done to achieve the national goals.[1] The cooperative nature of the legislation stands out—participation is voluntary, the adoption of standards and tests by states is voluntary, and school-improvement plans funded by Goals 2000 do not need prior federal approval or certification. Under Goals 2000, the federal government and the states act together in pursuit of systematic educational change and improvement.

Politically, what was to become Goals 2000 began as a bipartisan effort, an outgrowth of the 1989 National Education Summit held in Charlottesville, Virginia, among President George Bush and the 50 state governors. It was formulated as America 2000 under the Bush administration and was then recast and formalized as Goals 2000 under the Bill Clinton administration. It enjoyed the political support of both Democratic and Republican governors. Since its passage, vocal opposition has emerged on both the right and the left. Conservative critics of Goals 2000 express concerns over federal influence and direction of local schools, while liberal critics express concerns over the educational value of common standards and, especially, standardized testing of all students. Finally, the arrival of the year 2000 with all of the goals unmet has created the political question of whether and how to continue the efforts initiated by Goals 2000.

BACKGROUND

The fundamental purpose of the Goals 2000: Educate America Act was to promote "coherent, nationwide, systemic education reform,"[2] by establishing national goals, internationally competitive standards, and assessments and providing states flexibility to design programs to achieve the goals. At the heart of the act are eight national education goals to be achieved by the year 2000. Summarized, the goals are as follows:

1. All children will start school ready to learn.
2. The high-school graduation rate will be at least 90 percent.
3. All children will have demonstrated competence over a challenging curriculum in at least grades 4, 8, and 12.
4. All teachers will have access to professional development opportunities to maintain and improve skills.
5. U.S. children will be ranked first in the world in mathematics and science achievement.
6. All adults in the United States will be literate.
7. All schools will be safe, disciplined, and alcohol and drug free.
8. Every school will promote parental participation and involvement.

Several boards or panels were established to direct efforts toward achieving these goals. The National Education Goals Panel, which had previously existed as a voluntary organization, was codified in the legislation to monitor progress toward the goals. The National Education Standards and Improvement Council was established—though for political reasons it was never staffed or made operational—to create national curricular content and performance standards. Finally, the National Skills Standards Board was created to assist voluntary state efforts to create their own standards and assessments.

Various grant programs were established to provide federal resources to the states in pursuit of the national goals. Approximately $400 million has been appropriated each year to help fund state education-reform efforts. Beyond this main effort, smaller grant programs include monies to develop parent information and resource centers and to promote academic research related to the national goals.

The whole structure of Goals 2000 rests on several related assumptions. The first is a belief that systemic school reform can be achieved by setting ambitious standards. If the academic bar is set clearly and set high, everyone involved in education—teachers and administrators, parents and children—will be motivated and mobilized to achieve the standards. The act thus encourages the creation of internationally competitive national and voluntary state standards, detailing what students ought to master at each grade level in each content area, and the creation of assessment mechanisms to measure the extent to which students meet these standards. Second, the act assumes that systemic reform can reach every child, that every child can master challenging material, and that such reforms can be achieved quite quickly. Third, the act assumes that there is a variety of organizational and pedagogical ways to achieve the national goals. The federal government does not need to impose or mandate an approach, but, rather, states can experiment and take different routes as long as they are headed in the same direction, toward the same goals. Finally, the act assumes that the best and proper role for the federal government in education reform is to aid states with some organization, resources, and research.[3]

The standards approach at the core of Goals 2000 was motivated by the publication of A Nation at Risk in 1983. The work of the National Commission on Excellence in Education, chaired by David Gardner (then president of the University of Utah and president-elect of the University of California) the report documented numerous "indicators of risk," data indicating that there were substantial problems in American schools, and argued that there was a national imperative for fundamental reform.[4] Many governors, in particular, began to advocate education reform in the wake of A Nation at Risk, including Republican governors Lamar Alexander in Tennessee and Tom Kean in New Jersey and Democratic governors Bill Clinton in Arkansas and Richard Riley in South Carolina. The U.S. Department of Education, under the leadership of

Terrel Bell and William Bennett, was very supportive of state efforts, but was largely limited to providing strong rhetorical support.

In 1989, in an effort to provide a more coordinated approach to reforming American schools, the National Education Summit was organized in Charlottesville, Virginia. The summit included President Bush, federal education officials, and all 50 state governors. Governor Clinton played a leading role among the governors in working out a common approach with President Bush. The result was the first enunciation of national education goals. The federal government and all of the states committed themselves to achieving six national goals (the first six listed earlier).[5]

In 1991, building on the national goals, President Bush initiated America 2000, an education plan that called for national standards created through the voluntary National Education Goals Panel, annual "report cards" on progress in improving school quality, and funding for demonstration or model schools through the New American Schools Development Corporation (NASDC). This newly created public corporation was quickly funded with a charge to create a $1-million model school in each congressional district in the country.[6] The NASDC still operates today, and has spent over $145 million to conduct research on and develop demonstration projects for effective reform strategies.

Bill Clinton, an active participant in the National Education Summit and the establishment of the national goals, remained very supportive of the standards approach to education reform. When he succeeded President Bush, he was committed to the same basic approach in education policy. The Clinton administration took America 2000, expanded upon it, added two additional goals (goals 7 and 8, listed earlier), formalized the structure, added funding, and recast it as Goals 2000. The two programs were not identical—Goals 2000 was certainly more ambitious—but they were clearly related. There was a continuum from *A Nation at Risk* to the National Education Summit and the national goals, America 2000, and Goals 2000. Goals 2000 was the legislative culmination of the evolving state-federal standards-based approach to education reform.

The Goals 2000 legislation moved through Congress relatively easily. Two sections of the proposal raised concerns, however, both of which remained controversial and were later effectively repealed. The first was the creation of the National Education Standards and Improvement Council, which critics feared would become a "national school board" and a mechanism for the federal government to impose a curriculum on states and school districts. The second was the proposal for Opportunity-to-Learn (OTL) standards, intended to outline basic guidelines for plant, equipment, funding, and other resources needed to ensure that every child had an equal opportunity to learn. Critics on the left wanted OTL provisions to be stronger, moving in the direction of equalizing school resources. Critics on the right feared that OTL standards would become a large unfunded federal mandate forcing local schools to increase spending.[7] In the end, the standards were diluted to recommendations and were eventually eliminated entirely.

The bill passed the House easily, 306 to 121, but final passage of Goals 2000 was blocked by a filibuster mounted by Senator Jesse Helms (R-NC), who wanted strong language supporting school prayer in the legislation. A scheduled Senate recess had to be delayed to break the filibuster, and the final 63–22 vote took place at 12:30 A.M., March 26, to finish Senate business and begin the recess.[8] President Clinton signed Goals 2000 into law on March 31, 1994.

IMPACT

The Goals 2000: Educate America Act has reshaped the federal-state relationship in education. Republican Governor Tommy Thompson of Wisconsin has said that "the program has changed the face of education as we know it," and Henry Marockie, state superintendent of schools in West Virginia, has commented simply that "the Feds finally got it right."[9] The enactment of Goals 2000 was the culmination and codification of a truly cooperative approach to education policy and reform. The federal government and the states are pursuing the same goals, with the federal government structuring and funding much of the reform effort and the states exercising flexibility and designing their own routes to high academic achievement for all children.

The actual effectiveness of Goals 2000, with the arrival and departure of the year 2000, is now being debated. The U.S. Department of Education casts the program as a clear success, while others have concluded—not happily—that "there is precious little evidence the first federal foray into state and local school reform is paying big dividends."[10] Supporters tend to look at deeds accomplished and in progress, including the formalization and work of the National Education Goals Panel, the participation of 48 states,[11] the work individual states have undertaken to create standards, and the standardized testing of students. The Department of Education cites many case studies of particular state programs and school districts where real progress appears to be occurring.[12]

Rather than looking at such deeds accomplished or particular cases, others have looked at overall changes in student performance to evaluate the effectiveness of Goals 2000 and have found very little movement forward. The National Education Goals Panel publishes a progress report each year, with data and several measures for each of the eight national goals. The most recent report (1999) indicated some progress in improving children's health (part of goal 1) and mathematics achievement (part of goal 3), but little or no significant progress on the other goals.[13] Supporters recognize these results, but argue simply that the intended reforms are still in progress, and that the national commitment to student performance and achievement is itself a major success.

Since passage in 1994, Goals 2000 has been subjected to increasing political criticism from both conservatives and liberals. Conservative criticisms have mirrored those expressed during the congressional debate, only the voices have become louder and more numerous. Lamar Alexander, for instance, who, as governor of Tennessee and then as secretary of education in the George Bush administration, was supportive of the standards approach and was responsible for administering America 2000, became very critical of Goals 2000. He and others expressed concern that both the National Education Standards Improvement Council and Opportunity-to-Learn standards would or could be used by the federal government to exert control over state and local education policies. In response to these concerns, President Clinton agreed not to make any appointments to the council, rendering it moot, and Goals 2000 was amended in 1996 to eliminate the OTL standards entirely.

Voices of liberal criticism have also grown since 1994. Many liberal education advocates saw the OTL standards as the only mechanism to deal effectively with the "savage inequalities" that exist between rich and poor school districts. One point of criticism, therefore, is that the OTL standards were too weak when they were passed and then were eliminated.[14] The most passionate criticism, however, is aimed at the assessment component of Goals 2000. Many view extensive, standardized testing of students, at best, as useless and, at worst, as harmful: "For me, the real scandal is that our school leaders, under pressure from the mandates of Goals

2000, are subjecting young children to these tests in the first place. These are high-stakes tests, written by hack scribes who show no more savvy than a salad bar crouton about children."[15] The two criticisms, the loss of OTL and harmful testing, are often tied together—given gross inequities in resources, the national goals are unreasonable and unreachable, and testing to these standards only guarantees failure. Goals 2000, from this perspective, rather than improving education, will be no more "than a yardstick for measuring the disappointing performance of American schools."[16]

Despite the criticisms, left and right, Goals 2000 unquestionably represents a tremendously ambitious program. It seeks comprehensive, systemic reform of all American schools. It seeks to achieve high academic performance from every American child. Further, these ambitions are pursued through a new cooperative relationship between the federal government and the states. Unlike previous education policies, it does not rest on either a reverence of local control or top-down federal mandates. It is a shared program and commitment, with the federal government providing a framework and resources, and programmatic decision making remaining with the states. The act thus represents a major shift in education policy and structure in the United States. It can not be faulted for a lack of ambition, but, with the goals unmet in 2000, the future of Goals 2000 is uncertain.

18. Goals 2000: Educate America Act

An Act To improve learning and teaching by providing a
national framework for education reform; to promote the
research, consensus building, and systemic changes needed to
ensure equitable educational opportunities and high levels of
educational achievement for all students; to provide a
framework for reauthorization of all Federal education
programs; to promote the development and adoption of a
voluntary national system of skill standards and certifications;
and for other purposes.[17]

Be it enacted by the Senate and House of Representatives of the United States of America in Congress assembled,

Section 1. This Act . . . may be cited as the "Goals 2000: Educate America Act." . . .

Section 2. The purpose of this Act is to provide a framework for meeting the National Education Goals established by title I of this Act by—

(1) promoting coherent, nationwide, systemic education reform;

(2) improving the quality of learning and teaching in the classroom and in the workplace;

(3) defining appropriate and coherent Federal, State, and local roles and responsibilities for education reform and lifelong learning;

(4) establishing valid and reliable mechanisms for—

(A) building a broad national consensus on American education reform;

(B) assisting in the development and certification of high-quality, internationally competitive content and student performance standards;

(C) assisting in the development and certification of opportunity-to-learn standards; and

(D) assisting in the development and certification of high-quality assessment measures that reflect the internationally competitive content and student performance standards;

(5) supporting new initiatives at the Federal, State, local, and school levels to provide equal educational opportunity for all students to meet high academic and occupational skill standards . . .

(6) providing a framework for the reauthorization of all Federal education programs by . . .

(D) encouraging and enabling all State educational agencies and local educational agencies to develop comprehensive improvement plans that will provide a coherent framework for the implementation of reauthorized Federal education and related programs in an integrated fashion that effectively educates all children to prepare them to participate fully as workers, parents, and citizens;

(E) providing resources to help individual schools, including those serving students with high needs, develop and implement comprehensive improvement plans;

(F) promoting the use of technology to enable all students to achieve the National Education Goals;

(7) stimulating the development and adoption of a voluntary national system of skill standards and certification to serve as a cornerstone of the national strategy to enhance workforce skills; and

(8) assisting every elementary and secondary school that receives funds under this Act to actively involve parents and families in supporting the academic work of their children at home and in providing parents with the skills to advocate for their children at school. . . .

TITLE I—NATIONAL EDUCATION GOALS

Section 101. The purpose of this title is to establish National Education Goals.

Section 102. The Congress declares that the National Education Goals are the following:

(1) School readiness.—(A) By the year 2000, all children in America will start school ready to learn. . . .

(2) School completion.—(A) By the year 2000, the high school graduation rate will increase to at least 90 percent. . . .

(3) Student achievement and citizenship.—(A) By the year 2000, all students will leave grades 4, 8, and 12 having demonstrated competency over challenging subject matter including English, mathematics, science, foreign languages, civics and government, economics, arts, history, and geography, and every school in America will ensure that all students learn to use their minds well, so they may be prepared for responsible citizenship, further learning, and productive employment in our Nation's modern economy. . . .

(4) Teacher education and professional development.—(A) By the year 2000, the Nation's teaching force will have access to programs for the continued improvement of their professional skills and the opportunity to acquire the knowledge and skills needed to instruct and prepare all American students for the next century. . . .

(5) Mathematics and science.—(A) By the year 2000, United States students will be the first in the world in mathematics and science achievement. . . .

(6) Adult literacy and lifelong learning.—(A) By the year 2000, every adult American will be literate and will possess the knowledge and skills necessary to compete in a global economy and exercise the rights and responsibilities of citizenship. . . .

(7) Safe, disciplined, and alcohol and drug-free schools.—(A) By the year 2000, every school in the United States will be free of drugs, violence, and the unauthorized presence of firearms and alcohol and will offer a disciplined environment conducive to learning. . . .

(8) Parental participation.—(A) By the year 2000, every school will promote partnerships that will increase parental involvement and participation in promoting the social, emotional, and academic growth of children. . . .

TITLE II—NATIONAL EDUCATION REFORM LEADERSHIP, STANDARDS, AND ASSESSMENTS . . .

Section 202. (a) Establishment.—There is established in the executive branch a National Education Goals Panel . . . to advise the President, the Secretary [of Education], and the Congress. . . .

Section 212. (a) Establishment.—There is established in the executive branch a National Education Standards and Improvement Council. . . .

TITLE III—STATE AND LOCAL EDUCATION SYSTEMIC IMPROVEMENT . . .

Section 302. (a) Purpose.—It is the purpose of this title to improve the quality of education for all students by improving student learning through a long-term, broad-based effort to promote coherent and coordinated improvements in the system of education throughout the Nation at the State and local levels.

(b) Congressional Intent.—This title provides new authorities and funding for the Nation's school systems without replacing or reducing funding for existing Federal education programs. . . .

Section 303. There are authorized to be appropriated $400,000,000 for the fiscal year 1994, and such sums as may be necessary for each of the fiscal years 1995 through 1998, to carry out this title. . . .

TITLE IV—PARENTAL ASSISTANCE . . .

Section 401. . . . (b) Grants authorized.—

(1) In general.—The Secretary is authorized to award grants . . . to nonprofit organizations, and nonprofit organizations in consortia with local educational agencies, to establish parental information and resource centers that provide training, and support to—

(A) parents of children aged birth through five years;

(B) parents of children enrolled in elementary and secondary schools. . . .

TITLE V—NATIONAL SKILLS STANDARDS BOARD . . .

Section 502. It is the purpose of this title to establish a National Skills Standards Board to serve as a catalyst in stimulating the development and adoption of a voluntary national system of skill standards and of assessment and certification of attainment of skill standards. . . .

TITLE IX—EDUCATIONAL RESEARCH AND IMPROVEMENT . . .

Section 902. The Congress finds as follows with respect to improving education in the United States:

(1) A majority of public schools in the United States are failing to prepare students to achieve the National Education Goals. The Federal Government should support an extensive program of educational research, development, dissemination, replication, and assistance to identify and support the best responses for the challenges ahead. . . .
Approved March 31, 1994.

NOTES

1. See Albert Shanker, "A Do-It-Yourself Kit" (American Federation of Teachers, http://www.aft.org/stand/previous/1994/100994.html, 1994).

2. P. L. 103–227: "Goals 2000: Educate America Act" (108 Stat. 125; 3/31/94). Text from *United States Public Laws*, available from *Congressional Universe* (online service). (Bethesda, MD: Congressional Information Service), p. 5.

3. For a general discussion of the basic assumptions behind the standards approach to reform, see David K. Cohen, "Standards-based School Reform: Policy, Practice, and Performance," in *Holding Schools Accountable: Performance-based Reform in Education*, ed. Helen F. Ladd (Washington, DC: Brookings Institution, 1996), pp. 100–102.

4. National Commission on Excellence in Education, *A Nation at Risk: The Imperative for Educational Reform* (Washington, DC: U.S. Government Printing Office, 1983).

5. On the summit, see U.S. Department of Education, "Goals 2000: Increasing Student Achievement through State and Local Initiatives" (Washington, DC: http://www.ed.gov/G2K/GoalsRpt/intro.html, 2000).

6. On America 2000, see Diane Ravitch, *National Standards in American Education: A Citizen's Guide* (Washington, DC: Brookings Institution, 1995), pp. 138–139, and David Stoesz, *Small Change: Domestic Policy under the Clinton Presidency* (White Plains, NY: Longman, 1996), pp. 129–131.

7. On the critics' arguments, see Ravitch, *National Standards in American Education*, pp. 148–155, and Joel Spring, *Political Agendas for Education: From the Christian Coalition to the Green Party* (Mahwah, NJ: Lawrence Erlbaum Associates, 1997), pp. 78–80.

8. On the final vote, see Congressional Quarterly, "Goals 2000 Bill Clears Senate in Early-Morning Session," *Congressional Quarterly Weekly Reports* 51, no. 13 (April 2, 1994): p. 804.

9. Governor Thompson is quoted in U.S. Department of Education, "Goals 2000: Increasing Student Achievement through State and Local Initiatives," p. 6, and Superintendent Marockie in U.S. Department of Education, "Goals 2000: Reforming Education to Improve Student Achievement" (http://www.ed.gov/pubs/G2KReforming, 2000).

10. Robert Holland, "A Goals 2000 in 2001?" *Education Week on the Web* (http://www.edweek.org/ew/ewstory.cfm?slug=07hollan.h19&keywords=robert%20holland, 2000).

11. Oklahoma and Montana are the two states that have made the decision to stay out of Goals 2000, but both allow individual school districts to participate.

12. See, for instance, U.S. Department of Education, "Goals 2000: Increasing Student Achievement through State and Local Initiatives."

13. "Progress Report on National Education Goals," *Education Week on the Web*, (http://www.edweek.org/ew/vol-18/18goalss1.h18, 2000).

14. On the issue of disparities between rich and poor districts, see Jonathan Kozol, *Savage Inequalities* (New York: HarperPerennial, 1991). On the inadequacy of the OTL standards in addressing the disparities, see Spring, *Political Agendas for Education*, pp. 79–80.

15. Susan Ohanian, "Goals 2000: What's in a Name," *Phi Delta Kappan* 81, no. 5 (January 2000): 344.

16. Stoesz, *Small Change*, p. 205.

17. P.L. 103–227.

Bibliography

Advisory Commission on Intergovernmental Relations. *The Evolution of a Problematic Partnership: The Feds and Higher Ed.* Washington, DC: Advisory Commission on Intergovernmental Relations, 1981.

————. *Intergovernmentalizing the Classroom: Federal Involvement in Elementary and Secondary Education.* Washington, DC: Advisory Commission on Intergovernmental Relations, 1981.

Allen, Hollis P. *The Federal Government and Education.* New York: McGraw-Hill, 1950.

Aronowitz, Stanley, and Henry Giroux. *Education under Siege: The Conservative, Liberal, and Radical Debate over Schooling.* South Hadley, MA: Bergin and Garvey, 1985.

Babbidge, Homer D., Jr., and Robert M. Rosenzweig. *The Federal Interest in Higher Education.* New York: McGraw-Hill, 1962.

Bailey, Stephen K., and Edith K. Mosher. *ESEA: The Office of Education Administers a Law.* Syracuse, NY: Syracuse University Press, 1968.

Bailyn, Bernard. *Education in the Forming of American Society.* Chapel Hill: University of North Carolina Press, 1960.

Baker, Keith A., and Adriana A. de Kanter, eds. *Bilingual Education: A Reappraisal of Federal Policy.* Lexington, MA: Lexington Books, 1983.

Bank, Barbara J., and Peter M. Hall, eds. *Gender, Equity, and Schooling: Policy and Practice.* New York: Garland Publishing, 1997.

Berke, Joel S., and Michael W. Kirst. *Federal Aid to Education: Who Benefits? Who Governs?* Lexington, MA: Lexington Books, 1972.

Berliner, David C., and Bruce J. Biddle. *The Manufactured Crisis: Myths, Fraud, and the Attack on America's Public Schools.* Reading, MA: Addison-Wesley, 1995.

Best, John H., ed. *Benjamin Franklin on Education.* New York: Teachers College, Columbia University, 1962.

Bestor, Arthur. *Educational Wastelands: The Retreat from Learning in Our Public Schools.* 2nd ed. Urbana: University of Illinois Press, 1985.

Binder, Frederick M. *The Age of the Common School, 1830–1865.* New York: John Wiley, 1974.

Botstein, Leon. *Jefferson's Children: Education and the Promise of American Culture.* New York: Doubleday, 1997.

Brademas, John. *The Politics of Education: Conflict and Consensus on Capitol Hill.* Norman: University of Oklahoma Press, 1987.

Brubacher, John S., ed. *Henry Barnard on Education.* New York: McGraw-Hill, 1931.

Brubacher, John S., and Willis Rudy. *Higher Education in Transition: An American History, 1636–1956.* New York: Harper and Row, 1958.

Bullock, Henry A. *A History of Negro Education in the South, from 1619 to the Present.* Cambridge, MA: Harvard University Press, 1967.

Butts, R. Freeman. *Public Education in the United States: From Revolution to Reform.* New York: Holt, Rinehart, and Winston, 1978.

Butts, R. Freeman, and Lawrence A. Cremin. *A History of Education in American Culture.* New York: Henry Holt and Company, 1953.

Cobb, Henry E. *Report on an Examination of the Developing Institutions Program.* Washington, DC: U.S. Office of Education, 1977.

Cohen, Sheldon S. *A History of Colonial Education, 1607–1776.* New York: John Wiley, 1974.

Commission on the Reorganization of Secondary Education. *Cardinal Principles of Secondary Education.* Bulletin No. 35. Washington, DC: U.S. Bureau of Education, 1918.

Conant, James B. *Thomas Jefferson and the Development of American Public Education.* Berkeley: University of California Press, 1962.

Crawford, James. *Bilingual Education: History, Politics, Theory, and Practice.* Trenton, NJ: Crane, 1989.

Cremin, Lawrence A. *The American Common School: An Historic Conception.* New York: Teachers College, Columbia University, 1951.

———. *The Transformation of the School: Progressivism in American Education, 1876–1957.* New York: Knopf, 1961.

———. *American Education: The National Experience, 1783–1876.* New York: Harper and Row, 1980.

———. *American Education: The Metropolitan Experience, 1876–1980.* New York: Harper and Row, 1988.

Cronan, Marion. *The School Lunch.* Peoria, IL: Chas. A. Bennett Company, 1962.

Culver, Raymond B. *Horace Mann and Religion in the Massachusetts Public Schools.* New Haven: Yale University Press, 1929.

Devine, Robert A., ed. *The Johnson Years.* Vol. 1, *Foreign Policy, the Great Society, and the White House.* Lawrence: University Press of Kansas, 1987.

———. *The Sputnik Challenge.* New York: Oxford University Press, 1993.

Dewey, John. *The School and Society.* Chicago: University of Chicago Press, 1974.

Downs, Robert B. *Horace Mann: Champion of Public Schools.* New York: Twayne, 1974.

Doyle, Denis P., and Bruce S. Cooper, eds. *Federal Aid to the Disadvantaged: What Future for Chapter 1?* New York: Falmer Press, 1988.

Du Bois, W.E.B. *Black Reconstruction in America, 1860–1880.* New York: Harcourt, Brace, 1935.

Eddy, Edward Danforth, Jr. *Colleges for Our Land and Time: The Land-Grant Idea in American Education.* New York: Harper and Brothers, 1957.

Finn, Chester E., Jr. *Scholars, Dollars, and Bureaucrats.* Washington, DC: Brookings Institution, 1978.

———. *We Must Take Charge: Our Schools and Our Future.* New York: Free Press, 1993.

Fishel, Andrew, and Janice Pottker. *National Politics and Sex Discrimination in Education*. Lexington, MA: Lexington Books, 1977.

Fretwell, Elbert K., Jr. *Founding Public Junior Colleges*. New York: Teachers College, Columbia University, 1954.

Gearheart, Bill R. *Special Education for the '80s*. St. Louis: C.V. Mosby Company, 1980.

Ginzberg, Eli, and Robert M. Solow, eds. *The Great Society: Lessons for the Future*. New York: Basic Books, 1974.

Gladieux, Lawrence E., and Arthur M. Hauptman. *The College Aid Quandary: Access, Quality, and the Federal Role*. Washington, DC: Brookings Institution and the College Board, 1995.

Gladieux, Lawrence E., and Thomas R. Wolanin. *Congress and the Colleges*. Lexington, MA: Lexington Books, 1976.

Graham, Hugh Davis. *The Uncertain Triumph: Federal Education Policy in the Kennedy and Johnson Years*. Chapel Hill: University of North Carolina Press, 1984.

Graham, Patricia Albjerg. *Progressive Education: From Arcady to Academe: A History of the Progressive Education Association, 1919–1955*. New York: Teachers College Press, 1967.

Gutek, Gerald L. *Basic Education: A Historical Perspective*. Bloomington, IN: Phi Delta Kappa Educational Foundation, 1981.

———. *Education in the United States: An Historical Perspective*. Englewood Cliffs, NJ: Prentice-Hall, 1986.

Hansen, Allen O. *Liberalism and American Education in the Eighteenth Century*. New York: Macmillan, 1926.

Hawkins, Layton S., Charles A. Prosser, and John C. Wright. *Development of Vocational Education*. Chicago: American Technical Society, 1951.

Heslep, Robert D. *Thomas Jefferson and Education*. New York: Random House, 1969.

Heward, William L., and Michael D. Orlansky. *Exceptional Children: An Introductory Survey of Special Education*. 4th ed. New York: Merrill, 1992.

Hirsch, E. D., Jr. *The Schools We Need and Why We Don't Have Them*. New York: Doubleday, 1996.

Hofstadter, Richard, and C. DeWitt Hardy. *The Development and Scope of Higher Education in the United States*. New York: Columbia University Press, 1952.

Holmes, Dwight Oliver Wendell. *The Evolution of the Negro College*. New York: AMS Press, 1970.

Hyman, Harold M. *American Singularity: The 1787 Northwest Ordinance, the 1862 Homestead and Morrill Acts, and the 1944 G.I. Bill*. Athens: University of Georgia Press, 1986.

Kaestle, Carl. *Pillars of the Republic: Common Schools and American Society, 1780–1860*. New York: Hill and Wang, 1983.

Kantor, Harvey, and David B. Tyack, eds. *Work, Youth, and Schooling: Historical Perspectives on Vocationalism in American Education*. Stanford: Stanford University Press, 1982.

Karier, Clarence J. *Shaping the American Educational State, 1900 to the Present*. New York: Free Press, 1975.

Karier, Clarence J., Paul Violas, and Joel Spring. *Roots of Crisis: American Education in the Twentieth Century*. Chicago: Rand McNally and Company, 1955.

Keppel, Francis. *The Necessary Revolution in American Education*. New York: Harper and Row, 1966.

Kirk, Samuel A., and James J. Gallagher. *Educating Exceptional Children.* 6th ed. Boston: Houghton Mifflin, 1989.

Kirp, David L., and Donald N. Jensen. *School Days, Rule Days: The Legislation and Regulation of Education.* Philadelphia: Falmer Press, 1985.

Labovitz, I. M. *Aid for Federally Affected Public Schools.* Syracuse, NY: Syracuse University Press, 1963.

Ladd, Helen F., ed. *Holding Schools Accountable: Performance-based Reform in Education.* Washington, DC: Brookings Institution, 1996.

Lapati, Americo D. *Education and the Federal Government: A Historical Record.* New York: Mason-Charter, 1975.

Lee, Gordon C., ed. *Crusade against Ignorance: Thomas Jefferson on Education.* New York: Teachers College, Columbia University, 1961.

Levitan, Sar A. *The Great Society's Poor Law: A New Approach to Poverty.* Baltimore: Johns Hopkins Press, 1969.

McConnell, T. R. *A General Pattern for American Public Higher Education.* New York: McGraw-Hill, 1962.

Meranto, Philip. *The Politics of Federal Aid to Education in 1965: A Study in Political Innovation.* Syracuse, NY: Syracuse University Press, 1967.

Midwinter, Eric. *Nineteenth Century Education.* New York: Harper and Row, 1970.

Nasaw, David. *Schooled to Order: A Social History of Public Schooling in the United States.* New York: Oxford University Press, 1979.

National Commission on Excellence in Education. *A Nation at Risk: The Imperative for Educational Reform.* Washington, DC: U.S. Government Printing Office, 1983.

National Education Association. *Report of the Committee of Ten on Secondary School Studies.* New York: American Book Company, 1894.

National Education Goals Panel. *National Education Goals Report: Building a Nation of Learners.* Washington, DC: U.S. Government Printing Office, 1992.

Nevins, Allan. *The State Universities and Democracy.* Urbana: University of Illinois Press, 1962.

Olson, Keith W. *The G.I. Bill, the Veterans, and the Colleges.* Lexington: University Press of Kentucky, 1974.

Parker, William B. *The Life and Public Services of Justin Smith Morrill.* New York: Da Capo Press, 1971.

Peirce, Paul Skeels. *The Freedmen's Bureau: A Chapter in the History of Reconstruction.* New York: Haskell House, 1971.

Pottker, Janice, and Andrew Fishel, eds. *Sex Bias in the Schools: The Research Evidence.* Rutherford, NJ: Fairleigh Dickinson University Press, 1977.

Pulliam, John D., and James Van Patten. *History of Education in America.* 7th ed. Upper Saddle River, NJ: Merrill, 1999.

Radin, Beryl A., and Willis D. Hawley. *The Politics of Federal Reorganization: Creating the U.S. Department of Education.* New York: Pergamon Press, 1988.

Rainsford, George N. *Congress and Higher Education in the Nineteenth Century.* Knoxville: University of Tennessee Press, 1972.

Ravitch, Diane. *The Troubled Crusade: American Education, 1945–1980.* New York: Basic Books, 1983.

———. *National Standards in American Education: A Citizen's Guide.* Washington, DC: Brookings Institution, 1995.

————. ed. *Brookings Papers on Education Policy, 1998.* Washington, DC: Brookings Institution, 1998.

Rebell, Michael, and Arthur Block. *Educational Policy Making and the Courts.* Chicago: University of Chicago Press, 1982.

Reigeluth, Charles M., and Robert J. Garfinkle, eds. *Systemic Change in Education.* Englewood Cliffs, NJ: Educational Technology Publications, 1994.

Rickover, Hyman. *Education and Freedom.* New York: Dutton, 1959.

Rippa, S. Alexander. *Education in a Free Society.* 8th ed. New York: Longman, 1997.

Rivlin, Alice M. *The Role of the Federal Government in Financing Higher Education.* Washington, DC: Brookings Institution, 1961.

Ross, Earle D. *Democracy's College: The Land-Grant Movement in the Formative Stage.* Ames: Iowa State College Press, 1942.

Rothstein, Laura F. *Special Education Law.* 3rd ed. New York: Longman, 2000.

Sharpes, Donald K. *Education and the US Government.* New York: St. Martin's Press, 1987.

Shor, Ira. *Culture Wars: School and Society in the Conservative Restoration, 1969–1984.* Boston: Routledge and Kegan Paul, 1986.

Sizer, Theodore R. *Horace's Compromise: The Dilemma of the American High School.* Boston: Houghton Mifflin, 1984.

Smith, Gilbert E. *The Limits of Reform: Politics and Federal Aid to Education, 1937–1950.* New York: Garland Publishing, 1982.

Spring, Joel. *American Education: An Introduction to Social and Political Aspects.* 4th ed. White Plains, NY: Longman, 1989.

————. *Conflict of Interests: The Politics of American Education.* 3rd ed. Boston: McGraw-Hill, 1998.

————. *The American School, 1642–2000.* 5th ed. Boston; McGraw-Hil, 2001.

————. *Political Agendas for Education: From the Christian Coalition to the Green Party.* Mahwah, NJ: Lawrence Erlbaum Associates, 1997.

Stevenson, Harold W., and James W. Stigler. *The Learning Gap: Why Our Schools Are Failing and What We Can Learn from Japanese and Chinese Education.* New York: Touchstone, 1992.

Summerfield, Harry L. *Power and Process: The Formulation and Limits of Federal Educational Policy.* Berkeley, CA: McCutchan, 1974.

Sundquist, James L. *Politics and Policy: The Eisenhower, Kennedy, and Johnson Years.* Washington, DC: Brookings Institution, 1968.

Taylor, Howard Cromwell. *The Educational Significance of the Early Federal Land Ordinances.* New York: Arno Press and The New York Times, 1969.

Tenenbaum, Samuel. *William Heard Kilpatrick: Trail Blazer in Education.* New York: Harper, 1951.

Tewksbury, Donald G. *The Founding of American Colleges and Universities before the Civil War.* New York: Teachers College, Columbia University, 1932.

Thomas, Norman C. *Education in National Politics.* New York: David McKay Company, 1975.

Thwing, Charles F. *A History of Higher Education in America.* New York: Appleton, 1906.

Tiedt, Sidney W. *The Role of the Federal Government in Education.* New York: Oxford University Press, 1966.

Toch, Thomas. *In the Name of Excellence: The Struggle to Reform the Nation's Schools,*

Why It's Failing, and What Should Be Done. New York: Oxford University Press, 1991.

Turnbull, H. Rutherford, and Ann Turnbull. *Free Appropriate Public Education: Law and Implementation.* Denver: Love Publishing Company, 1978.

Tyack, David, ed. *Turning Points in American Educational History.* Waltham, MA: Blaisdell, 1967.

Tyack, David, and Larry Cuban. *Tinkering toward Utopia: A Century of Public School Reform.* Cambridge, MA: Harvard University Press, 1995.

Tyack, David, Thomas James, and Aaron Benavot. *Law and the Shaping of Public Education, 1785–1954.* Madison: University of Wisconsin Press, 1987.

Tyack, David, Robert Lowe, and Elisabeth Hansot. *Public Schools in Hard Times: The Great Depression and Recent Years.* Cambridge, MA: Harvard University Press, 1984.

Unger, Irwin. *The Best of Intentions: The Triumphs and Failures of the Great Society under Kennedy, Johnson, and Nixon.* New York: Doubleday, 1996.

U.S. Department of Health, Education, and Welfare. *Land-Grant Colleges and Universities, 1862–1962.* Washington, DC: U.S. Government Printing Office, 1962.

Wade, Steven C. and Robert D. Hay. *Sports Law for Educational Institutions.* New York: Quorum Books, 1988.

Warren, Donald R. *To Enforce Education: A History of the Founding Years of the United States Office of Education.* Detroit: Wayne State University Press, 1974.

———, ed. *History, Education, and Public Policy.* Berkeley, CA: McCutchan, 1978.

Webb, L. Dean, Martha M. McCarthy, and Stephen B. Thomas. *Financing Elementary and Secondary Education.* Columbus, OH: Merrill, 1988.

Webster, Staten W. *The Education of Black Americans.* New York: John Day, 1974.

Williams, E.I.F. *Horace Mann: Educational Statesman.* New York: Macmillan, 1937.

Williams, Roger L. *The Origins of Federal Support for Higher Education: George W. Atherton and the Land-Grant College Movement.* University Park: Pennsylvania State University Press, 1991.

Wirth, Arthur G. *Education in the Technological Society: The Vocational–Liberal Studies Controversy in the Early Twentieth Century.* Scranton, PA: Intext Educational Publishers, 1972.

Zigler, Edward, and Sally J. Styfco, eds. *Head Start and Beyond: A National Plan for Extended Childhood Intervention.* New Haven: Yale University Press, 1993.

Zigler, Edward, and Jeanette Valentine, eds. *Project Head Start: A Legacy of the War on Poverty.* New York: Free Press, 1979.

Index

All **boldface** page numbers refer to the annotation of each law entry.

About the Author

DAVID CARLETON is Associate Professor of Political Science at Middle Tennessee State University. He has published extensively on gubernatorial politics and on human rights issues. He worked previously in government and in political campaign positions. He is currently preparing a textbook on state and local government.

DATE DUE